W9-CBO-295

"We owe Ms. Sapinsley a debt for rescuing the fascinating Mrs. Packard from obscurity and reminding us that, even a century and a half ago, the personal was political."
—Regina Morantz-Sanchez, *The New York Times Book Review*

"Sapinsley mines all the riches inherent in this compelling drama: the struggle between the sexes, religious intolerance, the arbitrariness of definitions of insanity, and the barbarity of the treatments for mental illness, creating a vivid and stirring portrait."
—*Booklist*

"[Sapinsley] has . . . created a vital portrait of a remarkable woman, ingeniously piecing it together from family records, contemporary newspaper clippings, and Packard's own writings. An eye-opener."
—*Kirkus Reviews*

"A fascinating biography of a pioneering crusader who heretofore has been ignored by historians."
—*Library Journal*

"Ms. Sapinsley's account of how she lobbied and pamphleteered, how she financed her work, and how well she succeeded, makes a thoroughly interesting piece of Americana."
—Phoebe-Lou Adams, *The Atlantic*

The Private War of
Mrs. Packard

The Private War of Mrs. Packard

Barbara Sapinsley

Foreword by Eric T. Carlson, M.D.,
Clinical Professor of Psychiatry and Director of the
Section on the History of Psychiatry and Behavioral
Sciences, Cornell University Medical College

With a new Introduction by Phyllis Chesler

KODANSHA INTERNATIONAL
New York • Tokyo • London

Kodansha America, Inc.
114 Fifth Avenue, New York, New York 10011, U.S.A.

Kodansha International Ltd.
17-14 Otowa 1-chome, Bunkyo-ku, Tokyo 112, Japan

Published in 1995 by Kodansha America, Inc.
by arrangement with the author.

First published in 1991 by Paragon House, New York.

This is a Kodansha Globe book.

Library of Congress Cataloging-in-Publication Data

Sapinsley, Barbara.
The private war of Mrs. Packard / Barbara Sapinsley.
p.   cm.—(Kodansha globe)
Originally published: New York : Paragon House, 1991.
Includes bibliographical references and index.
ISBN 1-56836-106-8 (pb)
1. Packard, E. P. W. (Elizabeth Parsons Ware), 1816–1897.
2. Psychiatric hospital patients—Illinois—Biography.   3. Women
social reformers—Illinois—Biography.   4. Insane—Commitment and
detention—United States.   5. Husband and wife—United States.
I Title.   II. Series.
[RC464.P33S26   1995]
362.2'1—dc20
[B]   95-41362

Book design by Virginia Norey

Printed in the United States of America

95 96 97 98 99   Q/FF   10 9 8 7 6 5 4 3 2 1

To Emmy Lou Packard

who introduced me to her remarkable great-grandmother
and most generously lent me valuable family documents,
letters, diaries, and mementos.

Contents

Introduction to the

1995 Edition

*J*discovered Elizabeth Parson Ware Packard in 1970, while researching my first book, *Women and Madness*. It was Elizabeth who made the analogy between institutional psychiatry and the Inquisition, she who fought for a woman's right to express her opinions in public, without being incarcerated in an insane asylum by male relatives who disagreed with her views. I applaud Barbara Sapinsley's first-ever biography of this amazing American heroine, whose daring deeds and indomitable spirit have, for too long, been forgotten.

In 1969, I cofounded the Association for Women in Psychology (AWP). I held a Ph.D. in psychology but I had learned nothing in graduate school or during my internships about the psychology of oppressed peoples—including women. Most of what we take for granted today was not even whispered about behind closed doors back then.

For example, I and everyone else in my generation were taught that biology *was* destiny: that women were different from and inferior to men; and that women—especially ambitious women (ourselves included)—were penis-envying monsters. None of my professors ever told us that women were oppressed: feared, hated, exploited, sexually traumatized, and then blamed for their own victimization. None of my clinical supervisors ever taught me how to administer a test for mental health—only for mental illness.

Nevertheless, inspired by the visionary, radical, grass-roots feminist movement, I began to study women as psychiatric patients, and to identify the double standards and sex-role stereotyping in psycho-therapeutic theory and practice. I planned to present some of my preliminary findings at the 1970 annual convention of the American Psychological Association (APA) in Miami.

Meanwhile, I immersed myself in the psychoanalytic literature, located biographies and autobiographies of women who had been psychiatrically misdiagnosed or hospitalized; read novels and poems about sad, mad, bad women; and absorbed both the mythology and anthropology of Goddesses and Amazons.

I read about European women who had been condemned as witches (including Regine Pernoud's account of Joan of Arc), and about women who had been imprisoned in psychiatric hospitals. I read selections of Elizabeth Packard's writings (they were available only in the Library of Congress); I read about some of Freud's patients, most notably Anna O (who became the feminist crusader Bertha Pappenheim), and Dora. I learned that in the twentieth century, some well-known and accomplished women—Zelda Fitzgerald, Virginia Woolf, Frances Farmer, Sylvia Plath, among others—had all been punitively labeled and hospitalized.

I began analyzing the nation's "mental illness" statistics and the relevant psychological and psychiatric studies. I also began identifying and interviewing the experts: women patients. I was starting to document what patriarchal culture and consciousness had been doing to women for thousands of years. No more, no less.

In the midst of this work, I arrived at the 1970 APA convention. On behalf of AWP, I asked the assembled APA members for the token sum of one million dollars "in reparations" for those women who had never been helped by the mental health professions but who had, in fact, been further abused: punitively labeled; ordered to "adjust" to their lives as second and third class citizens, and blamed when they failed to do so; overly tranquilized; sexually abused while in treatment; hospitalized, often against their will; given lobotomies or shock and insulin coma therapy; strait-jacketed, both physically and chemically; and used as slave laborers in state mental asylums. "Maybe AWP could set up an alternative to a mental hospital with the money," I suggested, "or underwrite a shelter for runaway wives."

Two thousand of my colleagues were in the audience. They were shocked. Many laughed. Loudly. Nervously. Some looked embarrassed, others relieved. Quite obviously, I was "crazy." Afterward, someone told me that jokes had been made about my "penis envy." Friends, this was 1970—not 1870. And I was a colleague.

I published *Women and Madness* in 1972. It was instantly embraced by other feminists and by many mainstream reviewers, both male and female. It would go on to sell nearly three million copies worldwide. However, my analyses of how diagnostic labels were used to stigmatize women and of why more women than men were involved in "careers" as psychiatric patients, were either ignored, treated as a sensation, or sharply criticized by those in positions of power within the professions. They accused me of having incorrect statistics and theories, of wildly overstating my case. Moreover, they said, I (or my book), was "strident," "hated men," and was "far too angry." I was just about to gain tenure at a university, and luckily, no father, brother, or husband wanted to imprison me because my ideas offended them.

It is inconceivable, even outrageous, but that is *all* Elizabeth T. Stone of Massachusetts (first hospitalized in 1842), Elizabeth Parsons Ware Packard of Illinois (first hospitalized in 1860), and Phebe B. Davis of New York (first hospitalized in 1865) did: They expressed views that angered their husbands or brothers. They spent years in state asylums for this reason and for no other.

Phebe B. Davis's crime—as she saw it—was daring to think for herself. Davis wrote: "It is now 21 years since people found out that I was crazy, and all because I could not fall in with every vulgar belief that was fashionable. I could never be led by everything and everybody." Adeline T. P. Lunt of Massachusetts (first hospitalized in 1871), noted that within the mental asylum, "the female patient must cease thinking or uttering any 'original expression.' She must 'study the art of doffing [her] true character . . . until you cut yourself to [institutional] pattern, abandon hope.' "*

Elizabeth Packard's crime was that she taught her Sunday school students that we are all born "good," not "evil." In addition, she privately believed in spiritualism and in the existence of a spiritual Mother. Elizabeth's husband, the Reverend Theophilus Packard Jr., strongly disagreed with her views—and even more strongly, with his wife's right to hold or to publicly

---

* Jeffrey L. Geller and Maxine Harris, *Women of the Asylum: Voices from behind the Walls, 1840–1945* (New York: Anchor Books, 1994).

express *any* views. In his opinion, wives were supposed to obey and be subordinate to their husbands; if they weren't, that proved they were mentally ill.

Elizabeth wrote: "I regarded the principle of religious toleration as the vital principle on which our government was based and I, in my ignorance, supposed the right was protected to all American citizens, even to the wives of clergymen." In Sapinsley's words, "In nineteenth-century America, a husband exercising his authority no matter how was not 'wrong'; a wife's attempting to resist it was."

In 1860, when their sixth and youngest child, Arthur, was eighteen months old, Theophilus Jr. exercised his *legal* right to have Elizabeth committed to an insane asylum. Theophilus forbade the children, whose ages ranged from eighteen months to eighteen years, to communicate with or talk about her. He kept her inherited income from her, deprived her of her clothes, books, and personal papers, and misrepresented her situation to her father and brothers. Dr. Andrew MacFarland, the psychiatrist-director of the asylum at Jacksonville, sequestered her outgoing mail and seized her few books and the writing paper she smuggled in.

Elizabeth was not the only nineteenth-century woman who had been imprisoned by her husband; she was, however, among the first who became crusaders against the practice. Battering, drunken, philandering, and psychotic husbands could *legally* have their wives imprisoned as a way to punish them, gain control of their dowries and real property, and live with or marry other women. In 1860, Susan B. Anthony and Elizabeth Cady Stanton wrote:

> Could the dark secrets of those insane asylums be brought to light we would be shocked to know the countless number of rebellious wives, sisters and daughters that are thus annually sacrificed to false customs and conventionalism, and barbarous laws made by men for women.

Elizabeth and other similarly legally kidnapped women feared that they might be driven mad by the brutality of the asylum itself, and by their utter lack of legal rights, both as women and as prisoners. Their fear was justified. Female psychiatric patients were routinely beaten and deprived of sleep, food, exercise, sunlight, and all contact with the outside world. They were sometimes even murdered, and some women tried to kill themselves as a way of ending their torture.

Elizabeth T. Stone of Massachusetts (first hospitalized in 1842) described the asylum as "a system that is worse than slavery"; Adriana Brinckle of Pennsylvania (hospitalized 1857–1885) described the asylum as a "living death," filled with "shackles," "darkness," "handcuffs, straightjackets, balls and chains, iron rings and other such relics of barbarism"; Tirzah Shedd of Illinois (first hospitalized in 1862) wrote: "This is a wholesale slaughter house . . . more a place of punishment than a place of cure;" Clarissa Caldwell Lathrop of New York (first hospitalized in 1880) wrote: "We could not read the invisible inscription over the entrance, written in the heart's blood of the unfortunate inmates, 'Who enters here must leave all hope behind.' " Adriana Brinckle of Pennsylvania wrote: "An insane asylum. A place where insanity is made." Sophie Olsen (first hospitalized in 1862), also of Jacksonville, wrote: "O, I was so weary, weary; I longed for some Asylum from 'Lunatic Asylums!' "* According to Olsen:

> *The faces of many [women] were frightfully blackened by blows received, partly from each other . . . but mostly from their [female] attendants. . . . I have seen the attendant strike and unmercifully beat [women] on the head, with a bunch of heavy keys, which she carried fastened by a cord around her waist: leaving their faces blackened and scarred for weeks. I have seen her twist their arms and cross them behind the back, tie them in that position, and then beat the victim till the other patients would cry out, begging her to desist . . . I have seen her strike them prostrate to the floor, with great violence, then beat and kick them.†*

Tirzah Shedd wrote that:

> *There is one married woman [here] who has been imprisoned seven times by her husband, and yet she is intelligent and entirely sane. . . . When will married women be safe from her husband's power?‡*

In 1860, the year Elizabeth was first imprisoned, Susan B. Anthony gave shelter to a "runaway" wife, Mrs. Phoebe Phelps of Massachusetts, whose violent husband (a state senator) had locked her away in a state asylum.

---

* Geller and Harris.
† Ibid.
‡ Ibid.

Freed by her brother, Phelps promptly fled the state with one of her children. Anthony's abolitionist friends ordered her to return Senator Phelp's legal property: his wife and daughter. Anthony refused to do so. She viewed the situation as analogous to returning a runaway slave to its master. Senator Phelps hounded Anthony. He also hired detectives. Within a year, Senator Phelps had repossessed his living "property."

However, to my joy, while reading Sapinsley's biography, I discovered that within five years, Phelps would join Elizabeth in testifying before the Massachusetts state legislature on behalf of married women, mental patients, and their rights.

Elizabeth endured the gravest persecution without becoming bitter or crazy. She ministered to her sisters in bondage. She washed them and their rooms daily, comforted them, and prayed with them. She tried to shield them from beatings and from suicide. Against all odds, Elizabeth never lost her wits. After three and a half years, she finally regained her freedom. She did not desert those she left behind. Like other wrongfully incarcerated nineteenth-century women—Alice Bingham Russell and Mrs. H. C. McMullen of Minnesota, and Mrs. L. C. Pennell of Indiana—she became a tireless and creative crusader on behalf of mental patients, married women, and mothers.

For her first reform, Elizabeth Packard proposed that: "No person shall be regarded or treated as an Insane person, or a Monomaniac, simply for the expression of opinions, no matter how absurd these opinions may appear to others". Packard was actually trying to enforce the First Amendment on behalf of women!

Packard also noted that: "It is a crime against human progress to allow Reformers to be treated as Monomaniacs . . . if the Pioneers of truth are thus liable to lose their personal liberty . . . who will dare to be true to the inspirations of the divinity within them?"

Phebe B. Davis (first hospitalized in 1865) was more realistic. She wrote that "real high souled people are but little appreciated in this world—they are never respected until they have been dead two or three hundred years."

Alice Bingham Russell of Minnesota (first hospitalized in 1898) was legally kidnapped by a sheriff on her husband's orders. After obtaining her own release, Russell spent twelve years trying to document and "improve the conditions of the insane." Russell described many women whose husbands imprisoned them in order to gain control of their wives' property.

Barbara Sapinsley has captured the high drama inherent in Elizabeth Packard's life. Elizabeth was no feminist firebrand; she was a God-fearing and dutiful Christian daughter, wife, and mother. She relied on "manly, Christian" men to come to her aid and some actually did. However, Elizabeth was also extremely well-educated, industrious, and in great good health. In Sapinsley's words, Elizabeth was "a keen thinker, a powerful speaker, and a very independent character."

In a sense, Elizabeth was not solely altruistic. She understood that obtaining justice for herself involved obtaining it for others in her situation. But *Elizabeth* also wanted to be sure that *Theophilus* had no legal right to hospitalize her again, no legal way of seizing her earnings or her real property, and no right to deny her visitation or to retain custody of their children. Elizabeth drafted and lobbied for countless bills on behalf of married women to retain their own wages, and to be heard by a jury or a judge before being locked away as "insane." She championed the rights of mental patients to send and receive mail. Elizabeth stubbornly, persistently, brilliantly, understood that she might have to change the laws for every mother in order to see her own dear children.

Does Elizabeth's account of institutional brutality and torture mean that mental illness did not exist or that those so afflicted needed no help? Not at all. What she and other ex-inmate crusaders did was to document that most women in asylums were not insane; that "help" was not to be found in doctor-headed, attendant-staffed, and state-run patriarchal institutions; that fathers, brothers, husbands, judges, physicians, and female attendants will do anything that We, the people, allow them to get away with; that women were as oppressed within the family as they were within asylums.

That oppression still exists today. In my view the themes of Elizabeth Packard's crusades are, unfortunately, not out of date. Psychiatric labels and diagnoses—the *institution* of psychiatry—are still used to stigmatize already traumatized populations of second-class citizens, *and* to punitively diagnose all those who dare to rebel, especially women. Even today, when women allege economic discrimination or sexual harassment, they are, incredibly, called "crazy" and often forced into psychiatric exams.

Hard to believe? What about the women in the American military who complained about being sexually harassed, *post*-Tailhook, and were punished for doing so? In 1994 women testified before the House Armed Services Committee that once they had filed grievances, they were ostracized, brutally questioned about their private sex lives, transferred to dead-end jobs, and forced out of the armed services. Lieutenant Darlene Simmons, a Navy lawyer, was ordered to take a psychiatric exam after she accused her commander of harassment in 1991 and 1992. A psychiatric exam? How absurd, how chilling, how familiar.

Many practicing therapists, both male and female, are profoundly phobic about feminist insights. Happily, there are exceptions. However, most mental health professionals who run medical, graduate, and psychoanalytic schools are not familiar with or do not respect feminist approaches to womens' mental health. This is truly astounding, given that contemporary mental health professionals did not learn about incest, rape, wife-beating, or child abuse from graduate or medical school textbooks but from feminist consciousness-raising; from grass-roots counselors, with and without degrees; and from the victims themselves, empowered to speak, not by psychiatry but by feminist liberation.

In a letter she once wrote to the Chicago papers, Elizabeth said:

> *It was once argued that the Negro slave must first be fitted for freedom before he could be trusted with it; but the more enlightened claimed that the very best way to fit him for freedom was to elevate him to the position of a free man. Responsibility does elevate.*

Elizabeth Packard has elevated us all.

Phyllis Chesler
May 1995

Foreword

Although physicians have struggled to treat the insane throughout recorded history, the birth of the specialty of psychiatry can only be dated to the late eighteenth and early nineteenth centuries. About the same time, the view that the mentally disturbed patient could best be treated away from home in an institutional setting was becoming increasingly accepted. This trend was associated with the steady increase in the construction of insane asylums or, as they were otherwise termed, state hospitals for the mentally ill. These institutions, in turn, required proper medical professionals to administer them. As the body of psychiatrically inclined professionals grew, they felt the need to organize their fledgling specialty, both for their own educational support and to share experiences in learning how to meet the needs of their patients. As a consequence, Western civilization spawned national psychiatric organizations between 1840 and 1855 in the United States, France, Germany and Great Britain. Interestingly enough, these societies often preceded the formation of any national medical society.

Along with this burgeoning expansion in the psychiatric field there were more and more investigations into and discussions of how patients should be treated medically. Other issues concerning hospitalization also came under examination. These discussions were legally necessary for many patients, who either did not recognize the extent of their own plight or even denied their problems and tried to refuse both their admission to the hospitals and the therapies recommended for them. The severity of their illnesses varied widely, and, in hindsight, some clearly may not have required inpatient treatment. Some were undoubtedly irritable and difficult to live with, and their admission was a major relief to their relatives. On other occasions, patients were at a risk of being manipulated by their relatives for financial gain. Gradually, each state in the United States developed its own laws regarding commitment procedures.

Many patients did not appreciate being hospitalized and were vociferous in their complaints. Some even published stories of their experiences. Most of these accounts were minor pamphlets with little subsequent impact, but three authors before 1910 stand out clearly: John Thomas Perceval (1803–76), Elizabeth Parsons Ware Packard (1816–97), and Clifford W. Beers (1876–1943).

Perceval was only nine years old when his father, Spencer Perceval, then the prime minister of Great Britain, was assassinated by John Bellingham, an insane person who was tried and executed within eights days of the assassination. Perceval grew up suffering from emotional problems, was hospitalized in two different asylums and apparently recovered. He wrote two books about his experience (1838 and 1840) and turned to defending "the rights of lunatics." He became one of the founders of The Alleged Lunatics' Friends Society and later its secretary. He subsequently testified before the House of Commons committee on issues involving the insane. The last named patient-reformer, Beers, was hospitalized in June 1900 and spent most of the next three years in three different mental institutions. He went back to work in late 1903, but was so excited about his reform ideas for the insane that he needed a month-long hospitalization for his elated state. Beers then decided to dedicate himself full-time to his cause. First he wrote a book, *A Mind That Found Itself*, which was published in 1908 and continued in print for the rest of his life. His goal was not only to improve mental hospitals, where he felt cruelly treated, but also to work for the prevention of emotional problems. Beers founded a local organization for this purpose in Connecticut in May 1908 which led the following year to the National Committee for Mental Hygiene, which continues to our day as the National Association for Mental Health.

The most famous American woman's account of her hospitalization was written almost fifty years earlier by Mrs. Packard. Among her other qualities, Mrs. Packard was an intelligent, verbal, aggressive, and independent woman, irrespective of any emotional problems she might have had. One challenge facing the reader of this fascinating volume by Barbara Sapinsley is whether Mrs. Packard even needed to be hospitalized. There is, however, her early brief hospitalization at age nineteen for "brain fever" at the Worcester State Hospital under the distinguished Samuel B. Woodward, one of the thirteen founders in 1844 of what became known as the American Psychiatric Association. Mrs. Packard seemed to recover well from this episode, and her next hospitalization did not occur until twenty-four years later, at age forty-three, in the context of a difficult marriage. By then her domestic life was far from tranquil. Her marital discord was clearly evident, and this presents readers with an opportunity to analyze how they would have judged such a marital situation. Part of the problem was a religious one. Her husband, Reverend Theophilus Packard, Jr., a fervent minister, nearly fifteen years older than his wife, was dedicated to his Calvinistic beliefs, inflexible in his views, and had little tolerance for the different ideas his wife was expounding. Another source of friction was the question of the "inalienable rights of women" (as well as men) as Mrs. Packard phrased it. This idea was underlined by an Illinois law that allowed a husband to hospitalize his wife for insanity with the superintendent's approval without going through any further medical or legal procedures to protect her rights. This fact naturally incensed Elizabeth Packard and became the sustaining stimulus for her campaigns to change popular views and the law— campaigns that eventually took her to thirty-one states. It is her story and much more that Barbara Sapinsley explores in vivid detail and that will absorb the reader's attention with its continuing human drama.

Eric T. Carlson, M.D., clinical professor of psychiatry and director of the Section on the History of Psychiatry and Behavioral Sciences, Cornell University Medical College.

Preface

S*ome twenty-odd years ago* a friend of mine married Emmy Lou Packard, the great-granddaughter of Elizabeth Parsons Ware Packard, or Mrs. E. P. W. Packard, as she became known during her crusading years. Emmy Lou asked if I would be interested in writing about her great-grandmother, whose life she related to me in all its drama. I tried it out on my agent. He thought it had "everything"—religion, marital discord, false imprisonment, a courtroom scene, kidnapping, illicit love, persecution, politics (not necessarily in that order) and public success at the expense of private happiness.

Emmy Lou's mother, Emma L. Packard, really wanted to write the story herself but she realized she never would and generously gave me all the anecdotal material and reminiscences she had been collecting through the years. She also lent me Mrs. Packard's books plus the Reverend Packard's priceless diary and journal and their son Samuel's journal (which I immediately copied for hours on end on my typewriter—their spines were too fragile to open them flat on copy machines—so I could return the originals as quickly as possible). And over the years, as I pursued the story through old newspapers, in the archives of historical societies and hospitals, and letters to descendants of people who figured in Mrs. Packard's life, Emma Packard kept me supplied with contemporary newspaper reports of developments that would have delighted Elizabeth Packard and for which she probably would have claimed some credit. Sadly, Emma Packard did not live to see the book in print.

At the suggestion of Herman Gollub, then an editor at (I think) Little, Brown, who read my one-page summary, I read *The Day They Shook the Plum Tree*, the story of Hetty Green, a legendary eccentric millionaire in New York City. It opened with Hetty Green's law firm finally distributing her vast estate. Then it flashed back to where the money came from, how her father had accumulated it and how Hetty lived as virtually a shopping-bag lady despite her wealth. I took the book as my model. Only instead of starting at the end, as *Plum Tree* did and flashing all the way back, I started with the turning point in Elizabeth Packard's life, her trial on charges of insanity, flashed back to her beginnings, brought the story up to the trial and then carried it forward from the trial to its conclusion.

In the course of my research, I kept running into dead ends, a few of them fires that left nothing but ashes behind. The courthouse in Kankakee City, Illinois, where the *Packard vs. Packard* trial was held, burned down twice; no records of the trial survived. Emmy Lou was under the impression that when Elizabeth Packard first settled in Chicago she had tutored the children of the first Marshall Field, but the warehouse in which the Field family's papers were stored had burned down and no records survived.

In addition, there were no records of the floor debates of the Illinois legislature. Until recently, it did not keep such records, printing only who introduced and who seconded bills, the dates and number of yeas and nays, largely, I was told, to conceal the hanky-panky that was part of Illinois legislative procedure. Loella S. Young, then director of public relations at the Jacksonville (Illinois) State Hospital, deplored her predecessor's lack of historical sense: The earlier public relations director had tossed out all the records of inmates who were no longer alive. The Rock Island Railroad, for whom Elizabeth Packard's youngest son had worked for an unknown number of years before his untimely death, informed me that because of the Railroad Retirement Act which required enormous numbers of records, it was forced to discard all data pertaining to its deceased employees to make way for the retirees to come. (Perhaps the advent of the computer and the mushrooming of miniaturization in methods of record keeping will make for more preservation of more less-than-world-shaking information.)

At one point, I went through the phone books of Manteno and Kankakee City, and wrote to everyone with the same name as anyone mentioned in connection with the Packard trial. I was one generation too late. Some didn't answer. Some wrote that they either were not related or they *were* related but had never heard dinner-table mention of the Packards. One, Myra B. Beedy, a descendant of Mrs. Packard's friend Daniel Beedy, knew nothing about Mrs. Packard or the trial but she worked in the Kankakee County courthouse and took it upon herself to look for any relevant documents. All she could find was the petition for divorce that Elizabeth Packard had always claimed she did not want and never asked for. The most memorable, though not the most helpful, among the responses was the phone call that woke me at 1 A.M. New York time (midnight in Manteno) from one woman who demanded to know what I *really* wanted; she did not believe a word in my letter and warned me that if I ever contacted her again she would turn me in to the FBI and the CIA.

During all this time, my manuscript (first, the first chapter, then other chapters one by one) was making the rounds. I received more rejection letters than Margaret Mitchell. Two were downright nasty, but most were encouraging, kind, regretful and sometimes flattering. My favorite went something like this: "My! Isn't Mrs. Packard a fascinating woman, and my! didn't Ms. Sapinsley do a good job. But she isn't well known." I still don't know to whom the "she" referred. But I *did* know I had a good story and that if I lived long enough it would be published.

Now all that is history. After three rewrites, one of them an attempt, by request, at fictionalizing the story (which is really not my style), and more than one change of agent, *The Private War of Mrs. Packard* is alive and well, and I trust no one will ever again say that she or I "is not well known."

The Private War of
Mrs. Packard

1.

On Trial

he time: January 1864. The place: Kankakee City, Illinois, fifty miles south of Chicago, seat of the twentieth judicial circuit court, Judge Charles R. Starr presiding. The event: the trial of *Packard vs. Packard.*

As he toasted in the New Year that January 1, Judge Starr had no idea that within two weeks he would be trying the case of his career. His usual judicial fare was petty larceny, boundary disputes, unpaid bills, unfulfilled contracts and an occasional horse thief. A drama of marital strife involving charges of false imprisonment at home, false confinement in an insane asylum, religious conflict over Calvinist doctrine and whether women had rights to their own thoughts, let alone their own property, was more than he, Kankakee County or the state of Illinois was prepared for.

Kankakee City (population 3,800, most of them farmers), for all it was the county seat, did not anticipate the influx of people that the trial would bring. They came from Manteno, the neighboring town where the Packards lived, and they came for the newspapers they worked for, from all over the state. The few inns and rooming houses would be crammed and many a tired, hungry husband would have to wait for his supper because his wife had been among the two hundred good ladies who crowded onto spectator benches, alternating between weeping and applauding as one of their own, one hundred years before Betty Friedan, fought for justice under the law. Had the Civil War not been monopolizing the national news, there would have been reporters from much farther afield and *Packard vs. Packard* would have made history instead of becoming merely a footnote.

Until 1860 Mrs. Packard was an unlikely figure for a cause célèbre. During her first forty years, she had led a thoroughly ordinary life. She was born in western Massachusetts, still frontier territory by Boston standards, to descendants of Pilgrim stock. She was a preacher's dutiful daughter, another preacher's dutiful wife and a devoted mother of five. She varied from the norm only in being more charming and better educated than most. With her inquiring mind and strong ego she would have been more at home in the twentieth century. She made the mistake of marrying a man who held fast to the theology of the eighteenth century and believed a wife should be an echo. But unlike myriad other women who were similarly mismatched, she did not suffer the incompatibility in silence. Neither did her husband.

In spite of losing out to the Civil War as news, the trial of Mrs. Packard cast a long shadow. It was one of two events* that brought to public attention the flagrant and frequent abuses attendant on commitment of people to mental institutions. The conditions in mental hospitals and the treatment of inmates often made news; how the patients got there seldom did—until after the Packard trial—and the psychiatric profession was not pleased.

It all started when Mrs. A. C. Haslett of Manteno, whom Elizabeth Packard referred to as her "most efficient friend," came to Judge Starr with a problem. Her dear friend, Mrs. Theophilus Packard, Jr., wife of the local Presbyterian minister, was being held incommunicado in her bedroom by her husband. Mrs. Packard was convinced that her husband was making plans to transport her to an insane asylum in their home state of Massachusetts. He had already committed her to the Illinois State Hospital for the insane at Jacksonville, Illinois, where she had spent three years. Only recently had she come home, where Sarah Haslett felt she should always have been.

Mrs. Haslett and her husband had tried to get in to see Elizabeth and had been turned away either by Theophilus himself or by one of their young sons on orders from his father. Other friends and neighbors had had similar experiences. The back door was padlocked and the windows of Elizabeth's room nailed shut.

---

* The other was a novel, *Hard Cash*, by Charles Reade, based on an actual case of wrongful commitment.

The Hasletts were prepared to organize a posse and storm the Packard house, but friends had voted that down. Someone suggested that Mrs. Packard break her bedroom window and jump out whereupon the posse, assembled below, could rescue her, but Elizabeth voted *that* down. (No one ever made clear how the message about the plan had been sneaked past the minister's security system.) Elizabeth reasoned that should she break the window but fail in her attempt to escape, she would have given her husband grounds, which she maintained he lacked, for committing her—doing damage to his property, namely, his house and herself. So Mrs. Haslett appealed to Judge Starr for advice.

The judge told her that if Elizabeth were indeed a prisoner in her own home and if there were people willing to swear to it in writing, he could issue a writ of habeas corpus and guarantee Elizabeth her day in court. State law allowed a husband to commit his wife to an insane asylum if the superintendent of the asylum agreed "without the evidence of insanity required in other cases." But state law did not allow him to hold her prisoner in her own home.

There were enough friends who had tried to visit and been turned away and had seen the padlocked back door and the nailed-shut bedroom window to so testify. While they were at it, the four men who signed the affidavit threw in an additional complaint against the Reverend Theophilus Packard, Jr.—information obviously gleaned from their wives. They said he "cruelly abuses and misuses her" by "depriving her of her winter's clothing, this cold and inclement weather."

On January 11, 1864, Judge Starr issued the writ ordering Theophilus Packard to produce his wife at the judge's chambers at 1 P.M. the next day "together with the day and cause of caption and detention by whatsoever name the same may be called."

Years later, reflecting in tranquility, Theophilus Packard tried to describe for his children and their children the troubles he had lived through. His account of the trial began: "Four intermeddlers in town got a writ of Habeas Corpus. . . . On the 12th of January about 10 o'clock A.M. I was served . . . to appear before Charles R. Starr, Judge at Kankakee, 12 miles distant at one o'clock P.M., the *same* day—in three hours time . . . as though I was falsely imprisoning her."

But a clergyman of all people must obey the law. So at the designated hour, in righteous indignation, he produced Elizabeth at the Kankakee courthouse. He had obviously obtained legal counsel on short notice because he produced a statement in lawyer's language justifying his actions. His wife, his response said,

> *is and has been for more than three years past insane, and for about 3 years of that time was in the Insane Asylum of the State of Illinois . . . that she was discharged from said Asylum without being cured and is incurably insane . . . that since the 23rd of October, the undersigned has kept the said Elizabeth with him in Manteno, in this county, and while he has faithfully and anxiously watched, cared for, and guarded the said Elizabeth, yet he has not confined and imprisoned her in a close room, in the dwelling house of the undersigned, or in any other place or way, but on the contrary, the undersigned has allowed her all the liberty compatible with her welfare and safety.*

He also denied depriving her of her winter clothing* and refuted her suspicions about his planning to commit her to a Massachusetts asylum by claiming he was about to move his *whole* family back to Massachusetts. Finally he presented the judge with a letter from the superintendent of the state insane asylum at Jacksonville, Dr. Andrew McFarland, refusing to readmit Elizabeth since she was incurable.

The judge issued a call for a jury, saying to Theophilus in effect, "Prove it." Elizabeth was confident that her husband could not. To her, the judge's action was only the first step toward Right and Justice, capitalized in her mind, prevailing.

During her childhood and adolescence in western Massachusetts, Elizabeth had automatically assumed she would follow in her mother's footsteps—finish her schooling, teach small children for a while and, at the proper time, marry a suitable "manly" breadwinner and become, in her turn, a "womanly" housewife and mother. Should she marry a clergyman, she would walk in the footsteps of centuries of clergymen's wives, doing "women's work" among her husband's parishioners.

This, in fact, Elizabeth had done with the approval and approbation of

---

* His denial notwithstanding, there must have been something to the charge because nearly two years later Elizabeth's father felt it necessary to write to him: "Rev. Sir: I think the time has fully come for you to give up to Elizabeth her clothes."

her husband, his family and his parish. From a loving family she had moved into an appreciative community. Everyone spoke highly of Elizabeth. Yet there she was, in her middle years, in a midwestern county courthouse, charged by her own husband with being insane, largely because she disputed him on Calvinist theory, refusing to believe that her babies were born damned or that women had no right to hold and express their own opinions.

Theophilus, as his diary and retroactive journal show, worried his thoughts and feelings like a dog does a bone. He flaggellated himself for spiritual inadequacies and dwelt almost lovingly on his physical ailments and mental anguish. What happened on the outside interested him much less than what happened on the inside.

Elizabeth, unlike her husband, looked neither backward nor inward. She was much too eager to embrace the future and rush with full heart and open arms into whatever it might contain, especially if it contained more freedom of expression and action. One of the greatest frustrations of her years in the state asylum had been her inability to make a good citizen's contribution to the Civil War effort. But since she had been shut into her room and forced, by the unfamiliar emotion of fear of the future, into thinking about the past, she did sometimes wonder where her path had detoured. Yet even in those introspective moments she never wondered if *she* had done the detouring. Her ego would not let her.

With the trial pending and the hostilities out in the open, Elizabeth could hardly return to her husband's house. Her Manteno friends—Theophilus's "intermeddlers"—had retained a legal team to handle Elizabeth's defense. One of them, J. W. Orr, took her into his home for the duration. But first he took the precaution of having his own physician, (a onetime clergyman who could also judge her theology) examine her before he agreed to defend her. Mrs. Orr gave Elizabeth clothing from her own wardrobe that they altered together so she could appear in court in her usual fastidious fashion.

Another of her attorneys, Stephen Moore, constituted himself unofficial recorder of the proceedings. He took down testimony verbatim except when a witness spoke too rapidly or too volubly for his pen. Then he summarized. The Kankakee county courthouse has burned down twice since then and Moore's personal account is the only record extant of the trial.

Moore, by now, was half in love with Elizabeth, and it showed. "To make the case fully understood," he began, "I will here remark that Mr. Packard was educated in the Calvinist faith and for 29 years had been a preacher of that creed, and would in no wise depart from the religion of his fathers." (Theophilus's journal would, in time, verify Moore's statement.) Moore continued: "He is cold, selfish, and illiberal in his views, possessed of but little talent, and a physiognomy innocent of expression. He has a large self-will and his stubbornness is only exceeded by his bigotry."

As for his client:

> *Mrs. Packard is a lady of fine mental endowments, and blest with a liberal education. She is an original, vigorous, masculine thinker, and were it not for her superior judgment, combined with native modesty, she would rank as a "strong-minded woman.". . . Her views of religion are more in accordance with the liberal views of the age in which we live. She scouts the Calvinist doctrine of man's total depravity, and that God has preordained some to be saved, others to be damned. She stands fully on the platform of man's free agency and accountability to God for his actions.*

These ideas, he wound up, produced continual contention between Elizabeth and her husband, the latter claiming they "were emanations from the devil" and "the vagaries of a crazed brain." For these ideas, Theophilus denounced her from his pulpit, expelled her from the Bible class, refused to let her participate in family prayers at home and shut her away from her friends. He persuaded his sisters and their husbands, and even Elizabeth's father and two brothers back in Massachusetts that she was, indeed, insane.

So, although the rationale for the trial was whether or not Elizabeth had been held prisoner in her own home, the arguments debated her mental health and turned on arcane points of theology.

Theophilus's lawyers considered asking for a change of venue since popular opinion was already against their client. But in the end they did not. Moore took this to mean that they doubted it would be granted, presupposing insufficient grounds. At any rate, the trial took place at once in Kankakee City. Both sides rounded up medical testimony from local physicians and lay opinions from friends and relatives. Neither Packard took the stand. Theophilus hardly even communicated with his lawyers. Elizabeth whispered occasionally to hers. Her calm confidence broke only twice. He was neither calm nor confident but he managed to maintain a stony exterior.

The prosecutor opened the trial. His first witness was a doctor, Christopher Knott, from Kankakee City, not Manteno. Elizabeth had seen him once before. He had paid her a visit at Theophilus's request in 1860 before she was taken to Jacksonville. He testified that he had thought her "partially deranged on religious matters" and had given Theophilus a certificate to that effect, which was what Theophilus had consulted him for. "Her mind appeared to be excited on the subject of religion," Dr. Knott said. "On all other subjects she was perfectly rational. . . . She was what might be called a 'monomaniac,'" a common condition among the religious, he thought.

Dr. Knott continued: "I take her to be a lady of fine mental abilities, possessing more ability than ordinarily found. . . . I would say she was insane the same as I would say Henry Ward Beecher, Spurgeon, Horace Greeley and like persons are insane." He added that he thought all she needed was rest, that confinement or restraint of any kind would be the worst treatment for her.

The next witness was Dr. J. W. Brown, also of Kankakee City. His appearance occasioned Elizabeth's first shock. She remembered him well, a strange little man who had come calling only the month before and made her thoroughly uncomfortable. She had no idea he was a doctor. He had introduced himself as a salesman of the new treadle-operated sewing machines.

He and Elizabeth had discussed sewing machines, he said, and he found her entirely rational. She realized how much easier and more efficient housekeeping would be, especially with small children, if she could stitch up clothing on these new models and she looked forward to the day when she could have one. Then the discussion turned to the status of women and "she exhibited no special marks of insanity on *that* subject although she had many ideas quite at variance with mine." Next they moved on to politics and the Civil War. Elizabeth drew analogies between her differences with her husband and the differences between the Union and the Confederacy. She said the South was waging war for two wicked purposes—to overthrow a good government and to establish the principle of human slavery, which she considered despotism. Mr. Packard, she said, was opposing her to overthrow free thought in women so "the despotism of man may prevail over the wife." Still no indication of insanity. Finally Dr. Brown brought up the subject of religion and "then I had not the slightest difficulty in concluding that she was hopelessly insane."

Dr. Brown based his conclusion not so much on any one thing Elizabeth said as on her conversation as a whole, but he did pick out one statement as a sample: She said she was "the personification of the Holy Ghost." He did not know what she meant. There followed a complex colloquy with the defense counsel who offered a possible metaphysical explanation. Dr. Brown agreed the defense could be right even though he did not understand metaphysics. (No one asked Elizabeth what she meant.) But Dr. Brown found other indications of an unsound mind: "She found fault that Mr. Packard would not discuss their points of difference in religion in an open manly way instead of going around and denouncing her as crazy to her friends and to the church. She had a great aversion to being called insane. Before I got through the conversation she exhibited a great dislike to me."

The spectators tittered.

Dr. Brown had fifteen more reasons to bolster his conclusion, all carefully written down. He was eager to read them. He listed her aversion to being called insane and her rejection of the Calvinist doctrine of total depravity twice in slightly different words. Among the remaining reasons:

- *Her calling him a copperhead without proving it.*
- *Her feelings toward her husband.*
- *Her husband's description of her case.*
- *Her belief that some calamity would befall her because of his visit.*
- *Her refusal to shake his hand when he left.*

His final reason was a rambling incoherent sentence that Moore took down as follows: "Her viewing the subject of religion from the osteric standpoint of christian exegitical analysis and agglutinating the polsynthetical ectoblasts of homogeneous asceticism."

Whatever Dr. Brown actually said, he reduced the spectators to helpless laughter. "It required some moments to restore order in the courtroom," Stephen Moore recorded.

Then the prosecution called Theophilus's brother-in-law, Abijah Dole, husband of his younger sister Sybil, and superintendent of the Sunday school. In the latter capacity Abijah had had some problems with Elizabeth. But first he wanted to report a couple of domestic incidents.

Once, five years before, the Packards' only daughter, Libby, then nine, was ill with brain fever, an ailment common in nineteenth-century medical annals, attributed to a variety of stressful physical or emotional causes or both. Abijah Dole went to visit one morning. He found Elizabeth uncharacteristically in her nightclothes, her hair disheveled and her face "wild." Libby was "moaning and moving her head," typical symptoms of the malady. Abijah thought Elizabeth had cast a spell on the child but he conceded, under cross-examination, that she might have been distraught because she had been up all night with Libby and was afraid the child would die. On another occasion, Elizabeth had told him she could no longer live with Theophilus, obvious indication of an unbalanced mind.

Then came the experiences in the Sunday school Bible class. The students had been discussing Moses smiting the Egyptians. Elizabeth thought "Moses acted too hasty but that all things worked for the glory of God." Abijah knew Theophilus did not want her to discuss her ideas at the Sunday school so he silenced her.

Once she asked him to let her read a paper she had written in response to a question raised in class. (For some reason, Moore noted, this piece of testimony upset Abijah enormously; he started to cry. After a few minutes, he calmed down and proceeded.) "I was willing to gratify her all I could for I knew she was crazy, but I did not want the responsibility myself, so I put it to a vote of the school. . . . She was allowed to read it." Abijah could not remember the content of the paper, only that it proved to him that she was insane.

Later Elizabeth asked for a letter releasing her from membership in the Presbyterian church so she could join the Methodists, the only other Protestant sect in town.

"Was that an indication of insanity?" the defense asked.

"She would not leave the church unless she was insane," was Abijah's reply. He was a Presbyterian; he believed his church and it alone was right. "I do not deem it proper for persons to examine new doctrines or systems of theology," he said.

Did he also believe that everything in the Bible was right and true? Yes, indeed he did. In a preview of Clarence Darrow at the Scopes monkey trial in Dayton, Tennessee, in 1925, the defense asked: "Do you believe literally that Jonah was swallowed by a whale and remained in its belly three days and then was cast up?"

> Abijah: *"I do."*
> Defense: *"Do you believe literally that Elijah went direct up to Heaven in a chariot of fire, that the chariot had wheels and seats and was drawn by horses?"*
> Abijah: *"I do.*

In the middle of the afternoon Sybil Dole entered the courtroom with Libby, now nearly fourteen. As they passed the defense table, Libby broke away from her aunt and ran to her mother to hug and kiss her. Sybil pulled the girl back, saying audibly, "Come away from that woman. She is not fit to take care of you." Recorded Stephen Moore: "Not a mother's heart there but was touched, and scarce a dry eye was seen." Libby did not come to court again; the younger children didn't come at all. Sybil decided it was not wise to expose them to such sympathy for their mother.

Sybil, who had been close to Elizabeth since the latter married into the Packard family, testified that Elizabeth, who had always been so sweet and kind, seemed changed when she arrived in Manteno in the late 1850s. On occasion she talked "in a wild, excited manner. . . . She accused Dr. Packard very strangely of depriving her of her rights of conscience—that he would not allow her to think for herself on religious questions because they differed on these topics."

Sybil was at the Packard house one day when an unexpected visitor dropped in. Elizabeth was not prepared for company: "She was out of bread and had to make biscuit for dinner." At that point a man's voice came from the spectators' benches: "Wife, were you ever out of bread and had to make biscuit for dinner? I must put you in an insane asylum, no mistake!" Sybil was momentarily taken aback but she pulled herself together and continued.

She had spent that night at the Packard house and shared Elizabeth's room (which Theophilus was not doing). Elizabeth spoke of how much the family circle meant to her, of her husband's kindnesses toward her in the past, and the tenderness that once existed between them. Sybil found nothing strange in her behavior then, but on a later occasion Elizabeth seemed excited and said to her husband, "You regard me as insane. I will thank you to leave my room." She ordered Sybil out, too.

Sybil's final piece of evidence concerned one supper when Elizabeth spoke about religion and her husband chastised her. Elizabeth became angry and told him she would talk if and when she had a mind to. She took up her teacup and left the room, saying, "I will have no fellowship with the unfruitful works of darkness." This was shortly before Theophilus took Elizabeth to Jacksonville, and since she was aware of his plans, Sybil conceded to the defense that Elizabeth's attitude was perhaps understandable.

The final prosecution witness was Sarah Rumsey, a daughter of one of Theophilus's parishioners, who had been retained as a mother's helper about a week before Elizabeth's removal to the asylum. Sarah had known the Packards for two years. She had never "worked out" and did not think she would be doing so then, but when she arrived Mr. Packard dismissed their

French maid (herself a recent innovation in the household where Elizabeth had always done the major chores). "When [Mrs. Packard] found I was going to stay in the house and that the French servant had been discharged," Sarah testified, "she ordered me into the kitchen. Before that she had treated me kindly as a visitor. I thought it was an evidence of insanity for her to order me into the kitchen. She ought to have known that I was not an ordinary servant."

As additional proof Sarah offered the following:

> She liked to keep the house clean and have her yard and flowers look well. . . . She wanted the flower beds in the front yard cleaned out and tried to get Mr. Packard to do it. He would not. She put on an old dress and went to work and cleaned out the weeds. . . . It was a warm day and she stayed out until she was almost melted down with the heat. . . . Then she went to her room and took a bath and dressed herself and then lay down exhausted. She did not come down to dinner. . . . She was angry and excited and showed ill-will.

To Sarah such behavior seemed insane.

Sarah stayed until Elizabeth was taken away. "I approved of taking her away," Sarah said. "I deemed her dangerous to the church; her ideas were contrary to the church and were wrong." But when the sheriff and two doctors, both strangers, arrived unannounced to take her off, Sarah continued, "She did not manifest as much excitement as I would have done under the same circumstances."

The prosecution then asked for a ten-day adjournment so Dr. McFarland, who was attending a family funeral in Ohio, would be able to testify. The counsel for Elizabeth protested that it was unheard of for a case to recess midway so one side could hunt up additional evidence. Judge Starr ordered the trial to continue; he would decide about granting a continuance when the defense had concluded.

The prosecution then asked to read the letter from Dr. McFarland, dated December 1863, plus a certificate from the asylum signed by him in June 1863. The judge allowed it. Thus, Theophilus had the benefit of the doctor's testimony while Elizabeth's lawyers were denied the opportunity to cross-examine. Theophilus retained possession of both documents so Stephen Moore could not copy them for his record and had to summarize. He submitted the summaries to Theophilus's attorneys who agreed they were "correctly stated."

In brief, the June certificate stated that Mrs. Packard had been under treatment in the asylum for three years and had been discharged as incurable. The December letter said that no possible good could result from readmitting her.

With that the prosecution closed.

Dr. McFarland's letter caused Elizabeth's second shock, and a shattering one. In her three years under his supervision, she had transferred to the doctor the affection and admiration she had once had for her husband. She had thought of him as friend and protector, a "manly" man who appreciated her "womanliness," someone with whom she could and did converse almost as an equal and the sort of man she wished she had married instead of Theophilus. His taking his stand alongside her husband was to her nothing short of betrayal.

The defense was willing to go straight to the jury but the prosecution objected so Elizabeth's side opened with more doctors. Theophilus's doctors had been strangers to Elizabeth. Those who testified for her were family friends. Both had found no evidence of insanity before or since her stay in Jacksonville, though one had been preconditioned to find it before he examined her.

Now the defense wanted to read to the jury the controversial Sunday school paper that Abijah Dole had found so revealing. After the prosecution looked at it and admitted it was indeed the paper referred to, Elizabeth's lawyers changed their request: They wanted *Elizabeth* to read it. This the judge allowed. So Elizabeth stood up and in a clear, distinct voice read to the jury and spectators her essay, "How Godliness Is Profitable":

> Have we any reason to expect that a Christian farmer, as a Christian, will be any more successful in his farming operations, than an impenitent sinner— and if not, how is it that godliness is profitable unto all things? Or in other words, does the motive with which one prosecutes his secular business, other things being equal, make any difference in the pecuniary results?
>
> Mrs. Dixon gave it as her opinion, at the time, that the motive did affect the pecuniary results.
>
> Now the practical result to which this conclusion leads, is such as will justify us in our judging Mrs. Dixon's true moral character next fall, by her success in her farming operations this summer.
>
> My opinion differs from hers on this point: and my reasons are here given in writing, since I deem it necessary for me, under the existing state of feeling

toward me, to put into written form all I have to say, in the class, to prevent misrepresentation.

I think we have no intelligent reasons for believing that the motives with which we prosecute our secular business, have any influence in the pecuniary results.

My reasons are common sense reasons, rather than strictly Bible proofs, viz: I regard Man as existing in three distinct departments of being, viz: his physical or animal, his mental or intellectual, his moral or spiritual; and each of these three distinct departments are under the control of laws peculiar to itself; and these different laws do not interchange with, or affect each other's department.

For instance, a very immoral man may be a very healthy, long-lived man; for, notwithstanding he violates the moral department, he may live in conformity to the physical laws of his animal nature, which secure to him his physical health. And, on the other hand, a very moral man may suffer greatly from a diseased body, and be cut off in the midst of his usefulness by an early death, in consequence of having violated the physical laws of his animal constitution. But on the moral plane he is the gainer, and the immoral man is the loser.

So our success in business depends on our conformity to those laws on which success depends—not upon the motives which act only on the moral plane.

On this ground, the Christian farmer has no more reason to expect success in his farming operations than the impenitent sinner. In either case, the foundation for success must depend on the degree of fidelity with which the natural laws are applied, which cause the natural result—not upon the motives of the operator; since these moral acts receive their penalty and reward on an entirely different plane of his being.

Now comes the question, how then is it true that "godliness is profitable unto all things" if godliness is no guarantee to success in business?

I reply, that the profits of godliness cannot mean, simply pecuniary profits, because this would limit the gain of godliness to this world, alone, whereas it is profitable not only for this life, but also for the life to come. Gain and loss, dollars and cents, are not the coins current in the spiritual world.

But happiness and misery are coins which are current in both worlds. Therefore, it appears to me, that happiness is the profit attendant upon godliness, and for this reason, a practically godly person, who lives in conformity to all the various laws of his entire being, may expect to secure to *himself as a natural result, a greater amount of happiness than the ungodly person.*

So that, in this sense, "Godliness is profitable unto all things" to every department of our being.

Manteno, March 22, 1860, E. P. W. Packard

As she sat down, the crowd broke into applause. Again it took the sheriff to restore order.

Then one of the "intermeddlers," Daniel Beedy, took the stand. The Beedys were old friends. When he first heard rumors that Elizabeth was insane he and his wife had gone over to see for themselves. "We talked about religion, politics, and various matters such as a grey-haired old farmer could talk about," he said. "I saw nothing insane about her."

The next witness was a neighbor, Mr. Blessing. Elizabeth often visited the Blessings and after she started attending the Methodist church of which they were members, he saw her every Sunday. When Theophilus started saying publicly that she was insane, Elizabeth appealed to him to help her get a trial under the law. She claimed if either of them were insane, it was her husband. He personally never thought her insane, Mr. Blessing said, but "I did not like to interfere between man and wife." While she was at Jacksonville, the Blessings visited her and took a dentist friend with them. The dentist later told them he did not think her insane either.

Mrs. Blessing followed her husband to the stand. She told about their visit to Jacksonville. Elizabeth had been sewing a dress for Dr. McFarland's wife; she had the run of the large rambling building, including the keys, and she gave them a guided tour. After Elizabeth came home to Manteno, Mrs. Blessing went next door to see her. "She was at work . . . cleaning up the feather beds. They needed cleaning badly." Mrs. Blessing visited often until Theophilus locked Elizabeth in her room. However, "on Saturday before the trial . . . Mr. Packard . . . unlocked the door and let me into her room. . . . She had no fire. We sat there in the cold."

Then came Mrs. Haslett, the friend who had started the trial-ball rolling. She testified that neither before nor after Jacksonville had she noticed any signs of insanity in Elizabeth: "I called to see her a few days after she returned from Jacksonville. She was in the yard cleaning feather beds. I called again in a few days. She was still cleaning house. The house needed cleaning. And when I called again it looked as if the mistress of the house was *home.*"

But there came a day when Mrs. Haslett was turned away by George, the fifth child. (The two older boys had already left home. In fact it was because the oldest, Theophilus III, had turned twenty-one and could legally remove his mother from the asylum that she had been able to come home.) Mrs. Haslett talked to Elizabeth through the nailed-down bedroom window. "[It] was fastened with nails on the inside and two screws passing through the lower part of the upper sash and the upper part of the lower sash from the outside."

For some reason the prosecution had been waiving cross-examination. Now they chose to question Mrs. Haslett. She revealed that she and Elizabeth had discussed ways of freeing Elizabeth. Elizabeth had wondered if filing a bill of complaint would inevitably lead to a divorce; she did not want a divorce. She wanted to be married and protected by a husband. In the absence of protection *by* him, she wanted protection *from* him. Mrs. Haslett thought *that* was crazy. She thought Elizabeth should end the marriage.

The final witness for the defense was attorney Orr's doctor-cum-theologian, Dr. Duncanson, who had degrees in both fields from universities in Scotland. During Dr. Duncanson's diagnostic visit with Elizabeth, they had talked for three hours on subjects political, scientific and religious. It was his considered opinion that she was the most intelligent lady he had talked with in years. Even her position vis à vis the Holy Ghost as female, which had occasioned the prosecution's doctor such distress, followed an old theological doctrine, espoused by Socinus in the late sixteenth century although not widely followed.

"I did not agree with . . . her on many things," he said, "but I do not call people insane because they differ with me. . . . You might with as much propriety call Christ insane . . . or Galileo, or Newton, or Luther, or Robert Fuller, or Morse . . . or Watts. . . . I pronounce her a sane woman and wish we had a nation of such women."

That ended the case for the defense.

At 10 P.M. on Monday, January 18, seven calendar days but only five since Judge Starr first pounded his gavel, the jury, shepherded by the sheriff, retired. At 10:07 P.M. they were back with their verdict: "We, the undersigned, Jurors in the case of Mrs. Elizabeth P. W. Packard, alleged to be insane, having heard the evidence in the case, are satisfied that said Elizabeth P. W. Packard is sane."

The spectators cheered; the ladies waved their handkerchiefs and crowded around Elizabeth in decorous pandemonium with their congratulations, hugs and kisses. When order was finally restored, the defense attorneys moved that their client be discharged. Judge Starr complied: "It is hereby ordered that Mrs. Elizabeth P. W. Packard be relieved of all restraints incompatible with her condition as a sane woman."

So Elizabeth was free—as she had never doubted she would be. After all, didn't Right and Truth always prevail? She was free of the charge of insanity, but she was also free of husband, home, children and money. Theophilus had decamped after mortgaging everything he owned (which included everything his wife owned, too) to Sybil for train fare back to Massachusetts.

While Elizabeth had been returning at the close of each court day to the warmth and contentment of the Orrs' hearth, her husband had been going home to a cold, empty house (his children were staying with the Doles) to sit in solitude and wonder what sins he had committed to merit such grievous punishment. While Elizabeth sat relaxed and confident with her lawyers, he remained silent and suffering, later recollecting in his journal that he, "for five days attended upon the *form* of a trial—but the actual reign of mobocracy, insult, partiality, prejudice, injustice and malignity. Being in danger of violence and death by a mob, I withdrew from the mobocratic court before the last day of the trial, and on Monday, January 18th, took two of my young children and went to South Deerfield, Mass."

The reporters, too, were now free to wrap up their stories, which they did in splendid rhetoric. The *Illinois State Journal* of Springfield gave a staid if inaccurate account:

> Considerable excitement has been caused in Kankakee county by the case of Mrs. E. P. W. Packard, wife of Rev. Theophilus Packard of Manteno in that county . . . Her case was brought up on a writ of habeas corpus, and the jury, without leaving their seats, returned a verdict asserting her sanity. The Kankakee Gazette says that Mr. Packard, against whom feeling has been intense, since the trial has left for parts unknown. Some alleged eccentricities in theological views is said to have been the basis for the charges of insanity against Mrs. Packard.

The *Chicago Post* gave its editorial writer freer rein. After a brief introduction of the principals, it said:

> Mrs. Packard became liberal in her views, in fact avowed Universalist sentiments; and as her husband was unable to answer her arguments, he

thought he could silence her tongue by calling her insane, *and having her incarcerated in the Insane Asylum at Jacksonville, Ill. He finally succeeded in finding one or two orthodox physicians as bigoted as himself, ready to aid him in his nefarious work, and she was confined in the asylum under the charge (?) [sic] of Dr. McFarland, who kept her there three years. She at last succeeded in having a jury trial and was pronounced sane.*

Previous, however, to the termination of the trial, this persecutor of his wife, mortgaged his property, took away his children from their mother, and left her penniless and homeless, without a cent to buy food, or place where to lay her head. And yet he pretended to believe she was insane! If he believed his own story, . . . his heart full of love should have gone out towards the poor, afflicted woman, and he should have bent over her and soothed her, and spent the last penny he had, for her recovery!

The Kankakee Gazette wound up its purple-prosed report with some gratuitous advice: "It is to be hoped Mrs. Packard will make immediate application for a divorce and thereby relieve herself of a repetition of the wrongs and outrages she has suffered by him who for the past four years has only used the marriage relation to persecute and torment her in a merciless and unfeeling manner."

But Elizabeth, who was already on record as not wanting a divorce, had other priorities. First, she too would go back to Massachusetts. Unlike her husband, her trip would not be an escape but a mission to assure her father and her brothers, in person, that she was *not* insane. Next, she would figure out a way of supporting herself. Then she would sue to get back her children. After that, she would embark on what would be her life's work— trying to get the laws changed so no other wives could be committed to asylums solely on their husbands' say-so. And while she was at it, she would bring retribution down upon Dr. McFarland for his betrayal of her love and trust.

But first she allowed herself a moment of weakening under friendly persuasion and *did* file for divorce. Ironically, this application is the only document pertaining to the Packard case to survive the Kankakee courthouse fires and it reflects a move that she never carried to completion.

To the end of her long life Elizabeth remained Mrs. E. P. W. Packard, estranged wife of the equally long-lived Rev. Theophilus Packard, Jr.

2.

The Stage Is Set

Hindsight is always 20/20. It is easy to say today, nearly a century after Elizabeth Packard's life was completed, that she was born with the makings of a crusader. It is also easy to say that she was born too soon—most crusaders are—and that with a different husband she might have championed a different cause.

She chose her crusade out of personal experience and pursued it with such éclat that had it not been such a narrow aspect of the mental health field she might have been coupled with Dorothea Dix in reform literature. Instead, until now, she was known largely because of the hackles she raised—and still sometimes does—in the psychiatric profession.

Elizabeth Parsons Ware Packard was born on December 28, 1816, to the Reverend Samuel Ware, only son of a wealthy farmer, and his wife Lucy Parsons, in the shabby industrial town of Ware, Massachusetts. (The reverend was not a descendant of a founding father; the town's name had evolved from "Weare," the name of the river on whose banks it stood.) Lucy was thirty-seven at the time of Elizabeth's birth, two years older than her husband. By nineteenth-century standards theirs was a late marriage, contracted when the newly ordained Samuel was twenty-nine and his bride thirty-one. (The conventional marriage age for a nineteenth-century woman was twenty-two or twenty-three.) Elizabeth was their fifth-born child but the first to survive. As a result, she was thoroughly adored and indulged, especially by her father.

Her birth certificate read "Betsey," the same name as the firstborn who had died at birth. By the time she was in her teens she had renamed herself Elizabeth, her first stand for selfhood.

Two years after Elizabeth, Lucy had another child who clung to life for two months and then died. Two years after that, young Samuel was born, strong and healthy, and two years later, when Lucy was an aged forty-four, the last of the Ware children, Austin, was born and also survived.

Lucy was highly emotional, subject to spells of tears and prayers for the souls of her family and friends, a not-uncommon form of hysteria among Victorian-era women. During these bouts Elizabeth heard often about the four dead babies who preceded her and the one who died when she was two. The importance of health and strength, a subject just beginning to be publicly discussed, was impressed upon her early.

For four years after Austin's birth life in the Ware household was unremarkable except for the constant "open house" the Reverend Samuel held almost every evening. Since the railroad did not come to western Massachusetts until midcentury, travelers by stage coach or private carriage had to break their trips at the end of each day. In Ware, the lodging of choice for state and county dignitaries, clergy and men of letters was the home of Samuel Ware. The reverend delighted in the stimulating conversation—the exchange of ideas, not all of them theological, even the political, social and philosophical disagreements that he never let turn acrimonious. Elizabeth was allowed to sit quietly in the corner, "a silent listener to my father's guests." She attributed many of her later ideas on marriage, parenthood and a woman's purpose in life to what she had heard during those evenings in her father's parlor.

When Elizabeth was ten, her father's health failed. Having fulfilled his contract with his congregation by serving them for sixteen years (in 1810 the church had "voted to give [him] $590 settlement on condition he should be an ordained minister in the town of Ware 15 years"), he requested permission to resign amid the high praise of his parishioners. The governor of the church agreed. "He was abundantly blessed in his labors," said his successor. During his ministry there were three revivals; 197 new members joined the church, and his flock "voted unanimously that ... the Rev. Samuel Ware [is] an exemplary christian, and an able, judicious and faithful minister of the gospel." In April 1826 the Wares moved to Conway, Massachusetts. In 1828 Samuel's father, aged eighty-two, died and left his only son his fortune.

The Wares continued to move at intervals around Hampshire and Franklin counties. Samuel was an occasional guest preacher but thanks to his father he didn't need to work. He was free to spend his time in learned discourse, exploring new ideas that he might or might not accept, which opened intellectual doors for his eavesdropping daughter.

Much of the metaphysics was beyond her comprehension. Even the words were unfamiliar. But one thing puzzled her, that the God she had been taught to worship and follow as part of living should have decided before she was born whether she was to go to Heaven or Hell. She wondered why it was so important to follow his teachings if her eternal life had already been determined.

Discussions of the various interpretations of the Trinity shocked her. To the Christian young, the concept of the Father, the Son and the Holy Ghost or Holy Spirit, was a given. What was there to discuss? Yet here were her all-wise father and his guests talking about mysterious people like Socinus and Abelard and Grotius who had different ideas of the meaning, even the existence, of the Three and the relationships among them. Elizabeth stored it all away, undigested, in the recesses of her mind where it stayed hidden and forgotten until the frictions of her marriage brought it to the surface.

They stayed in Conway for five years, during which time Samuel's young sister, Susanna, died leaving six children and a husband who promptly disappeared. The abandoned children were distributed among their aunts and uncles. The fifth child, Angelina, came to live with the Wares. Angelina was about Elizabeth's age and Elizabeth referred to her always as "my adopted sister."

After Conway came several years in Amherst. Then the Wares moved to South Deerfield, where Elizabeth, aged twenty-two, got married. The Wares stayed in South Deerfield for six more years until Lucy, then aged sixty-five, contracted a fever and died. The local newspaper gave her a prominent and laudatory obituary, extolling her good deeds in the community, her piety and her concern for the spiritual welfare of family and friends. A few months later Samuel remarried. The new Mrs. Ware had been Olive Boltwood, the widow of one of Amherst's leading citizens. (There is a street in downtown Amherst named Boltwood.) The Wares moved to Shelburne where Elizabeth was now living in the bosom of the Packard family.

In 1853, by which time Elizabeth, Theophilus and their children had gone west, Samuel and Olive returned to South Deerfield where they stayed except for a brief spell in nearby Sunderland (to which Elizabeth returned after her trial), until Samuel died, ill health or no, at the ripe old age of eighty-five.

The early 1800s, when Elizabeth was born, were years of fermenting discontent, though few had yet recognized it.

The grip on the New England mind of the dead hands of Jonathan Edwards and Cotton Mather was beginning to loosen. Thinking people were beginning to question relationships that had been the foundations of early American society—those between man and God, man and government, man and church and man and woman, not necessarily in that order. At first they asked questions only of themselves. Then a few braver ones began to ask out loud. Mary Baker Eddy, five years younger than Elizabeth, stood up in church in her teens to challenge the Calvinist doctrine of the "secret elite" who would be saved by declaring that if she could not be sure she would find her sisters and brothers in Heaven when she got there, she didn't want to go. Margaret Fuller, six years older than Elizabeth, began to demand that women should have the right to their individual opinions though they might differ from those of their fathers or husbands. Such women were looked on as freaks of nature but many a nameless wife and mother was confiding similar "heretical" thoughts to her diary.

The Transcendentalists were emerging upon the literary and philosophical scene around Boston, chief among them Ralph Waldo Emerson and Henry David Thoreau. Their thesis was that man (as in mankind) could "transcend" reason by having faith in himself and his intuition as a guide to thought and behavior.

Abolitionists were attacking the theory that a man, if black, was property. Quakers had been preaching that message for half a century with some success. Massachusetts had declared slavery unconstitutional in the 1780s; Congress outlawed the slave trade in 1808, and by the 1820s all the northern states had abolished the system. A national organization, the American Anti-Slavery Society, was founded in 1833 and within four years, when Elizabeth was just twenty, there were local societies all over the country.

Three years later, Abolition spawned another equally momentous movement, the drive for votes for women. In 1840 there had been an international antislavery conference in London. Henry Stanton, an abolitionist leader from Boston, and James Mott, a Philadelphia Quaker, attended with their wives. The convention ruled that only men could sit as delegates and relegated their wives to the balcony. This did not sit well with two of them. Lucretia Mott and Elizabeth Cady Stanton, sitting on park benches in London, made plans and in 1848 called the first Women's Rights Convention at Seneca Falls, New York.

Avant-garde ideas were in the air.

During the closing years of the eighteenth century, the biggest question was man's relationship to government. An early minister of the Calvinist church at Ware wrote despairingly that "less was thought of Christ's kingdom than of gaining political independence of the country." From his point of view he was right to despair; the disorganizing consequences of the fight for independence altered beyond repair the structure of organized religion.

By the early 1800s ninety percent of the population had no church affiliation at all and those who did joined through choice rather than establishment pressure. The clergy felt threatened and worked harder than ever to save souls and bring them into their congregations. The vitality of the church began to be measured in numbers rather than the strength of commitment. Revivals, which had taken place at intervals throughout the eighteenth century, now became epidemic, sweeping in waves across the country, a replacement for teaching and preaching that had produced converts too slowly.

Revivals varied in form. They might be indoor meetings with sawdust-trail preachers arousing the people to such a pitch of emotional intensity that they would stampede down the aisles in their eagerness to "accept Christ." They might take place in open fields, weather permitting, where space allowed such bizarre behavior as barking, jumping up and down, running in circles, falling in fits and engaging in orgies of self-recrimination. Or they might assume the form of solitary agonized soul-searching—some people withdrew to the woods for their ordeals, others retired to their bedrooms— which would result in the penitents putting the devil behind them. Revivals made the recognition of sinfulness and the desire for forgiveness a public matter between man and his fellow churchgoers and sometimes even between man and the city council, since church and state, despite the Bill of Rights, frequently overlapped. In Massachusetts the separation of church and state was not constitutionally stipulated until 1833.

Elizabeth's mother was "saved" during a late eighteenth-century revival. Her bouts of prayers and tears dated from then. Theophilus "accepted

Christ" during an early nineteenth-century revival and, figuratively, beat his breast in despair over his sinfulness for the rest of his life. Elizabeth would make her own peace with God through ratiocination and disputations with her husband.

Samuel Ware had provided his children (and his niece, Angelina) with the best education New England had to offer.

Some scholars were beginning to point out that the education of children started at their mothers' knees and, in the words of Abigail Adams, "if we mean to have heroes, statesmen and philosophers, we should have learned women." But conventional wisdom still echoed Jean-Jacques Rousseau: Serious education robbed women of their charm and disrupted their contentment; in addition all knowledge except of domestic affairs was unbecoming.

Samuel Ware was ahead of his time. He sent Elizabeth to the Amherst Female Seminary where, while other girls at more traditional schools for females were learning the Three Rs plus such "accomplishments" as embroidery and piano, she studied the classics, algebra and French. Elizabeth was fond of saying that she had the same education as her brothers—she mentioned science, philosophy and literature—and she appreciated it more than they did.

She was intense. Elizabeth pursued her learning fervidly, incorporating classroom vocabulary into her daily language, the little biology taught into her daily regimen, and quotes from poets and philosophers into her conversation. She sought out new ideas and new thoughts with passion. She was fortunate in having a father who believed in educating girls as well as boys and who let her sit in on grown-up talk.

Elizabeth's teachers generally agreed that she was "the best scholar in their school." One wrote that her compositions "abounded in thoughts even if they didn't have drapery." (Elizabeth commented years later that she thought the bones beneath were more important than the drapery that could have covered them.) When Elizabeth was sixteen, she took the conventional next step. She began to teach small children.

In 1835 there occurred a watershed event that would alter a lot of Elizabeth's attitudes and give Theophilus a questionable justification for his actions twenty-five years later. At Christmastime, just after her nineteenth birthday, Elizabeth was struck down with what the doctors called brain fever.

Brain fever, shorthand for an inflammation of the brain, was a popular diagnosis in the nineteenth century with definite manifestations and, in medical minds, a panoply of causes. Its symptoms were listed as violent headaches, inability to tolerate light or noise, redness of the face and eyes, delirium and spasmodic twitching or convulsions that sometimes ended in coma. Some patients were restive and screamed aloud; most showed signs of mental confusion and could be irritable and forgetful. They were all difficult to care for.

By the twentieth century the term virtually disappeared from medical terminology as did many of its symptoms. Today there is no precise equivalent but some forms of meningitis or encephalitis come close. Consequently, it is hard to say what, exactly, Elizabeth suffered from. All we know is that she lay delirious for three weeks.

The usual medical treatment in the nineteenth century was bleedings plus purges and emetics. And these the Amherst doctors tried, but none helped. Finally, Elizabeth's parents decided they had to hospitalize her. They chose the three-year-old Worcester State Hospital, a stark gray-stone building on the outskirts of Worcester. It was New England's first public psychiatric institution, authorized by the state legislature some years before as "a humane alternative for poor lunatics." (The Wares were far from poor and Elizabeth was far from a lunatic, but the hospital was nearer to their home than any of the few private institutions then in existence in New England, and its director was famous.)

Worcester's director, Dr. Samuel N. Woodward, descended from a long line of Yankee physicians, had already made the hospital into a model for the nation. (He was so highly regarded that many a private hospital tried to lure him away with offers of higher pay and fewer patients. But he insisted on staying where he felt he was more needed.)

The hospital required a court order for admission, and to obtain one Samuel had to fill out an appallingly worded form: "Whereas, upon application of [*name and address*] it hath been made to appear to me [*name*], Judge of Probate for said County of [*name*] after a full hearing in the matter, that [*name*] is a Lunatic so furiously mad as to render it manifestly dangerous to the peace and safety of the community that the said [*name*] should continue at large. . . ." The form ended by ordering the sheriff, deputies, constables and the signer of the application to "carry him" (which was scratched out in this case and "her" substituted) "to the State Hospital at Worcester." Samuel filled in and signed the application on January 20, 1836, and on February 6 (without sheriff, deputies or constables), he took her there in his carriage. She was admitted as Case Number 404.

Her admission form read "female; age 19; single; ill for 5 weeks prior to admission; supposed cause, 'mental labor'; occupation, teacher." There was a line to indicate whether the illness was "hereditary or periodic" which was left blank, a rare but not-unheard-of omission that could lead one to question Theophilus's later assertion that his wife's mother had been "hopelessly insane." Worcester authorities today say that such an omission is not of itself significant, but had there been any mention of insanity in the family, it would have been noted "somewhere on the record" which it is not.

Samuel told the doctors he thought Elizabeth's illness resulted from her having "laced too tight" combined with "too much mental effort" at her job.

To today's readers, Samuel's explanation sounds quaint. But a century ago it was not farfetched. Apart from contagion, which early doctors had recognized through observation without yet knowing that bacteria could produce and spread disease, a mixture of emotional and physical factors were cited as causes: famine, fatigue and those events that cause severe shocks to the nervous system such as bad news, the death of someone dear and unrequited love, as well as lack of sleep, prolonged watching at a sick bed and "intense study." So Samuel was not so far off.

Many a fictional hero and heroine in nineteenth-century literature suffered from brain fever—Emma Bovary, Heathcliff's Catherine, Lucy Feverel, Ivan Karamazov and some of Sherlock Holmes's clients. But unlike real life, many of them died. Actually, brain fever was not a fatal disease.

Dr. Woodward was a phrenologist, a believer in the theory that the brain is divided into areas, each responsible for a specific cognitive, behavioral or emotional trait. Any of these areas could be under- or overdeveloped in relation to the others. Like muscles, they could be strengthened by exercise or atrophied by disuse. Insanity was thought to be one result of an imbalance that phrenologists could diagnose by feeling the shape of the skull. "Too much mental effort" as a diagnosis also fit nicely into phrenological thinking.

Elizabeth stayed at Worcester for six weeks. Here she was given opium and myrrh, also remedies of the time, and her progress was steady. According to her record on admission, "She is very pleasant at present, has amenorrhea and considerable excitement of the nervous system."

In the nineteenth century, they were satisfied with weekly reports:

Feb. 12: She tore her clothes some last night, today is some better. Takes the Mg. Sul. mixture and at night tinct opii.*
Feb. 16: Did not sleep too well last night. She is more calm. Her mind is rational on some topics, greatly insane on others. Takes the Mg. Sul. mixture and morphine.

(There was no mention of which topics produced which reactions but in her later life, her deviations from the norm were all theological and, without any documentation, Dr. McFarland would claim he traced one of them to her Worcester stay.)

Feb. 29: Is improving but occasionally disturbed. She wants indulgences and has doubtless had them to a great extent.

One of the things that disturbed her, which the report does not mention, was the fact that her beloved and, she had thought, loving father had put her in the hospital to start with.

The entries in March all indicated steady progress. On March 16 medication was stopped and on March 18 her father took her home. The final entry read:

Left the hospital this morning in a very favorable state, her mind free from insanity, her health restored, and all operations of the system going on favorably, her mind improved rapidly. She is an interesting and intelligent girl.

The effects of Elizabeth's stay at Worcester were more extensive than the record showed. She blamed the early bleeding and medication for the "derangement" that put her in Worcester in the first place and she developed a lasting antipathy toward any kind of medical treatment. She also developed an antipathy toward her father for "very needlessly and unkindly" committing her. Later, during the pressures of her ordeal in Illinois when Samuel seemed to be accepting Theophilus's version, she would write: "I do believe his degeneracy as a man may be distinctly traced back to that *misguided* act when Beezlebub [sic] first triumphed completely over the father in him." Perhaps her craving for a "manly" man to protect her derived from that disillusion with her father.

---

* Magnesium Sulphate mixture and tincture of opium

Nineteenth-century hospital records are bare bones compared to today. There is no mention of conversations between Elizabeth and Dr. Woodward. But since it is known that he made a point of visiting every patient every day, and since the final entry on Elizabeth's chart recorded that she was "an *interesting and intelligent* girl" (italics added), it seems likely that they chatted; given her intellectual curiosity, phrenology was probably discussed. Its concepts would have appealed to her.

Phrenology placed the blame not only for mental illness but also for criminal activity (which it considered mental illness) on environment and offered a concept of human perfectability based on changes in the environment. It thus provided an antidote to the Calvinist credo of man's inherent sinfulness, a tenet with which Elizabeth would in time take violent issue.

Three years after her return to health, Elizabeth married a man fifteen years her senior who had known her since she was ten, before and during her illness. He had also known her mother through many a spell of prayers and tears for those same twelve years.

Theophilus, in his old age, living at the Dole home in Manteno and expecting each day to be his last, wrote out the story of his life to be shown to his children after his death. Seen through the prism of time and the mellowing glow of being cared for by an adoring and uncritical younger sister, the events of his middle years became altered. He found the cause of his problems with Elizabeth to be her early hospitalization at Worcester, and his memory served his needs by informing him that her illness was hereditary. But he did not blame their many moves and his many lost jobs on Elizabeth as Dr. McFarland did. Theophilus blamed them on his health.

Though he may have confused dates and facts and misunderstood the motivations of others, his account—long after the fact—is probably an accurate-enough reflection of his feelings and rationale.

Theophilus Packard, Jr., was the son of the pastor of the Congregational church at Shelburne, Massachusetts, and Mary Tirrill, a deacon's daughter (who was also her husband's first cousin). He was born on February 1, 1802, in the shabby farmhouse that his father had bought three years earlier along with the acreage on which it stood. The year of Theophilus's birth his father built a larger house that the family occupied until 1865 when his mother, aged ninety, died.

The Reverend Packard was known and revered throughout the county as the Sage of Shelburne. A plaque in the entry of his church testified: "The longest single pastorate this church has ever had was held by the Reverend Theophilus Packard, D.D. who was settled here Feb. 20, 1799 and who continued in faithful service for a period of about 55 years. In the early part of his ministry when academies were few, Dr. Packard instructed students and prepared them for college. Thirty-one young men whom he educated in theology became preachers of the gospel."

The elder Packard was a strong believer in education for all. In addition to teaching, he served on the governing board of Williams College and helped to found Amherst and Mount Holyoke colleges. In fact, the decision to establish a college at Amherst was made at a meeting in the front parlor of his home. The Sage of Shelburne was a formidable model to emulate.

Theophilus was the oldest of eight children and, when he met the Wares in 1826, he was an only son. He had had a brother, Isaac, two years younger than he, who had died melodramatically six years earlier, at sixteen.

Statistically Theophilus was a child of the nineteenth century, but he was born into an eighteenth-century family. Despite the father's interest in education, which implied flexibility, the family did not make the transition to nineteenth-century ideas. Both parents were deeply religious and steeped their children in "religious truths" and the beauties of a life in Christ. They targeted Theophilus for the ministry and prayed over him regularly, especially since in his early years he let their exhortations flow over his head. He preferred childhood games and sports. Looking back, Theophilus decided he had been "growing up . . . exposed to everlasting ruin. . . . The principles of selfishness were the principles which reigned in my heart. . . . My mind was carnal, sinful, absolutely and completely depraved."

But life in the Packard household was not all homily and prayer. There were times of great conviviality such as the day each winter when loyal parishioners brought their pastor his yearly supply of wood, a fringe benefit to supplement his annual salary of three hundred dollars.

"I well remember what a joyous day was that," Theophilus wrote, "a warm supper at the close and a hot flip of beer and rum during the hours of the afternoon. That was before Temperance Reform reached Shelburne."

During the winter snows cold sledders also came to the Manse to get warm and sample the flip. In the front parlor "my hospitable excellent mother" served dinner to many a dignitary, among them, by Theophilus's count, four college presidents and that "Dictionary-maker of world-wide reputation, Noah Webster" plus a well-known native of the Sandwich

Islands (Hawaii) who inexplicably had made his way to western Massachusetts.

Theophilus tended to stress his shortcomings rather than his strengths, perhaps thinking that to list his strong points would sound boastful. He remembered being intimidated by crowds and experiencing "the most disagreeable emotions" when anyone engaged him in serious religious discourse. He worried more about his body than his soul, and with some justification. He was illness- and accident-prone.

In the year of his birth dysentery spread through Shelburne, striking down many of the town's one thousand people. Theophilus did not contract it until the epidemic was subsiding. Then he nearly died. A few years later he fell from a high fence and was laid up for months. At five he was nearly kicked in the head by a horse. In his teens he was sitting up with a sick neighbor when the house caught fire. The following year, just for the exercise, he was cutting down a small walnut tree when he accidentally gashed his leg. The wound never healed properly. He developed intestinal problems and a high fever and thought he was going to die. His father later told him he had said, "I have abused all my privileges and now I must die and go to hell." However, when he recovered, his fear of eternal damnation receded. "This one thing . . . I have learned from it," he later wrote, "viz: To be very suspicious of *death-bed* repentence."

A couple of years later, Theophilus went with some classmates to a swimming hole. He could not swim but he wanted to learn, so he ventured in beyond his depth, nearly drowned and had to be rescued by a fellow student. A few years after that, on a trip, some food got stuck in his throat. He stopped at the Medical Institution in Pittsfield where a professor, with the student body watching, "passed a prong down my throat . . . and thus removed the troublesome intruder." Some years later he damaged his inner ear.

All his life Theophilus complained of dyspepsia which he blamed on "too great an indulgence from an affectionate mother, in early years, in regard to diet." He also suffered from what he called catarrhal troubles and whenever he caught a cold he developed complications. When he could not identify an ailment, he would say he was in "ill health" or "weak in body" or that his health "was poor" or "quite variable." Year after year he anticipated an imminent end.

Theophilus did not take to education as early or as eagerly as did his future wife. He attended the local district school without distinction. Until he was twelve, his mother taught him and Isaac the Bible; then their father began to teach them Latin. At fifteen, Theophilus began to think about college and the following year he started to prepare, first at an academy where he took up Greek, then with a private tutor, both away from home.

During this period, Theophilus was exposed to his first revival. He went to some of the meetings but, given his reluctance even to discuss religion, they understandably made him nervous. When he came home for a visit, he found there had been a revival in Shelburne, too, and one of his sisters, his brother Isaac, and some friends had "obtained a hope" and joined the church.

"If sickness and a near prospect of death would not convert me," he wrote, "and the prayers and tears and entreaties of Parents would not do it, then the scenes of a revival occurring around me would not do it."

That fall, in 1819, Theophilus entered Williams, selected because it was nearest to his home and the least expensive. He chose a boardinghouse a mile from the campus so he would be forced to walk at least two miles each day. He made new friends and applied himself diligently to his studies. He decided he wanted to "obtain a vast fund of knowledge and to excel as a scholar."

In September 1820, while Theophilus was home on vacation, Isaac, now sixteen, was stricken with a fever. The Sage of Shelburne was away on a trip and Isaac's mother waited for him to return before calling the doctor. Isaac grew rapidly worse. He asked to have the Bible read to him and expressed great worry about the souls of his family. At the end of a week the doctor gave up. The family, except for the two youngest, gathered at his bedside. Isaac spoke to each individually. When it was Theophilus's turn, Isaac is reported to have asked him, "Are you prepared to meet your Maker?" Theophilus was not. "Then God have mercy on your soul," cried Isaac, and died. "This scene had a powerful indescribable effect on my mind," Theophilus wrote.

The next year there was a crisis of sorts at Williams. Its president, Dr. L. S. Moore, came into conflict with the legislature over the site of the college. He wanted it moved; the legislature did not. Dr. Moore resigned and went to the newly established Amherst. There is a lingering suspicion that he had the offer from Amherst before the dispute. Many of the students decided to leave with him.

Theophilus followed Dr. Moore to Amherst. There he kept careful track of every penny spent on college.

1823

June 24, Board for last fall term —	$ 14.00
June 28, Board for last spring term	$ 14.00
Aug. 27, for four term bills	40.00
Aug. 28, Expenses at Commencement	10.00
Total here	78.00

Expenses in Amherst Collegiate
Institution in 1822 & 1823, total   195.00

Expenses two years at Wms Col $211.20

The total expense of my collegiate education
including clothing, books, travelling expenses

$195.43
211.20
406.63

Theophilus found a vast difference between an old established institution and a newly founded one. At Amherst, there were not enough teachers, the library was small and poorly stocked, the chemistry department lacked apparatus, there were too few lecterns for the lecture hall and the students tended to be insubordinate. But Amherst did have an excellent telescope.

Theophilus became interested in astronomy. He spent many hours observing the heavens. He was especially impressed by Saturn's rings and Jupiter's belt. "Very curious and wonderful were their appearances," he wrote. "They declared most strikingly the greatness, skill and power of the Creator. Yet all this exhibition of the Divine Workmanship did not lead me to fear, love, and obey the Maker of heaven & earth. Truly it may be said, 'An undevout astronomer is mad.'" He also began to read philosophy.

At commencement in August 1822, the senior class was so small that some of the juniors were asked to take part in the exercises. Theophilus gave a speech on "Military Fame" and took part in a dialogue on "Turkish Oppression." But more significant, in light of his future relationship with his wife, was his third endeavor, a colloquy on "A Comparative View of the Native Genius of Males and Females." His partner in this colloquy was his classmate, Edward Dickinson, father of Emily. (Despite the prominence later achieved by the debaters, Amherst College either did not retain or subsequently lost their papers.)

In the spring of 1823 there was a revival at Amherst and some of his classmates were converted, including, to Theophilus's shock, one whom he had always considered "impenitent." This young man discussed his salvation with Theophilus and, although he made no attempt to proselytize, he disturbed Theophilus enough for the latter to develop an acute case of anxiety, more severe than his already acknowledged reactions to religious discourse. "It was not might or power that caused me to tremble," Theophilus wrote, "but a view of my sins and state and prospects."

For a whole week he talked to no one, stayed away from classes, ate little and slept less. He read the Bible and begged God for mercy. He wrote: "My agony of mind, in view of my corrupt nature and sinful heart and actual transgressions, was truly awful. . . . On Thursday, March 28, 1823, at about half-past four in the afternoon in my room . . . a sudden and instantaneous change in my feeling and state of mind took place. All at once, I seemed clearly to realize and most sensibly feel, *that it would be perfectly just for God to let me utterly perish forever.*"

After a week of self-recrimination, lack of food and sleep and the sensory deprivation that isolation can cause, Theophilus was born again. "God appeared to me not only good & merciful, but righteous, just and glorious." His week-long despair was succeeded by "such joy, calm, serenity and sweet peace as I never before experienced. . . . Death, Eternity & judgment were divested of their former terrors, and were pleasing themes of meditation."

Theophilus now found himself, as he wrote in his diary, "willing to prefer the Savior to all worldly good" and, in a remarkably Freudian slip, "to prefer sin to holiness." He scratched out "sin to" and added "to sin" at the end of the sentence, thus squaring the words with his rebirth. He decided on the spot to spend the rest of his life in the service of the Lord "anywhere God might call me to go" and so wrote to his delighted mother.

The Sage of Shelburne recommended Princeton Theological Seminary for his prodigal son, because of the presence on the faculty of Archibald Alexander, D.D., a scholar whom he had met in 1801 at the graduation of Daniel Webster from Dartmouth. (The two divines had ridden back together to Shelburne on horseback, and Dr. Alexander had remained for a few days to preach and convert. When Theophilus, Jr., was born five months later, his parents seriously considered naming him Archibald.)

On November 4, 1824, Theophilus left for Princeton. His father took him by "private conveyance" to Northampton. Then he went by stage to New Haven, from there by boat to New York, then by another boat to New

Brunswick, New Jersey, and finally by stage to Princeton. Theophilus liked his professors and fellow students, most of whom came from the southern and middle Atlantic states and offered him new views and attitudes. He boarded at a house "whose piazza was stained with the blood of soldiers wounded in the Princeton battle during the Revolutionary war." He visited the grave of Jonathan Edwards.

Converts being traditionally more devout and dogmatic than long-time believers, Princeton was an excellent choice for the newly saved Theophilus. It was a stronghold of strict Calvinists, or Old School, who neither could nor would accept the spreading liberalized version of their faith, known as New School, that had developed at Yale. New School, or New Haven, theology offered greater hope of divine grace to a wider segment of the population. It was willing to accept the possibility that other denominations could also validly preach the word of God and it cooperated in interdenominational missionary work. If a soul were to be saved—and the New School did not accept predestination as final—what matter which denomination saved it? To Old School adherents, this was heresy.

The factionalism was tearing the church apart. Under fire, each side dug in, the Old School more intransigently than the New, New School believers recognizing that time was their ally. Old School believers found danger in the most minute deviations, as Theophilus would demonstrate some thirty-five years later.

In 1826 Theophilus was licensed to preach. He filled vacant pulpits and substituted for vacationing preachers as far away as Martha's Vineyard to the east and Vermont to the north. In 1826 he also met Samuel Ware and became a regular visitor at the Ware home in Conway where he discovered a family far different from his—a beautiful, intensely curious young daughter and a mother who rode an emotional roller coaster, unlike his own steady, predictable mother and sisters who were content to leave intellectual decisions to the men of the household.

In 1828 the church at Shelburne invited Theophilus to join his father as colleague pastor. There was a lot of politicking before he was safely installed. A segment of the congregation had turned to Unitarianism (a deplorable faith, he thought) and were waiting for the Sage of Shelburne to die so they could install one of their own as minister. To have a Congregationalist (then interchangeable with Calvinist) assistant preacher waiting in the wings, as it were, was not to the Unitarians' liking.

Prior to 1827 the Congregational Society and the voting population of Shelburne were the same. The town voted in the pastor and the town paid his salary. If the Shelburne Unitarians, who had withdrawn from the Congregational Society, were to cast their votes for the pastor, they might well be able to elect a Unitarian. But in 1827 the Congregational Society reorganized separately from the town. Now only parish members could choose their pastor or colleague pastor. So Theophilus was safely elected. He kept a careful record of who voted for him and against him and who abstained. (The tally was ninety for and twenty-two against, among them some members of the families of his future brothers-in-law, and forty-two who did not vote at all, among them Theophilus himself and his father.)

Theophilus enjoyed preaching but had difficulty writing sermons. He deplored the "low state of religion in the church and the parish"; he lamented that he did not have the "revival spirit" in him and therefore got no help from the Holy Ghost in converting sinners and increasing the membership. He visited graveyards and read gravestones, noting recent additions and commenting on the unexpectedness of death and the possibilities of damnation. He worried that either or both might happen to him even though he had "come to God."

On January 1, 1829, he began to keep a diary, vowing on the first page to keep the following resolutions:

1. Resolved *to sleep only 6 or 8 hours in the 24, when well.*
2. Resolved, *to live rigidly temperate in diet and drink.*
3. Resolved, *to write in this* diary, *at least once a month.*
4. Resolved, *to fast the first day of every month, or monthly.*
5. Resolved, *to improve my time better, in* study or exercise, *or* visiting.
6. Resolved, *to live* nearer *to* God—*and be more prayerful.*

Theophilus's life and thoughts were now almost exclusively devoted to his church, his God and his spiritual future. Yet occasionally the secular world intruded.

In 1832 he helped the town School Committee examine applicants for a teaching post. One of the candidates, Noah S. Wells, had created some disturbances during public religious meetings the previous year so the committee turned him down, in writing. Wells's father was an ardent Unitarian, opposed to the Congregational church in particular and evangelical religion in general. He sued for libel. "The case was tried amid great sectarian prejudice and passion, and in the violation of some of the common usages of courts," wrote Theophilus in much the same language he would use about Elizabeth's trial. The verdict was one cent in damages. "The secret of the whole affair of the prosecution," he concluded, "was a wish to give a hard stab at Orthodoxy."

In February 1833 Theophilus reported that his third sister, Esther, who was teaching in Williamstown, "was taken deranged." On his birthday he and his father had gone to Williamstown to bring her home. He attributed her delirium, in a view considerably more sympathetic than he would show to his wife over her teenage illness, to "deep religious feeling—anxiety for her school," classic symptoms of brain fever. Esther recovered in a month.

In 1835 Theophilus took some time off to visit the Midwest. In Dayton, Ohio, he heard Dr. Lyman Beecher tried (and acquitted) for heresy before a Presbyterian synod. Later, at a boardinghouse in Cincinnati, he met and talked at length with William Henry Harrison, a future president. He crossed the Ohio River to Kentucky "and entered a *slave state* for the first time. Saw one slave."

To know about slavery and to abhor it from afar and to actually see what one has abhorred in theory are very different. Theophilus's first sight of a living, breathing man who was owned by another man, putting flesh onto the bones of the concept, was akin to a revelation. Now the idea of one man owning another, when "man" to him equaled "soul" and all souls belonged to God, became more than a moral outrage. It became an evil that it was his duty as a God-fearing Christian to eradicate. He came home to Massachusetts and began to write and lecture against slavery. "I was intent on doing what I could to aid in creating public sentiment against it. . . . I procured the formation of a County Anti-Slavery Society."

Theophilus never saw the parallel between a cotton planter "owning" the blacks who worked for him and a husband "owning" his wife and children. And if anyone had pointed it out to him he could well have replied in the words of a contemporary pastoral letter of the Massachusetts Congregational clergy: "The power of woman is in her dependence, flowing from the consciousness of that weakness which God has given her for her protection."

In 1836, aged thirty-four, Theophilus first mentioned thinking about marriage. Despite describing himself more than once as having had a carnal and sinful mind, he gave no clue in his journal of recollections or in his diary, then current, of an interest in any woman for any reason. The only love he ever expressed, and that by implication, was filial and brotherly. What his physical and emotional needs were he never said and how he coped with them he never revealed. His decision to get married seems to have been more pragmatic—a minister should have a wife—than romantic. In any event, he did nothing about it except to buy a house and six acres near his parents' home for $850. But he didn't move in.

Three years later, in 1839, as many of his contemporaries were taking second wives to replace their first who had died of too much childbearing, Theophilus finally moved toward taking the big step. He asked his old friend, Samuel Ware, for permission to court Samuel's twenty-two-year-old daughter, Elizabeth.

Elizabeth had attracted many men since she grew up as handsome physically as she was keen mentally. (Among them, according to family legend, was Henry Ward Beecher.) But she had turned them all down. She had once written: "I shall rule myself. And if I ever get a husband (which article I never yet had the good fortune to get but I am sure I shall sometime), I shall rule myself to obey my husband because 'twill be my pleasure to do so." The decision would be hers, not custom's.

What she valued most highly, she said, was a "manly nature" to complement and appreciate her "womanly nature." She never defined what she meant by "manly" but, again in hindsight, it seems to have been a combination of strength on which she could lean *when she wanted to*, respect for her ideas and opinions, a willingness to admit her to equality at the very least in conversation, a position in the community that would bring her reflected glory and a commanding appearance. In other words, part father, part companion, part lover and part hero. Elizabeth had set her sights high.

Her father's longtime friend, fifteen years older than she, pastor at his hometown church, son of the Sage of Shelburne whom she admired enormously, seemed to meet her requirements. He certainly met her father's.

All those years Elizabeth had thought of Theophilus as her father's "ministerial companion," never as a "social companion" for her. His proposal came as a complete surprise. She assumed he was a junior version of his father and would grow into another Sage; in her eyes, he was as stalwart a figure as had ever crossed the Ware threshold. He, apparently, did not think of her as a junior version of her mother.

The courtship was brief. They were married on May 21, 1839, at the Wares' new home in South Deerfield. They took a two-week honeymoon

trip in a new two-seater carriage, a gift from a devoted Shelburne parishioner, to all the towns in Massachusetts where she had lived and where either
of them had relatives. On June 3 they moved into Theophilus's brand-new
three-year-old house.

Theophilus, who after ten years was less diligent in keeping up his diary
and made many a retroactive entry, wrote with a strange sense of priorities:
"1839. This year I entered the married state, & left my father's house, which
had been my pleasant and happy home for 37 years, to live in my own house
nearby."

3.

The Blessings of Marriage

If Theophilus could decide retroactively that his problems with Elizabeth derived from her early hospitalization, Elizabeth could conclude that hers with him came from his parents having been first cousins and "perhaps they shouldn't have married." (And perhaps she was right.)

Lucy thought theirs was the strangest courtship she had ever witnessed, and Elizabeth's description bore that out: "We would sit on opposite sides of the fireplace and eye each other as closely as King and subject. I would kiss him after we were engaged when I met him at the door and that was it. He would not bend his head much to get it, but I would on tip toes reach his cheek and bestow it." They were literal illustrations of the old French proverb: "Il y a l'un qui baise et l'autre qui tend la joue."*

Theophilus was so undemonstrative that Elizabeth wondered if he actually loved her. Her father reassured her; he said Theophilus's diffidence was only because (despite twelve years of familiarity) he did not know her yet. Whatever her doubts, she was sure he had never loved anyone else. Years later she would comment: "He never was a natural boy, son, brother or husband."

Elizabeth enjoyed being married. If Theophilus was not the most ardent or active of lovers, Elizabeth was novice enough not to realize that anything

---

* "There is the one who kisses and the other who extends the cheek."

was lacking. She was now daughter-in-law to the Sage of Shelburne and wife to his colleague pastor. She was a personage in the community with duties to perform and admiration to receive. That was sufficient, at least for the time being. She did not yet recognize, as Alexis de Tocqueville and other visiting Europeans had noted, that "in America the independence of women is irrecoverably lost in the bonds of marriage."

Theophilus took his new wife around Shelburne and introduced her to each of his parishioners. They were delighted with their pastor's bride and relieved that he had finally taken one. Elizabeth took on as her special responsibilities the young people's activities and what was called the "Infant Class" at the Sabbath school, and, according to her husband, "she was very acceptable to the people." There was an occasional theological convention held in Shelburne during which they entertained many of the visiting ministers and Theophilus noted, "my wife performed her part most excellently."

Elizabeth was determined to be as good a wife and homemaker as her mother had been, to make her home the haven that custom demanded for a husband laboring in "a heartless and debasing world" (although the church hardly fit that contemporary description of the business world). According to one woman's magazine, a man would "find his reward in [his wife's] sweet tones and soothing kindness." Wives were to be selfless, to live for others. Elizabeth tried. Theophilus did not relinquish the purse strings but he was as generous as he thought prudent in the money he gave her to manage the household. And since she had churchly duties as well as wifely ones, he hired a young girl to help around the house.

Elizabeth's daily chores were not so different from those with which she had helped her mother. Such labor-saving devices as the sewing machine, the ice box and daily iceman, the washboard and the Mason jar, which made preserving perishable foods easier, were still ten to twenty years away. Elizabeth tended the vegetable garden, fed the hens and gathered the eggs. Even though there were now stores selling farm-grown produce it was still more economical to grow one's own. She also dipped candles, a tiresome and time-consuming job, although if one dipped enough at a time one did not need to do it again for weeks, perhaps even months.

Then there was the big bed to air, fluff and remake, the rooms to dust, the laundry and mending, especially of Theophilus's clothing. The hired girl could do the scrubbing and the dusting but Elizabeth insisted on tending to her husband's wardrobe herself. Every seam must be intact and straight, every button secure. As colleague pastor, her husband must be a role model for Shelburne's young men, in appearance as well as deportment and Christian piety.

Lucy Ware had always set a good table. Her husband's unending stream of guests not only dined adequately, they enjoyed the sight, smell and taste of everything she served. She was especially proud of her puddings. Theophilus did not host much more than afternoon coffee and cakes, but Elizabeth put complete dedication into the backstage preparations.

In time the novelty wore off and Elizabeth was sometimes homesick. Theophilus indulged her. As often as she wanted, she could go home for a visit. He frequently took her himself. Then, four years later, some months after Lucy had died, Samuel and his new wife moved to Shelburne to be near Elizabeth and his first two grandchildren.

Lucy worried about her daughter. She tried to find out, without raising questions in Elizabeth's mind, how Theophilus treated her, what he asked of her and mostly if Elizabeth was happy. Lucy, who obviously knew what life with a physically and intellectually stimulating man could be, hoped her daughter would be as fortunate. She hoped it was not a vain hope.

Elizabeth and Theophilus traveled a lot the first few years. They went to New York and Philadelphia for national "assemblies" of churchmen. Sometimes Theophilus was a guest preacher. They went to Boston for a ministerial meeting and Elizabeth, as Theophilus carefully noted, "had her teeth filled by a Boston dentist. The bill I paid was $30." By midcentury, the railroad reached western Massachusetts which made traveling easier.

During the fifteen years before they moved west, Theophilus listed visits to the Wares in South Deerfield, to some Ware cousins in Conway, to Amherst for a college reunion, and to twenty-two different New England towns and cities to make speeches or to exchange pulpits. "The cost of these journeys was doubtless quite a number of dollars, which was most cheerfully expended. I have probably expended in travelling in my life enough to buy quite a comfortable homestead." His only expressed regret was that he "did not introduce the subject of religion into conversation as much as I ought" in the early years of their marriage. Yet later, when Elizabeth tried to do just that, he refused to discuss it with her.

In March 1842, after nearly three years of marriage, their first child was born. Unlike her mother who, before Elizabeth's birth, seemed to get pregnant again almost as soon as she recovered from childbirth, Elizabeth's pregnancies were remarkably evenly spaced at two- and three-year intervals. Theophilus entered in his journal the day of the week and hour of the day of each birth, plus the prayers he offered up for the souls of the newborn.

Theophilus III, to be known as Toffy, was born on March 17, 1842, a Thursday, in midafternoon. On May 1 he was baptized. His Packard grandparents gave Theophilus two dollars for their new grandson, "to procure some *good* book for his benefit, with the charge that he should in time to come look on their graves and remember them and this their gift to him and prepare to meet them in heaven." (Twenty-five years later Theophilus, who apparently did not buy the book, sent the money, now grown to ten dollars, to his son along with the grandparents' instructions.)

Elizabeth was even more delighted with motherhood. Theophilus, too, enjoyed his new son. "It gave me great pleasure to witness the growth and development of our first born," he wrote. "I often took him with me when I visited schools and when I exchanged in neighboring towns. I felt a deep interest in his becoming a christian, and often did I talk with him about religious things. . . . One day, as I held him on my lap and talked to him about the solemn Judgment of the *Great Day*, he quickly got down and ran away to a retired spot to pray."

Elizabeth had mixed feelings about burdening one so young with such fearsome ideas as salvation and damnation but she was still in awe of the "goodness, piety and sincerity" of her husband. Theophilus still represented God on Earth and who was she to question him? Still, she remembered those evenings in her father's parlor and the convoluted conversations about "saved" and "damned." Her father's friends had questioned. She began to wonder whether her childhood wondering about predestination might have been valid after all. Then she had puzzled over the urgency of following divine guidance when her other-worldly future had already been determined. Now she began to ask herself how a just and loving God could judge a newborn infant, a *tabula rasa* as it were, as saintly or sinful, or, what was even more unlikely, how such a determination could be made while the infant was still within the womb, and how such a divine decree could have been decided upon before the Fall.

Elizabeth was far from alone in raising this question. During the first half of the century American Protestantism was changing. Women were playing a bigger part inside and outside church walls. Religious life was becoming less rigorous; children could be baptized much earlier, and the idea of infant damnation (which Theodore Parker, one of the country's best-known religious thinkers, had said would never have been accepted in the first place had women been in charge) died quietly around 1850.

There were changes in the interpretation of Christ, too. The new Christ was the exemplar of meekness and humility, a human dominated by love, sacrificing himself for others, asking nothing, giving everything and forgiving his enemies to boot. These were also quintessential female traits. Many minor sects began to give God a dual nature, male and female. They also began to say that since the world had failed its first test as the growth of godlessness and vice seemed to indicate, and since the world was male governed, it was male laws and male values that had failed. Thus, the second coming should produce a different and higher set of values, presumably female. (This belief contributed immeasurably to placing woman on a pedestal, which would, in the twentieth century, prompt another type of rebellion.)

For males like Theophilus Packard, Jr., product of an eighteenth-century upbringing, any tampering with the Calvinist God's law and His vengeance toward sinners was virtual heresy. Such ideas did not even bear discussion. Elizabeth, however, having begun to explore the roots of religion, kept right on going. She began to apply to church doctrine that scientific reasoning—what she called "the test of facts"—she had learned at school, and the results were remarkable. The pseudonymous Dr. Brown, multisyllabic witness for the prosecution at her trial in Kankakee, may have been right, at least in part.

Dr. Brown had called Elizabeth "hopelessly insane" because of what in today's world would be better defined as eccentric or unconventional or, in the vernacular, "far out."

Elizabeth, in probing her own attitudes toward the theology of her forebears, arrived at some novel (but not unique) interpretations of the Bible. They bore resemblances to the theories of Abelard, the twelfth-century French cleric and the sixteenth-century theologians Arminius of Holland and Socinus of Italy, though Elizabeth never mentioned having read any of them. Her ideas were probably sparked by long-forgotten, ill-digested and perhaps poorly recalled scraps of discussions about the Trinity (by scholars who were familiar with those theories) that she had overheard in her childhood. She came to the conclusion that there was a sexual component to the Trinity as there was to the Holy Family. Since the Trinity had a spiritual Father and a spiritual Son, it should also have a spiritual

Mother, and it seemed to her only logical that the spiritual Mother must be the sole remaining member of the Trinity, the Holy Ghost. In this view, Mary was the mother of the human Jesus and the Holy Ghost was the Mother of the heavenly Christ. From this concept it had to follow that womankind must be the Holy Spirit's representative on Earth and she, as a woman, as she metaphysically expressed it to Dr. Brown, was "the personification of the Holy Ghost." Later she rephrased the concept: "A spiritual woman is a living temple of the Holy Ghost."

This thesis, that the Holy Ghost was the Mother of Christ, is not so far from the Socinian idea that Christ had been conceived by the Holy Spirit, though Socinus did not specify whether that Spirit embodied the male or female element. Later sects, as mentioned earlier, straddled the issue by giving God a dual nature, male and female.

Largely because of Dr. McFarland's speeches and writings in which he referred to her case, this description of her theory was gradually whittled down to Elizabeth's having written that she herself *was* the Holy Ghost. Had she indeed written that, or even meant it, psychiatrists would be quite right in describing her as "psychotic" or "delusional." But she did not.

Medical dictionaries define *delusion* or *psychosis*, the words sometimes applied to Elizabeth, as "a system of false beliefs." But twentieth-century medicine also recognizes that a system of false beliefs can be limited in subject matter and the part that subject plays in daily life may be only occasional. In all other areas of activity the delusional person may function normally, perhaps even in exemplary fashion, and the particular variant may show up only rarely. Whether the delusion merits institutionalization, outpatient therapy or a "grin-and-bear-it" attitude depends largely on circumstances.

Had Elizabeth, for example, been married to a grain merchant, a tradesman or even a local office holder, say, her departure from religious norms might have gone unnoticed or at most been considered hugely eccentric. But in her case her husband was a preacher, and a Calvinist to boot, and religion was not an "occasional" subject. To Theophilus and at least some of his parishioners, she was a threat to his way of thinking and living, not to mention his way of earning a livelihood, whereas to her friends and neighbors she was just a remarkably brainy and unusual woman.

It never occurred to Theophilus, at a time when wives were not supposed to have original ideas, to discuss theology with her as a way of keeping her from spreading her doctrinal digressions beyond the family parlor. Theophilus's emotional and intellectual rigidity and Old School fear of *any* deviation from orthodoxy could not recognize the questioning of doctrine as worthy of discussion.

While Elizabeth was pregnant with her second child, her mother, then sixty-five, died. Elizabeth spent much of her pregnancy grieving for Lucy. On June 24, 1844, a Monday, in the morning, Isaac Ware, Isaac for Theophilus's dead brother and Ware for Elizabeth's maiden name, was born.

"Like all the human race," wrote his father, "he was born destitute of saving religion and must be born again by the Spirit of the Lord, to reach heaven. . . . My earnest continued prayer to God for him is, that he may see that his heart is wrong by nature, and *must* be changed by grace, to avoid the condemnation of God's law which he has broken." Elizabeth felt that her mourning her "sainted mother" for those seven months had affected Isaac in some way; he seemed to feel a "particular tenderness toward his mother."

Their third son was born on November 29, 1847, also a Monday morning. He was named Samuel for both his maternal grandfather and the first Packard to arrive at Plymouth in 1638 from Wyndham, England. Of this son Theophilus would write: "I fear infidel notions and fatal errors will prove the ruin of his soul. I have talked with him, written to him & prayed for him, but I fear he will perish." (Theophilus's fears proved groundless. Samuel was the only one of his children to follow in his fundamentalist footsteps.)

The following year marked the twentieth anniversary of Theophilus's service as a minister in Shelburne. He took the occasion to note two decades of changes in the community: "In the town 287 deaths have occurred—more than a quarter of the whole population! The deceased were of various ages, from one day to 93 years—some ripe for heaven & some stupid, and some driven away in their unpreparedness. . . . How many times have I gone into the five grave yards of Shelburne with circles of mourning relatives, and seen the dead committed to their long and silent home!" He also found it worth noting that "during this time . . . a Unitarian Society was formed, and afterwards a church, in hostility to evangelical religion, and both have become extinct."

The next year, on February 20, 1849, Shelburne commemorated the fiftieth anniversary of the elder Theophilus's ordination as pastor. The Sage of Shelburne was now eighty and feeble. He asked his son to prepare the

sermon for the occasion and, in the end, Theophilus, Jr., had to deliver it for
him, too.

In 1850, on May 10, the Packards' only daughter was born. They christened her Elizabeth Ware and called her variously Lizzie or Libby. "It is
exceedingly pleasant to have one daughter in a family of children," wrote
Theophilus. "May the Lord . . . make her a rich blessing to our family and to
all with whom she may be associated in life, give her a safe and peaceful
death in the faith of the gospel, and through grace admit her to the
presence of the redeemed in heaven."

Along with her new ideas about theology, Elizabeth was also developing
theories of child rearing. With a nod to Ecclesiastes, she wrote: "Train your
children that there is a time to eat and a time to refrain from eating, and that
time is when they have eaten enough and not before. Don't tell a child he
isn't hungry when he knows you lie in saying he isn't. . . . Let us teach him
things he does not know, but don't let us call in question what he does know."

She established a timetable: chores followed by play, then lessons, dinner,
then more play until bedtime. She kept a record of their academic achieve-
ments and the children kept their own tally of good and bad behavior.
Every three months Elizabeth awarded a prize based on the final score. It
was a complex arrangement. As the child Samuel explained it to a visitor:

> We choose to do a good deal for she gives us a credit mark when we do, for
> extra good behavior; and the good marks cancel out bad marks. . . . Whenever
> ma thinks we try very hard to do right she gives us a good mark . . .
> "disobedience" is the hardest line to cancel, for one "disobedience" counts six
> common "misdemeanors," and it takes a very good mark to cross out some of
> them. She marks us "disobedient" when we do wrong on purpose, or get angry,
> and speak cross to each other. Other misdemeanors are only when we forget,
> and don't mean to do wrong.

Elizabeth drew a distinction between presents and prizes. Presents were
bestowed for good schoolwork—proper punctuation, correct sums, neat
copybooks, and so on—so *each* child could get a present each quarter but
only *one* could get the prize. Thus, the children acquired their toys, pocket
handkerchiefs, hair- and toothbrushes, story books such as *Uncle Tom's Cabin*
and *Robinson Crusoe*, and a subscription to *Youth's Companion*.

"We always like to have mother choose our presents for us," explained
Samuel, "for she always gets something that we can amuse ourselves with.

But pa most always gets something good to eat, and we soon eat it up and then it's all gone. Ma don't approve of our having confectioneries; she says they are not healthful and she don't like to have us get an appetite for such things." (Theophilus was probably remembering his childhood craving for "such things" but forgetting that he blamed them for his ever-present dyspepsia.) Elizabeth was also emphatic about the importance of the children cleaning their teeth after eating and saying "thank you" whether they felt thankful or not.

Samuel had more complaints about Theophilus than his father's choice of presents: "Pa gives me so little on my plate. . . . But I keep asking for more until I get all I want. Pa says I don't want any more but . . . Ma says I may eat all I want at the table but I mustn't eat anything between meals." Samuel also complained that "Pa has such long praying times." The children were supposed to keep their eyes shut and hands folded during prayer. "I can't help peeking out of one eye sometimes before he gets through," Samuel confessed. That would produce a demerit, so Samuel's bad marks mounted "every time Pa prays at home, or in church. I like to have Pa exchange with Mr. Harris of Conway for he prays so short. . . . I could go to eating so much quicker than I could when Pa asked the blessing."

Elizabeth, aware of the children's attitude toward their father, wrote: "I think my children would never have reverenced their father's authority without [my] requiring subjection to it, for the fitful, unstable and arbitrary government he exercised over them was only fitted, naturally, to inspire contempt rather than reverence."

She thought Samuel "was the most interesting, fascinating child I had and the many compliments I received through his demeanor made me almost proud of being the mother of such a cherub boy." He was the only one of her children who could qualify as handsome, she reported, but "he soon outgrew his beauty . . . as for my only daughter, Dr. Chandler of Greenfield said, 'She is a perfect image of Dr. Packard [the Sage] . . .' [but] she is as lovely as she is homely, as sweet as she is coarse, as good and gentle in temper as she is bad in looks." (Despite such an inauspicious start in life, young Libby grew up to be considered a handsome woman.)

On July 18, 1853, the fourth Packard son was born. He was named George Hastings for the husband of Theophilus's youngest sister, Lucy Jane.

It took some time, years to mature and years for the experiences of marriage and motherhood to settle into habit, before Elizabeth admitted to herself that Theophilus was not a junior version of his father and was not about to grow into a senior version. Now his agonizing over a child's soul was almost more than she could tolerate.

Theophilus noted: "When I have talked with [George] about securing the salvation of his soul by faith in Christ the savior, as he has set on my lap, he has often wept, and inquired what he would do to be saved. . . . I have heard him say in his sleep, *'Do you think the Holy Spirit has left striving with me?'*" Elizabeth also heard him talk in his sleep and she wept for George, especially since she, as a representative of the Holy Spirit on Earth, had not left striving with him.

Theophilus was also acknowledging silently that the young, eager, hopeful, admiring girl he had married had grown into a woman with ideas of her own and, unlike his sisters, was not to be influenced against her inclinations by his authority as legal husband and spiritual mentor. In fact there were times when he wondered whether Elizabeth even recognized that he *had* authority. To him this was almost as heretical as questioning Calvin.

Theophilus needed to hold fast to his beliefs. Therein lay his sense of security. This need spread to holding fast to his possessions. He began to pinch pennies. He had always been cost conscious, as his tabulations of his college expenses years before showed. His diary was filled with references to major expenses. Now he was entering such trifling expenditures as postage. There were times when he protested Elizabeth's hospitality to uninvited visitors because they would be eating the food he had provided for his family. Elizabeth, beginning unconsciously to act the martyr as a form of getting even, would scrimp in feeding herself and the children to make up to Theophilus—and make sure he knew it—for the food she had served to guests. Samuel's complaint that "Pa gives me so little on my plate" may have been a sign of things to come. Theophilus also begrudged Elizabeth's giving outgrown baby clothes to one of his impoverished cousins.

Other marital cracks were beginning to show. Elizabeth's cooking had not relieved Theophilus's dyspepsia. Not long after young Isaac's first birthday he went off to Saratoga Springs for two months. He had been there in his bachelor days and felt the waters benefited him. He continued to fret about his digestion, his coughs and colds, and general malaise. In 1850 he was really ill, with typhoid. Other clergymen had to fill in for him for which he paid them five dollars a Sunday. (Once, he reported, "a *colored* man preached for me one half of a Sabbath without any uproar among the people.") It wasn't necessary for him to actually *be* sick. In 1854 he wrote in his journal that he "came near to having the prevailing cholera."

Because he was the only son of the revered Sage of Shelburne, the members of his church would never raise a voice in complaint. But Theophilus's increasing gloom and doom and the severity of the strictures he now rained down on them from the pulpit were becoming counterproductive. Where Elizabeth was on the verge of taking issue with the teachings of Calvin himself, members of the church at Shelburne limited themselves to rumblings of discontent with their pastor. Theophilus was only aware that life was not as pleasing to him as it had been. He thought a change of climate might help.

When George was a few months old, a decision was made to move. "My wife had become urgent for a dismission," Theophilus wrote, "and I thought it best." Elizabeth did not feel the decision to relocate had been hers but she did feel the move could be good for all of them and her father concurred. He thought they could prosper in the Midwest. But he added a word of caution: "See to it that prosperity don't prove your ruin." Ruin would indeed descend upon them, but not from prosperity. Theophilus asked the church for leave to resign. Sadly for sentiment's sake, they let him go. "Had I been more spiritual & faithful as a pastor, more souls might perhaps have been converted & saved," he commented.

Theophilus took an exploratory trip west during the summer of 1854. He was a guest preacher at Lyme, Ohio, where his sister Sybil Dole was now living, then moved on to Princeton, Illinois, where he preached for several Sundays. The Princeton Presbyterian church offered him a permanent post and the Lyme church asked him to serve there for a year.

He came home to consult with friends before he made his decision. But he had already, if unconsciously, chosen. He would go where his sister was. He seemed to consider home an extension of his childhood family, and that meant at least one sister at hand. His wife was still an afterthought, as his diary entry at the close of the honeymoon suggested. But before leaving for the Midwest, he finished a task he had been at for seven months— collecting and preparing materials for a history of the churches and ministers of Franklin County. He had it published in Boston and five hundred copies printed "costing $500," he noted in his diary. "I sold enough to pay the expenses, but received nothing for my time and labor." Then they were ready to move.

*   *   *

The whole venture started off badly. They sold their house and land and many of their household goods at a loss. "My homestead sold at auction for $425, for which I paid in 1836 $850," Theophilus wrote. "Personal property sold for about $150." Elizabeth noted that it had all been "insured for $600 at Mutual Insurance office."

In mid-September 1854, after two days of farewells to family and friends, they "took the cars for Lyme, O."

"The cost of my first journey [in 1835] to Ill. and home," wrote Theophilus, "was $65. The car fare etc. for us seven to Lyme, Ohio was $57. The cost of freight of 6735 pds. of goods to Lyme, O. was $83. When I removed West in 1854, my whole property was $2700."

The Presbyterians of Lyme welcomed the Packards, and the Doles took them in until their furniture arrived. "Had a convenient parsonage, and a pleasant, generous people during the year we were there," Theophilus recalled. His most concrete achievement was to acquire for his congregation a church bell.

In June 1855 Theophilus returned to Shelburne to attend the ordination of his successor, all expenses paid by the Shelburne congregation. He saw his old, sick father for the last time. Three months later, the Sage of Shelburne aged eighty-six, died. During that summer Toffy attended summer school at Oberlin, and at the close of the summer, as his year at Lyme drew to a close, Theophilus went job hunting again.

Elizabeth continued to try to engage her husband in discourse. She asked him, for instance, "If human nature is necessarily of a sinful nature, how could Christ take upon himself human nature and know no sin?" He responded that "a holy God might make a holy human nature for Christ and a sinful nature for the rest of the human family." His answer provoked Elizabeth to wonder, "Can a holy God make sin?" She finally decided He could not.

She was now convinced that the doctrine of total depravity conflicted with "reason, common sense and the Bible." She had also decided that her conscience was a safe guide for her. "Conscience is God's viceregent in the soul," she wrote. "I never dare to do what I conscientiously believe to be wrong; neither will I be deterred from doing what I consciously believe to be right." She also departed from conventional theological wisdom in not holding others to her standard. "I do not feel at liberty to judge any other's conscience than my own. . . . We must all stand or fall for ourselves in judgment. Therefore I claim Freedom of Conscience for all the human family." She was unaware that she had made one exception, her husband. She felt quite free to judge Theophilus's conscience and judgment.

The only questions Theophilus had ever asked were would he or would he not be saved and what could he do to improve his chances. He had never questioned doctrine, he had never questioned society; he had never wondered why things were as they were, except in the instance of slavery, and even then he had never seen a parallel between a man treating another man as property and a husband treating a wife as chattel.

When Elizabeth raised theological questions—all she was asking at first—she frightened him on two fronts. She was questioning his view of God and his heavenly future, but she was also questioning his position as lord and master of his household—his husbandship—and his worldly future. Theophilus had never learned to roll with the punches. He stood staunch and upright and each blow, no matter how slight, landed extra hard. But since his God was Right, Elizabeth had to be Wrong. And Wrong in one who once spent a few weeks in a mental institution indicated a relapse. Theophilus wondered aloud to Sybil and Abijah Dole if they had noticed any signs of insanity in Elizabeth.

Sybil always looked to her big brother for guidance. Elizabeth once tried to discuss New Church theory with her but Sybil could not. "I can't tell whether they are true or not for I dare not trust . . . reason to decide. I want Brother to judge for me." She allowed Brother to judge for her in other areas, too. If Theophilus saw signs of insanity in Elizabeth, then signs there must be.

Elizabeth had always been fond of Sybil. This wary, watchful attitude of Sybil's combined with Theophilus's growing detachment from her was alarming. Elizabeth noticed that some of Theophilus's favorite parishioners were looking askance at her, too. Since Theophilus had signed on at Lyme for only one year, they could move away without causing a disturbance and she could escape those whom he seemed to be turning against her.

"My wife was strenuously opposed to our remaining at Lyme more than the year for which I had engaged," Theophilus noted in his diary. If he knew why he didn't say. Nor did Elizabeth.

Having decided for their various reasons to leave Lyme, Theophilus visited Dubuque and Mount Pleasant, Iowa, and was invited to preach for a year at Mount Pleasant. In October they moved: "Cost of moving for our passage $48. Cost for 13,335 pds. of Freight, apples, goods, etc. $178." Tonnage and price had more than doubled in the one year.

They found society this far west vastly different from that of the East. The church was "small and feeble." Theophilus bought a house for $1,200 and spent another $1,000 building additions to it. Again his major achievement was to acquire a church bell.

They stayed in Mount Pleasant for two years. The schools were good and the children did well. The three older boys learned public speaking and performed to their father's satisfaction. But the pay was poor and "Congregationalism was not in very good order." Also, though Theophilus was unaware of it, a local gentleman named Abner Baker, probably the visitor to Manteno for whom Elizabeth baked the biscuits that figured at her trial, fell in love with her, and in Elizabeth's later writings there is a hint that it may have been more than a platonic love. Love, emotional and physical, was something Elizabeth craved, and both were in short supply at home.

Theophilus noted that "only a meagre support was furnished for the minister," which may have referred to the pay but more likely referred to the attitude of the congregation which did not seem to take to his brand of Calvinism. He blamed Elizabeth for his congregation's dissatisfaction, a diagnosis Dr. McFarland would adopt in discussions of her in later years. "A trouble-maker," he would call her.

"My wife was unfavorably affected by the tone of society, and zealously espoused almost all new notions and wild vagaries that came along," Theophilus wrote. As was becoming more and more the case, Elizabeth saw the situation differently. Far from being the cause of his changing jobs, she was convinced that she had been responsible for his getting and holding them for as long as he did. After all, had not more than one parishioner actually credited her "efficient and self-sacrificing efforts" with keeping Theophilus on in the pulpit?

This could have been true. The man to whom they rented their house when they decided to leave Mount Pleasant said to Theophilus, "Mr. Packard, you are doing more to damn souls than all your preaching does to save them."

By now Elizabeth had given up trying to discuss anything with her husband. She decided he was "lost to reason" and simply did what she believed and her conscience confirmed was right without consulting him first.

A man of more flexibility might have made use of Elizabeth's attempts to discuss with him her developing opinions in order to keep her questioning rather than disputing. He could thus have maintained an amicable relationship. But Old School and flexibility were mutually exclusive. Isaac, at age sixteen, would say of his father in surprisingly adult language: "He is like a man struggling as in a death-grapple to smother and keep out of view the pent-up forces of an immense volcano . . . the raging fires of an accusing conscience have long been consuming all except the exterior man."

Elizabeth wrote with a mixture of pride and unease, "I have marked all my children with my own image, and [Theophilus] knows enough to see that that image . . . incapacitates them to be ministers of the Calvinistic order. We have too much respect for our own identity—our inalienable rights." Thus, she gave her husband a rationalization for his increasing fury at her. She was endangering the salvation of their children. Theirs had clearly become a mismarriage made in heaven.

"I believe," Elizabeth wrote, "that the moment a husband begins to subject his wife, that moment the fundamental law of the marriage union is violated. . . . The husband has taken the first step towards tyranny, and the injured wife has inevitably taken her first step towards losing her natural feelings of reverence toward her husband."

The tenderness she had once felt toward Theophilus was gone. She had been standing up to him on behalf of their children for so long that it had become almost second nature. Standing up for herself was now easy. She continued to act the dutiful wife but the duties were done as a matter of principle, rather than "the impulse of true conjugal love." No longer would she "rule myself to obey my husband because 'twill be my pleasure to do so,'" as she had written in her teens.

Erich Fromm, in his book, *The Heart of Man,* in a handy if sweeping generalization, divided mankind—at least Western mankind—into two personality types, the biophiles and the necrophiles. Necrophiles, he said, are attracted to everything that is not alive; they love to talk about sickness, death, funerals; they dwell in the past, not the future; they cherish the feelings they had (or believed they had) yesterday; memory rather than experience is what counts. They are ardent devotees of law and order. The necrophile can relate to objects (including people) only if he possesses them, and any threat to that possession is a personal threat. He craves certainty, but life cannot be certain; only death is certain.

The biophile, Fromm continued, loves life and the processes of life, is capable of wondering and questioning, and would rather see something new than see the old confirmed. He does not need the security of confirmation. To the biophile all that serves life is good and all that stifles and narrows it is evil. He wants to mold and to influence by love, by reason and by example—never by force. Unlike Freud, who believed that love of life and the death wish (eros and thanatos) exist simultaneously in everyone and that their respective strengths are relatively constant, Fromm considered the love of death, or necrophilia, "the most malignant pathology that exists in man."

He could have been describing Theophilus and Elizabeth. Theophilus was obsessed with death and damnation; he clung to his cherished beliefs and increasingly to his pennies and possessions. He was threatened by deviations from orthodoxy. Elizabeth, by contrast, questioned everything including Calvin's God and Woman as Wife but not as person. She opened her arms to new experiences and new ideas, as Theophilus complained in their Iowa years. She tried to mold and influence her children through "love, reason and example—not force."

Once Elizabeth began to think of herself as a person in her own right, not the possession Theophilus believed her to be, and challenged his God besides, a confrontation was inevitable. The only question was how soon.

In early 1857, a few months before their eighteenth anniversary when Theophilus was fifty-five and Elizabeth was forty, the Packards moved again. The Doles were now settled in Manteno, Illinois, and Theophilus had visited there twice during the previous summer. The Manteno Presbyterian church offered him a contract, renewable each year, and he accepted. He bought a house on ten acres near the church for $2,500. "Our fare was $33; and freight of 8,775 pds. was $77." Their freight had been halved since the last move and the rates had gone down. Though neither he nor Elizabeth realized it, it was the beginning of the end.

Life in Manteno got off to a shaky start. Still, "my brother and sister Dole being very kind to us, it is much more pleasant to live in this place," Theophilus wrote. His sister was there; there were echoes of childhood. There were also drawbacks. He found a "small, feeble" church which had no building of its own and used the Methodist church part of the time, and "a society in a very loose state. . . . Sabbath greatly desecrated."

Elizabeth,, thwarted on so many levels, began to express herself by becoming almost as inflexible as her husband. There was almost a Hegelian phenomenon at work. Theophilus's passionate defense of Calvinism, the *thesis*, prompted Elizabeth to a contentious insistence on her contradictory views, the *antithesis*. But their struggle could never work itself out to the ultimate *synthesis*.

Elizabeth was not a feminist in the suffragist sense of the word. She was not looking for independence or rights and opportunity in political or professional arenas. She would have settled happily for a husband of moral strength (not stubbornness) and sufficient self-confidence to respect her intelligence, respect her opinions even when they differed from his, be influenced by her woman's instincts and at the same time shield and protect her from the hardships of daily life.

In 1858, the year their last child was born, a leading woman's magazine of the day said that "woman's instinct never hesitated in its decision, and is scarcely ever wrong where it has even chances with reason." All Elizabeth wanted was that even chance, though the slimmer her chance of getting it, the more she seemed to be asking for a better-than-even chance.

They had been in Manteno barely six weeks and not yet, in Theophilus's words, "much acquainted with our people," when the pressures apparently piled up. Elizabeth felt an acute need to get away, not just geographically. She needed to travel in time also, to a happier part of her life. She took Libby and George, aged 6½ and 4½, and returned east to Lyons, New York (near Rochester) to visit her cousin and "adopted sister" Angelina, now Mrs. David Field and a mother of four. She stayed for three momentous months.

Some sixty miles east of Lyons, in Cazenovia, New York, lived more cousins, Dr. Fordice Rice and his wife, Laura. They were spiritualists.

Spiritualism was a phenomenon that flourished in mid-nineteenth-century America. Latter-day historians attribute its appeal to such unsettling social conditions as the flood of immigrants fleeing both the revolutions sweeping Europe in the 1840s and the potato famine in Ireland plus the rapidly increasing industrialization and the new scientific and technological marvels. Communion with spirits from the past was one way people could reanchor themselves and accept these apparent scientific miracles. Spiritualism attracted some eminent members of the literati, abolitionists and other reformers. And, indeed, there appeared to be a kinship between spiritualists and reformers, the former voting ten times as often as nonbelievers for such reforms as abolition and temperance. Both these movements apparently bridged the gap between the pre–Civil War tradition of pushing for immediate purification of the nation's morals and the postwar, more relaxed approach of the Darwinian evolution's path toward improvement.

For some unexplained reason the movement began in a rapidly changing section of western New York that also gave birth to the Mormons and the Shakers. Although Spiritualism had a theology of its own, it is best known for seances during which the recently departed sent messages to those present through a medium who utilized table rappings, automatic writing, slate writing and an alteration in her voice.

Spiritualism's most dedicated foe was Calvinism, and many of the religious considered it a hospitalizable aberration. Medium-transmitted messages from "beyond" called into question the sovereignty of God, the depravity of man, predestination and the final judgment. It opened the gates to heterodoxy and challenged the authority of the church—and its spokesmen, the clergy—to be the sole interpreter of Scripture. It was an affront to the Bible. It would also be Elizabeth's first active step away from Calvinism.

Elizabeth spent some time with her spiritualist cousins, and for her benefit they organized a seance. As Elizabeth described it, the guest who was acting as medium began to shiver and said, "A spirit wants to communicate with someone." Laura got a pencil and paper. Then the table tipped toward Elizabeth, alarming her. She began to cry. The medium wrote, then read: "Don't be frightened, my daughter! We are your friends, come to communicate with you and help you." The message was from Elizabeth's mother, who had died fourteen years ago.

"My daughter, you did right to come on this journey," the medium continued. "You needed the rest of body and refreshment of spirit it is to impart. . . . And, my daughter, you need all these helps to fit and prepare you for the great work God in his providence has assigned you. You are living in a very dark, benighted community. You are to become a light to this community and a blessing to many others. But my child, prepare for Persecution! Persecution! Persecution!"

The following Saturday Laura held another seance with a different medium. This time the message came from Lucy Jane Hastings, Elizabeth's favorite among her Packard sisters-in-law. Lucy Jane had died the year before. Said Lucy Jane through the medium: "Brother's mind is in darkness. His spirit gropes in regions where the light cannot enter . . . he has been taken captive by false doctrines . . . he cannot extricate himself. Therefore, pity him! but fear not to expose the errors of his creed for these false doctrines must be overthrown to prepare the way for the teachings of Christ."

Considering Elizabeth's pent-up feelings and her need to unburden herself to any sympathetic ear, the Rices must have heard in some detail the frustrations of her life with Theophilus. It would have been easy for a practicing psychic to pick up whatever clues were necessary to supply Elizabeth with an appropriate message. However it was done, these spirit messages were balm to Elizabeth.

While she was in Cazenovia, Elizabeth also met Gerrit Smith, a local political leader, abolitionist, cousin of Elizabeth Cady Stanton, and a believer in spirit communication. (He was also the father of the young woman who actually first wore the garment popularized by and named after Amelia Bloomer; he was regarded by many husbands and fathers as a dangerous radical because he let his daughter romp as freely and dress as comfortably as a boy.)

As would happen to her frequently in years to come, Elizabeth found solace in the words of a worthy man. After listening to her description of life in the Packard household, Smith was quoted by her as having said, "Mrs. Packard, your husband is a monomaniac on the treatment of a wife." (She probably picked up from Gerrit Smith the word, *monomaniac*, which she would later use to describe herself on Calvinism even as she sought to have it removed from the lexicon of mental disorders.)

If Elizabeth had been looking for corroboration for her feelings toward her husband and his church, she had found it from Gerrit Smith and from the spirit messages delivered to her by her cousin Laura's medium friends.

But to accept these messages, she had to find a place in her theology for Spiritualism. She decided it could be a Biblical doctrine, that the Holy Ghost used spirit friends as agents. However, she would not accept a message from a spirit without subjecting it to reason and she would reject it if it conflicted with "gospel truth" or "scientific truth."

Spiritualism, she concluded, was itself a science with fixed laws that were still beyond man's ability to comprehend. As those laws became more developed and as mankind acquired new scientific knowledge, a practical and intelligent use of those laws would help achieve knowledge of things spiritual. She gave as examples the butterfly and the telegraph: "Had we never seen or known that a caterpillar could be changed into a butterfly we should call it a miracle. The facts occurring daily on the telegraphic wires would have been considered miracles to past generations. . . . I think it will continue to be a fact that supernatural events will continue to take place, because they are laws of our spiritual existence of which we are at present comparatively ignorant."

Theophilus was horrified. "She returned . . . a zealous spiritualist to my great grief and annoyance." What was even worse, she imparted her new theories to the children, the oldest of whom eventually subscribed to them.

But before Theophilus discovered her new belief, they had a passionate reunion. Elizabeth felt they had entered the "happiest two years of married life." She became pregnant with their sixth and last child, a boy, who was born on December 18, 1858, 5½ years after George's birth and ten days before her forty-second birthday.

Isaac, now fourteen, urged his mother, "Name it Arthur or Herbert. Don't name it after other folks as we all are. Give it something new this time." Theophilus presumably agreeing, the baby was christened Arthur Dwight. At least one of Elizabeth's children had adopted her feelings for individuality.

Elizabeth may have remembered the period of her pregnancy and Arthur's infancy as the happiest of her married life. Theophilus had a radically different perception: "This year I passed through such scenes of trial, anguish and agony that I was unfitted to a great degree for service. . . . Eternity alone will fully reveal what I have passed through. . . . God be praised for sustaining me."

4.

The Road to War

Theophilus attributed the "trials, anguish and agony" to Elizabeth's behavior and, indeed, she was not being the traditional helpmate. But there were other reasons, too. He was deeply in debt. Because of the financial panic of 1857 Theophilus had been unable to sell the Mount Pleasant house when he decided to move on. He did rent it, but not for much. The church in Manteno paid him five hundred dollars a year, barely enough for his family of seven—which was about to grow to eight with the birth of Arthur.

After years of listing parsimoniously the most trivial expenses, Theophilus was remarkably silent in the face of a real money pinch as if it were too painful to confront and would have revealed some personal weakness. There was a single reference, sandwiched between real and fancied grievances against his wife, that he had been "obliged to hire money, sometimes at 30 or 40 percent interest. At times I have had the burden of 3,800 dollars of debt on my shoulders at once."

With the inadequate salary and small rental return on the Iowa house, he could meet neither his interest payments nor the annual one hundred dollar installment on his life insurance. Yet, in character, he could not admit, especially to a wife, that there was a problem beyond his ability to solve. Had Elizabeth known the burden he was carrying, there was a chance that, after taking it in and perhaps mentioning that it was God's punishment for his treatment of her, her innate sympathy for creatures in distress, maternal warmth and need to be needed would have temporarily overcome her hostility. And temporarily they might have been able to work in tandem instead of at odds. But she did not know. It seemed as if Theophilus were determined to suffer.

The only bright spot for him during the Manteno years was the birth of Arthur. Theophilus baptized the baby in a public ceremony and admitted thereafter to a particularly "tender" feeling for this last of his children.

For Elizabeth, too, the event was a high mark. No one, not even a hostile husband, could deny her her importance as a nursing mother. Even the law allowed a mother the final word about her baby until it was weaned. For the first time since they had left Massachusetts, Elizabeth felt loved, wanted and cared for. She basked in those "happiest years of marriage," unaware that Theophilus did not share in them.

The church at Manteno seemed to coast along, showing little vitality but little deterioration either, so Theophilus felt it safe to take a holiday. His brother-in-law, Abijah Dole, deacon of the Sunday school, could be trusted to keep matters in hand until his return. Early in 1860 Theophilus, with young George, made his own refreshing pilgrimage back East. He preached at a few of his old pulpits in western Massachusetts, visited Mount Holyoke Seminary which his father, the Sage, had helped found, and "greatly enjoyed my visit with my aged, venerable, pious, beloved mother."

In an uncharacteristic move, before he left for the east, Theophilus provided Abijah with a spur for the latter's languishing Bible class, namely his own wife. Believers in conspiracy theory might credit him with laying a trap for Elizabeth. More likely it was someone else's idea, perhaps Abijah's, that she could enliven the moribund class with her propensity for talk and her provocative ideas, which Theophilus, preoccupied with his debts and his planned trip to see his beloved mother, shortsightedly agreed to. Theophilus probably reasoned that as long as the class discussed *only* the Bible, a subject on which Elizabeth was admittedly knowledgeable, there would be little opening for her to introduce what he considered her heresies. Because he had steadfastly refused to discuss with her her questions and doubts about his God and because she had been keeping her thoughts to herself (around the house), neither he nor Abijah realized how far she had strayed from their truth.

At any rate, once Arthur was weaned, Abijah approached Elizabeth: "Since you, sister Packard, have some views a little different from our own, I wish you would bring them forward and see if we can't get up an interest in our class."

At first Elizabeth could not believe she had heard correctly. Was Theophilus actually conceding that she *did* have the right to her own ideas on religion? Was he ceasing to equate a difference of theological opinion with an unsound mind?

Once she was convinced that the invitation was sincere and that Abijah, presumably with Theophilus's blessing, really thought her ideas would help his class, she took up the challenge with gusto. She went to the class; she spoke up, without fear or favor, not only on the Bible but on Calvinist doctrine, raising questions about such staples of Calvinist orthodoxy as total depravity (her particular bête noire), freedom of will, God's immutability, foreordination and predestination. The class became, in her words, "a lively discussion group." It also grew. From the six pious men who were there the day she joined it, it mushroomed to forty-six men and women, all of whom chimed in if only to question Elizabeth. "I can never recollect a time when my mind grew into a knowledge of religious truths faster than under the influence of these free and animated discussions," she wrote. Debate and discussion flourished; Abijah's wildest hopes came true. And before anyone realized what was happening heterodoxy had emerged.

Unlike occupants of pulpits, Elizabeth had a way of illustrating her points with down-to-earth examples that even the least learned among the Manteno farmers and housewives could grasp. For example, Elizabeth described the Bible as such a unique book that one need not be learned or talented to interpret it correctly any more than one needed experience and education to judge correctly the needs of nature. Her illustration of her point: An adult might choose strong drink to slake his thirst where a child would prefer cold water. But that need not lead one to conclude that strong drink is the best thirst quencher just because a mature man chose it. The man might well have "perverted his natural appetite" so that his choice was less in accord with nature than were the instincts of a child.

Some of her other ideas, even without homely illustrations, were expressed so succinctly that they frightened the pillars of the established order. On freedom of will: "Candor and honesty, it seems to me, compel us to admit that there is a mixture of truth and error in the creeds of all denominations ... not even excepting the creed of the Presbyterian church. ... Let us throw off the blinding influence of prejudice and sectarian zeal and [become] simple, sincere, charitable, honest seekers after the real, simple, naked truth." On total depravity: "God's work as he made it was perfect. It needed no regeneration to make it right. Regeneration was necessary only when we had become unnatural or different from what God had made us." On predestination: "Can God's *intentions* be thwarted? If they cannot . . . and God intended all mankind for happiness, will not all men be saved? If God intended it, and does not accomplish it, is He omnipotent?"

There emerged among the deacons a legitimate fear of potential discord and a threat to orthodoxy, not to mention the effect on their wives of the pastor's wife openly challenging her husband. That way lay heresy and hellfire.

When Theophilus came back from his visit east, he found his congregation in turmoil and his wife at the core of it. The church had become her arena of choice. A century later a therapist, had one been consulted, might have dug deeper and found that Elizabeth's fight was not so much against her husband's Calvinism as against the inability of women to fulfill themselves outside of the domestic scene. She was convinced she had the right to express herself. She wanted the freedom to do so. Her husband did not recognize the right and would not grant the freedom. It was all Calvin's fault.

Elizabeth, wherever they lived, had always gathered a circle of admiring men and women around her. Her charm and bearing, her learning, the ease with which she held forth on subjects literary and scientific as well as Biblical, inevitably made her a leader. Few around her, especially in the still-raw pioneer midwestern states, were as well educated or as articulate as she. Though they might disagree in their hearts with some of her ideas, they were hard put to marshal evidence to refute her. As a result, she had ardent partisans, ardent antagonists and quite a few acquaintances who were thoroughly confused.

Theophilus listened to his zealous parishioners first. Agreeing with the panicky elders, he replaced the easygoing Abijah as head of the Sunday school and its Bible class with a hard-liner, Deacon Smith, who decided that instead of tackling the problem head on by arbitrarily ending the popular free discussion, he would pursue a subtler long-range tactic. He would "put down Mrs. Packard."

"I regarded the principle of religious toleration as the vital principle on which our government was based," wrote Elizabeth, "and I, in my ignorance, supposed this right was protected to all American citizens, even to the wives of clergymen."

The change in the leadership of the school and its Bible class meant little to her at first. She continued to speak out. But after a few of Deacon Smith's put-downs, she caught on to what was happening. She also realized that her opponents in the congregation (with no opposition from her husband) could use her unorthodox views to revive the old innuendos about her sanity. The new situation became a challenge. Elizabeth had been asked to join the Bible class for a purpose; her usually obstructionist husband, for whatever reason, had concurred; the class, as Deacon Dole hoped, had come alive. This was not the time to sound retreat; it was a time to maneuver and protect her flank.

She began to write out her ideas for class discussion and what she planned to say on each. She first read them to Theophilus for his approval or, at least, the absence of disapproval. She hoped thus to forestall misquoting. She noted that some of her suggestions were rejected but, except for one—a paper entitled "Spiritual Gifts" which was "refused a hearing lest it be found to favor spiritualism"—she did not identify which were accepted and which were turned down.

Among the questions she proposed for class discussion were the following:

- *Does truth ever change?*
- *Can people have a difference of opinion on the same subject and yet all be correct?*
- *What causes diversity of belief?*
- *How ought we to treat those whom we think teach error? Should we concede them the same right of opinion as we do the advocates of truth?*
- *Are we to expect new moral truths to be developed in the present day, since the canon of scripture is complete?*
- *Does progress in knowledge necessarily imply a change of views?*
- *Does the motive with which we prosecute our secular business have anything to do with the pecuniary result? If not, how is godliness profitable?* (This last suggestion we know was not rejected since Elizabeth's paper on it was offered as evidence for the defense in her trial four years later.)

Elizabeth would recognize that her memory sometimes played her false on dates and times. She was more concerned with the sweep of events than with the details along the way. In later and calmer years she reconstructed the chronology of her last days as housewife and homemaker. If the incidents were occasionally out of sequence, the overall picture, as matched with Theophilus's later recollections, was in essence true.

The beginning of the end started when Deacon Smith finally gave up on his put-down tactic. The deacon went to see Theophilus and they conferred for two hours. After he left Theophilus asked Elizabeth to quit the Bible class.

As she recalled it, he started out using husbandly affection. It was a method that had worked in the past—"a few kind words and a little coaxing would always set her right," he had written. But that had been years before and except for her return from her visit east, husbandly affection had not been much in evidence for some time.

"I went into his extended arms and sat upon his lap and encircled his neck with my arms," Elizabeth reported, delighted at what seemed to be both a reconciliation and a concession. Then he suggested mildly that she give up the Bible-class discussions. "Deacon Smith thinks you had better and so do some others, and I think you better, too."

Elizabeth was agreeable, "if I can do so honorably, but I do not like to yield . . . to the dictation of bigotry and intolerance." She was perfectly willing to tell the class that since her husband and Deacon Smith had asked her to withdraw she would do so in the interests of peace. But Theophilus did not want that; he wanted her to say it was her idea to quit.

"But, dear, it is not my choice!" said Elizabeth.

"But you can make it so, under the circumstances."

"I can't be telling a lie."

Theophilus insisted that her withdrawal from the class should appear to be voluntary. Elizabeth, belatedly recognizing manipulation, made a strenuous plea for husbandly behavior as she saw it: "Oh, husband, how can you yield to such an evil influence? . . . Do be a man and go to the class, in defiance of Deacon Smith, and say . . . 'My wife has just as good a right to her opinions as you have to yours, and I shall protect her in that right.' . . . Then you will be . . . a protector of your wife—and you will deserve honor—but if you become my persecutor . . . you will deserve dishonor. . . . Don't fall into this fatal snare."

But Theophilus did fall—back onto his old standby: Elizabeth was exhibiting signs of mental illness. "Never before had [she] persistently refused my will or wishes . . . she seems strangely determined to have her own way, and it must be that she is insane."

Elizabeth reacted strongly to the accusation. The more vehemently she objected to being called insane, the more he cited her vehemence as proof of the charge. It was a Catch-22 situation.

About this time the smaller children fell ill with fevers. Libby was the sickest of all. She was diagnosed as having brain fever. In the twenty-four years since Elizabeth had been similarly diagnosed little new had been learned about it. Elizabeth remembered what had happened to her—the bleedings, the drugs, the physical restraint and especially the hospitalization—and was determined to protect Libby from anything similar. She sat up with her daughter night after night, fearing the child would die, sometimes so distraught by morning that she did not have the emotional strength to change out of her nightclothes. For the usually punctiliously groomed Elizabeth this was radical behavior that Abijah would later cite as one indication of derangement.

Theophilus and Sybil worried aloud about Elizabeth's state of mind and permitted their worries to seep out into the congregation. At one point Theophilus invited a couple of doctors to drop in, presumably for social visits. He managed to steer the conversation toward the church, and Elizabeth, exhausted though she was, reacted true to form: She took grave exception to the teachings of Calvin, especially the doctrine of total depravity and Theophilus's espousal of it. (On at least one occasion she admitted to being tempted to say aloud, "Well, Mr. Packard, I do not know but that you are what you claim to be, a totally depraved man." But she bit her tongue, knowing full well that Theophilus would take the statement not as a conversion to his belief but as more grist for his mill.) The doctors thought she was a bit intense on the subject but hardly insane. Later one of them would use Gerrit Smith's word, "monomaniac," thus opening a whole new area of disputation.

The question of quitting the Bible class had become moot. The children's illnesses gave Elizabeth the out she needed. She could withdraw without lying about her reasons for so doing and incidentally spare Theophilus the blame. (The class rapidly slumped to its original enfeebled state.)

Theophilus claimed that some of his congregation suggested that he hospitalize Elizabeth and, indeed, some might have. There were those who agreed with their pastor that no one—least of all the pastor's wife—could rationally challenge church dogma. Theophilus had built up a case against her that convinced him. Convinced, he was able to argue it more compellingly than ever and managed to bring around to his way of thinking his sisters and their husbands and Elizabeth's father and brothers. All except Sybil accepted his word by mail; Sybil alone could use her eyes. But she didn't. Sybil was used to taking her big brother's word; she saw what she expected to see and what she expected to see was what he told her was there to be seen. The only one he failed to convince was Elizabeth's cousin and "adopted sister" Angelina, though Angelina's husband, David Field, did waver.

Theophilus recalled that he "tried in vain to have some of [Elizabeth's] father's family take her for a while." He wrote the Reverend Samuel Ware and young Samuel and Austin "giving them a true account of her case." He also pressed Elizabeth to write them, presumably confessing to insanity or asking for refuge. "She declined to write and they declined to take her."

Elizabeth remembered it differently. She said her husband had suggested she visit her brother Samuel at Batavia, New York. She agreed provided she could take Arthur and Libby with her. She asked for ten dollars of her patrimony for spending money but Theophilus refused. He said he could not trust her with money. If she could not be trusted with money, she reasoned, how could she be trusted with children? She decided not to go. But Theophilus did not want her at home. He gave her an ultimatum: Batavia without money or the state insane asylum at Jacksonville.

At first Elizabeth did not believe he meant it. She thought Theophilus was just flexing his husbandly muscles again. However, for reassurance, she consulted a neighbor, Mr. Comstock, a lawyer. Mr. Comstock guaranteed that she could not be hospitalized without a trial and that no jury would commit her. Feeling safe, she resumed jousting with Theophilus, each of his rebuttals reinforcing her convictions.

Elizabeth was thinking along the same lines as the women at the second Women's Rights Convention of 1851 at Worcester, Massachusetts, though there is no written evidence that she even knew of the gathering. Elizabeth, in fact, showed little awareness of the women's movements that were going on around her, something that some latter-day psychiatrists consider a symptom of mental illness. However, these psychiatrists are not taking into account the fact that women were not yet identifying themselves by gender or finding common ground for their individual causes. Such organizing as they did centered on single issues—more educational opportunities for women, control of their own money, the vote, abolition and temperance. Few challenged the basic structure of society; what they sought was equity, not equality. Equality would be the cause for the next century.

Today's psychiatrists are right, however, in noting that Elizabeth was not a team player (although that does not necessarily indicate insanity). She seemed more comfortable working with and through sympathetic men, and she had little trouble finding them. She spoke up for women as women only in contending that the Declaration of Independence, in stating that all men were created equal meant *mankind* and that the "inalienable rights" of "life, liberty and the pursuit of happiness" with which they were endowed by their Creator meant *all*, not just *half* the human race. Elizabeth's war between the sexes remained a highly personal and individual one, at first only against her husband and later against her doctor.

Did she not have a right to her own opinion, she asked Theophilus? Yes, she did. And did not the U.S. Constitution protect her as a citizen in exercising that right? As a married woman, Theophilus assured her, she was *not* a citizen; she was not even a person. *He* was her only protection under the law. But she *was*, was she not, entitled to a trial before she could be committed?

Unfortunately, she had been misinformed. Mr. Comstock had not read the fine points of the Illinois commitment law enacted nine years earlier. Theophilus had. The law (subsequently declared unconstitutional) said flatly: "*Married women* and infants who, in the judgment of the medical superintendent of the state asylum at Jacksonville, are evidently insane or *distracted*, may be entered or detained in the hospital at the request of the husband of the woman or the guardian of the infant, *without* the evidence of insanity required in other cases." [Italics added.]

In the eyes of the law, Theophilus assured her, the decision was his, neither a judge's nor a jury's. Elizabeth still found it hard to believe he was serious, but the possibility began to drive all other thoughts from her head and monopolized her conversation.

Elizabeth's troubles were now coming in battalions. Her secret admirer, Abner Baker of Mount Pleasant, had been writing to her at infrequent intervals since the Packards had moved to Manteno. Now Theophilus found secreted in the folds of a tablecloth Baker's correspondence, which Elizabeth herself described as love letters. (To Theophilus they were almost worse than love letters; they discussed Swedenborgianism, which, to him, was more perfidious than infidelity.)

Emanuel Swedenborg, Swedish scientist, philosopher and mystic of the eighteenth century, founded the Church of the New Jerusalem in response, he claimed, to a revelation from God for a new age of truth and reason in religion. Many divines found him as much a threat to orthodoxy as Spiritualism. In fact, many thought he was himself a medium although he reversed the medium's role: In his church men were admitted into the spiritual world. The Spiritualists believed that spirits of the deceased visited the material world.

Though he had no indication that Elizabeth had answered Baker's letters, Theophilus assumed the worst. His wife was disloyal not only to his church, but to him. He extended his fury from Baker to all Mount Pleasant and demanded that Toffy, now aged eighteen, and working there as a postal clerk, return at once to Manteno. Elizabeth insisted that an eighteen year old was able and entitled to make his own decisions. Thus one more log was added to the fires of friction in the Packard household.

About this time Elizabeth extended her antipathy toward her husband and Calvin to the entire Presbyterian church. She stood up one Sunday and requested a letter of release from the church so she could join the Methodists. From then on she went to Sunday services at the Methodist church with her friends and neighbors, the Blessings.

Her new fellow churchmen and women, if they thought Elizabeth's behavior bizarre, were discreetly silent in public. Perhaps the Blessings had explained away this extraordinary change of faith. Certainly her neighbors, who were able to see at close range her domestic situation and Theophilus's practice of his religion at home, were all on her side. But in the church where Theophilus had been pastor for less than two years and had not yet shown much of his dark side, parishioners were vociferous in their disapproval. With few exceptions, they saw Elizabeth's act either as behavior unbecoming in a woman and a wife, or disloyalty to their spiritual leader, or even heresy. For Theophilus, as events would show, it was the last straw.

Elizabeth's first realization of the danger she was in came when her husband, as she put it, "left my bed without giving me any reason other than 'I think it best.'" Over the years Elizabeth had learned to accept Theophilus's passivity in bed, but she was used to his physical presence. There was something shocking and frightening about his removing himself from the room itself. She felt that it was *she* who was being removed from her familiar surroundings. A few days later he took from her charge the family medicine box, again saying only, "I think it best."

Then he became "unaccountably considerate of [her] health" and insisted on hiring a mother's helper (the French maid), something she had been asking for in vain for a long time. But just as the girl was trained to Elizabeth's satisfaction, he just as unaccountably dismissed her. Later she was told by a neighbor that the girl had said publicly, "I can't see what Mr. Packard means by calling his wife insane for she is the kindest best woman I ever saw."

Next Theophilus brought home the daughter of one of his parishioners, Sarah Rumsey. He told Elizabeth he had invited Sarah for dinner and, the French maid having just departed, she "offered" to stay on and help out. Elizabeth promptly showed Sarah to the kitchen, to Sarah's long-lasting indignation.

Now Theophilus began to accuse Elizabeth of neglecting her family, failing to cook meals or attend to the children's clothes. Elizabeth had thought Sarah was taking over those chores. The plot against her was obviously moving along as planned. For the first time since her father had taken her to the hospital at Worcester she knew fear to the point of paranoia. She reacted typically by taking her case to anyone who would listen.

Theophilus must have had qualms about what he was about to do even though it was within state law and even though he had already managed to get approval from his sisters and Elizabeth's father and brothers. He felt the need for public sanction and acted accordingly.

"Since [Elizabeth] had gone out among the French Catholics, Universalists and such like people in the town," he explained, and made "horrible representations" of his treatment of her, arousing a "rabid excitement" against him, he decided to invite to a meeting at his home some twenty townspeople from all the churches in town to discuss and judge Elizabeth's state of mind and his treatment of her. This was a remarkable act—one that raises questions about Theophilus's own state of mind.

Theophilus told Elizabeth of his plan. In fact, he gave her a formal written notice and offered to let her choose who should be invited. Elizabeth flatly refused to have anything to do with such proceedings. So Theophilus drew up his own guest list: "minister, postmaster, depot master, doctors, merchants, Justice of the Peace, males and females."

For whatever motives, most of those he invited came. They spent an entire afternoon discussing Elizabeth. The subject of their discussion was not there. Not only did she refuse to meet any of them, she left the house, an action that Theophilus took as a further indication of her unsound mind.

According to Theophilus, none of his panel of twenty said anything to show they thought Elizabeth was being mistreated and all but one, according to their host, agreed with him that she was "deranged." The holdout was a Dr. Simington—a "quack," Theophilus called him—who declined to cast a vote because he had not been consulted in her case.

Theophilus found nothing out of the way in convening such a gathering. Illinois law had made him the arbiter of his wife's mental state; God's law made him the guardian of her soul. He was committing her to save her soul, to keep her from endangering the souls of their children, and to shield his creed from her criticism. (He also said in passing that she had become impossible for him to live with. Around town, she was saying the same about him.)

During the week that followed, on three occasions Samuel, now aged thirteen, arrived at Elizabeth's bedside at midnight in tears. "They have been telling lies about you and I can't sleep 'til you forgive me," he sobbed. Why had he believed what he now called lies? Elizabeth asked. "Father paid me," Samuel replied. However, Samuel must have begun to balk because on his third midnight visit he reported that Theophilus had upped the amount of the bribe.

Isaac, now sixteen, was the most worried of all the children. (Toffy, at Mount Pleasant, didn't know what was happening.) Isaac went around town trying to enlist support for Elizabeth among friends and neighbors.

Elizabeth worried equally about Isaac. He was spitting blood. (The problem turned out to be transient; it cleared up and did not recur.) Theophilus had forbidden Isaac to speak to his mother so, in obedience, as he had been taught by his mother since childhood, he refused to answer her queries about his health, resorting to a head shake or a finger to his lips until Libby, aged ten, began to act as intermediary. Theophilus had not forbidden Isaac to *write*, so he sent a letter to Toffy. Toffy wrote back promising to free Elizabeth should she indeed be committed.

By now it was spring and the children were finally recovered from their fevers. Sybil offered to take Arthur for a while so Elizabeth could get a few good nights' sleep after the strain of sitting up by sick beds for so long. Elizabeth missed him dreadfully. On Saturday, June 16, 1860, she went to see him, hoping to bring him home with her. Sybil would not let him go "yet."

On Sunday, June 17, Sarah Rumsey's parents invited Libby to visit their youngest for a day or two. It would do her good, they said. Thus, seven-year-old George was the only little one left at home.

That night Elizabeth was more uneasy than ever. She could not sleep. Around midnight she got up and went looking for Theophilus. She had tried appealing to his manhood and his marriage vows; she had tried intransigence; she had tried threats and standing on her rights. Now she wanted to try sweet reasonableness. She found her husband surreptitiously searching through her trunks and boxes looking for Lord knew what. In a panic, she crept away.

The next morning, Monday, June 18, she rose early and even before dressing sought out Isaac. He might have been forbidden to speak to her; no one could prevent her from talking to him. She asked him to fetch Arthur and Libby home and to save her Bible-class papers which she had secreted behind a drawer in her wardrobe. She was counting on them to provide a defense when Theophilus cited her behavior in the class as evidence of her insanity. Isaac departed on his mission and George went out to the garden to pick a saucer of ripe strawberries for her breakfast. Theophilus then took George off "to the store to buy some sugarplums." Elizabeth, still in her nightclothes, was alone in the house.

Suddenly the front door opened. In came Theophilus (who had sent George on alone for the sugarplums), two physicians who knew Elizabeth as a member of the Bible class but not as a patient, and the sheriff of Kankakee County. As they approached her bedroom, Elizabeth hastily locked the door to give herself time to dress. But the men broke in. As these intruders invaded her bedroom she scrambled into the bed and pulled up the sheets as protection. The doctors positioned themselves at either side of the bed and each seized a wrist to take her pulse. Her heart—and pulse—pounded in fright. "Insane," the doctors each pronounced solemnly. Theophilus had thus satisfied the "forms of the law." He was now ready to take her off to the asylum at Jacksonville.

Elizabeth wanted to dress in private, partly because of her sense of dignity and partly so she could retrieve her Bible-class papers unobserved, but Theophilus refused. He sent Sarah Rumsey to her to act as lady's maid and spy. Sarah was surprised at the calm Elizabeth manifested; she, Sarah, would have been terrified and hysterical and she had expected the same reaction from Elizabeth, but Elizabeth could be self-contained when she felt the occasion demanded it as this one certainly did. She could not give any credence to the diagnosis, "insane." She asked for solitude to pray. That request Theophilus also denied; she could pray only if she left the door open. In retrospect Elizabeth remembered having prayed an unlikely prayer—that Theophilus be forgiven for what he was about to do.

*   *   *

The story of what was happening at the parsonage spread rapidly through the town and crowds began to gather at the depot. Some came out of morbid curiosity and a desire not to miss any excitement; others were going to try to fulfill their promises to Isaac.

Presently the wagon from the parsonage arrived with Theophilus, a couple of church deacons, and Sheriff Burgess, the men surrounding Elizabeth. The doctors, having spoken their lines, had retired from the stage. Elizabeth was now dressed in her traveling best, her hair groomed, her hat firmly in place. She carried only a small suitcase. Theophilus, it developed, had permitted her to bring along only the bare bones of her wardrobe.

Elizabeth refused to move from the wagon. She would fight fire with fire. She would certainly not cooperate in her own imprisonment. If her husband intended to put her away he must literally do it himself. So the men lifted her bodily from the wagon and carried her into the Ladies' Parlor at the depot.

Theophilus begged her to walk to the train. She refused. He brought in Mr. Comstock, the lawyer to whom she had turned for advice some weeks earlier. He urged her to cooperate since she could not stop Theophilus. She refused. The crowd outside was growing restive. Deacon Dole assured them all that everything was legal, the sheriff had the proper papers for transporting Elizabeth. He warned them that if they tried to prevent Theophilus from exercising his husbandly right of taking his wife to the asylum, they would be liable to arrest.

But Deacon Dole was wrong although no one in the crowd discovered it in time. The sheriff had no papers. He had gone to the probate court to get the necessary documents and had been refused because the proof of insanity he offered did not satisfy the court. He had decided to take action without them.

The train, whistle blowing, pulled up to the platform. Elizabeth still refused to move. A couple of the deacons attempted clumsily to lift her from the bench and carry her out to the platform. Her skirt was being pulled awry, her hat dislodged, her dignity threatened. Finally Elizabeth suggested they form a seat of hands by clasping each others' wrists. Thus, there would be no bodily harm to her and her demeanor, she hoped, would put Theophilus to shame.

By this time Isaac and George were returning from their errands, Isaac without the two young children and George with the sugarplums. A man from the station crowd broke the news to them. Both boys burst into tears, crying out, "We have no mother! We have no mother!" Isaac reproached everyone within the sound of his voice for not keeping their promises to help Elizabeth, then headed straight for home to find the Bible class papers. They were gone; Theophilus had beat him to the hiding place. George ran on to the station.

Elizabeth, from her perch on the deacons' seat of hands, looked down at the sea of faces, some stony, some curious, but most helpless and stricken. It was obvious that her friends and admirers were many. Mrs. Blessing was weeping, wringing her hands and crying, "Is there no man in this crowd to protect this woman? Will you let this mother be torn from her children?" Samuel stood in the crowd sobbing, "Oh, Mother! Mother! Forgive me!" At last Elizabeth, dry-eyed 'til now, began to cry, but not for herself. She wept for her children and what might happen to them without her.

George reached the platform as Theophilus and the sheriff were finally getting Elizabeth aboard and climbing into the train after her. As the train pulled out, he ran after it crying, "I will not go home without my mamma! I will get my dear mamma out of prison!" Friends had to pursue him and hold him back to keep him from running on and on down the track.

The aftermath was traumatic. Libby wept for days, damaging her fragile health and her reason. Isaac came down with a fever that produced delirium. Arthur, fortunately, was too young to realize what had happened. He could sense tension but, at eighteen months, he could also adjust. For Libby the problem was more acute and, in the long run, more damaging. As the only girl in the house, even though she was only ten, she suddenly found herself responsible for the cooking, housecleaning, diaper changing, laundry and such maternal disciplining of her little brothers as her father would have left to Elizabeth. Aunt Sybil did help out, but Aunt Sybil had her own home, husband and children, and devoted as she was to Brother, the Doles had to come first.

For Theophilus, life did not become the bed of roses he expected once his wife was gone. Home was less comfortable, less clean and less hospitable. Friends and parishioners dropped in less and less often. There was a gradual turning away from the pastor.

Theophilus was determined to wipe out Elizabeth's influence over their children, past, present, and future, by wiping out all contact, even by mail, with their mother. But his plan did not work. He would later complain: "I never saw children so attached to a mother . . . I cannot by any means wean them from her nor lead them to disregard her authority in the least thing. . . . She seems by some means to hold them in obedience to her wishes just as much in her absence as in her presence."

When he could not influence them away from their mother's teachings by gentle persuasion he turned to discipline. They obeyed, as their mother had taught them to, but they kept their own counsel. His pastoral work suffered. Apparently, the Lord was not as fully on his side as he thought and would confidently proclaim on the train ride to Jacksonville.

A nineteenth-century teenager was considered grown, his habits, his values and his mind-set pretty well formed. Toffy and Isaac, both in their late teens at the time of Elizabeth's removal to the asylum, were sure their father was wrong. Toffy, already working away from home, was free to write to his mother as often as he liked. Isaac could also manage to write freely, if less often. The others were severely circumscribed. Samuel was torn. He loved and believed in his mother but he also loved and respected his father in spite of his childhood complaints about long premeal sermons and short servings of food. He wavered and suffered; whichever way he leaned, his conscience would trouble him. As for George, Elizabeth would later write that his love for her was so deep that Libby, now surrogate parent, could easily control him by saying that an act would please mother, in which case he did it, or "it will make mother feel bad," in which case he did not. So much for Theophilus's attempts to protect them from their mother's "harmful influence."

Sheriff Burgess left the train at Kankakee City. Theophilus and Elizabeth continued the journey alone. It was a long ride, the better part of a day. At some of the stops it was possible to get a bite to eat and a cup of tea. The monotonous clicking of train wheels on rails for so many hours gave Elizabeth time to pull herself together and marshal her forces to cope with the immediate threat. Obviously Theophilus was going to put her in the insane asylum. But with pluck and brains she might be able to get herself released, especially since she was certain that the superintendent, whoever he might be, would soon realize that if either Packard were insane, it was not she.

They sat with the regular passengers and, as usual, Elizabeth talked freely to anyone who would listen. Many did and were appalled. Theophilus realized the hostility to him among the passengers and made no attempt to explain himself to them. He did try to argue down his wife: "You say, wife, that the Lord prospers those whose ways please him. Now, judging by this test, who is prospered in their plans, you or I? You see, I succeed in all I undertake while all your efforts are defeated. Now, isn't the Lord on my side?"

The Lord may have been on his side, but the passengers were not. A few offered to hide Elizabeth and help her escape at one of the way stops. But she declined. She was going to prove her husband wrong. An escape, especially if it failed, could be interpreted as an indication of derangement; she would be the weaker and Theophilus the stronger for her having tried.

It was after dark by the time the train reached Jacksonville, forty-five miles due west of Springfield, the state capital in central Illinois, and nighttime by the time a carriage delivered them to the front door of the ugly red brick building in the middle of rolling farmland where the state's impecunious insane or "distracted" were housed. The superintendent of this asylum was Dr. Andrew McFarland, who had come to Jacksonville in the early 1850s from the New Hampshire Asylum at Concord where he had established an enviable reputation as one of the pioneers in treating insanity as a curable illness.

Dr. McFarland was out of town, attending the triennial meeting of the Association of Medical Superintendents of American Institutions for the Insane (founded in 1844, which is now the American Psychiatric Association). His absence that day may have changed history. At the very least, it delayed Elizabeth's meeting with this man who would play such a prominent role in her life. His assistant, Dr. Tenney, greeted the Packards. In accordance with Illinois law, the superintendent had to be willing to accept her. Dr. Tenney was willing. There is some evidence to indicate that Dr. McFarland may not have been so willing so fast.

Elizabeth was duly "entered" as an inmate, and an indigent one to boot. Theophilus had persuaded Dr. Tenney (who, in turn, persuaded the trustees) that he needed every cent he had to educate his children. Thus, the state would foot the bill. (When Elizabeth later learned she was a charity patient, she was outraged. The older children had already left home and the younger ones were being supported by their wealthy uncle, George Hastings. To what depths, she asked herself, would Theophilus not sink?)

The new inmate and her suitcase were turned over to a female attendant who escorted her to a temporary bed in the female wing of the building; supplied her with a washbowl, a towel and a pitcher of water and wished her a good night's sleep, as if that were possible. Theophilus remained in the reception area where Dr. Tenney provided him with a warm meal and a comfortable bed for the night.

It was the end of a long road from the white clapboard house with its six acres in Shelburne, Massachusetts, into which the young Elizabeth, with her life ahead of her, had moved as a bride twenty-one years and two weeks before.

The form Theophilus had filled out that night, duly recorded in the Jacksonville hospital ledger, was a remarkable understatement of his carefully constructed case against his wife:

> *June 19, 1860: Elizabeth P. Packard, Kankakee Co. Married. Aged 44.*
> *Native of Massachusetts. In this state three years. Slightly insane for two*
> *years. Was in Worcester Hospital twenty-five years ago. Present attack more*
> *decided the past four months. Supposed cause is excessive application of body*
> *and mind.*
> *(Signed) Rev. Theophilus Packard, Manteno*

(Beneath, in a different handwriting, is the terse notation: "June 1863, Dis. order Trustees." But that was three years in the future.)

5.

Skirmishes

There had not been much change in dealing with what were then known as "mental maladies" since 1836 when Elizabeth was in Worcester. In 1860 Sigmund Freud was only four years old, Carl Gustav Jung and Alfred Adler yet to be born. Mental illness was thought to result from a breakdown in morality caused by the stress of civilization and by the failure of the community, family and church to properly "mold" an individual. Mental institutions were supposed to be instruments of social control. Incarceration would rectify the failures of the community so the unfortunate sufferer could, in time, be returned home a responsible citizen.

Elizabeth claimed that the only treatments administered at Jacksonville were "a little ale and/or the laying on of hands."

Actually there was more. There was medication: sedatives such as opium and myrrh. And there were restraints such as straitjackets, plus cold baths and isolation. Prior to the development of psychiatric treatment around the turn of the century, the asylum—an architectural convenience, Dr. McFarland once described it—was itself a therapeutic tool. For those who were disturbed to the point of violence to themselves or to others, a hospital was the logical resort. It separated the patients from an environment in which self-control—which they had lost—was required and allowed rest, good food and time to work their own cure. (If they did not, the patients would probably become lifelong residents.)

In cases of delusional or aberrational behavior, the institution provided a remedial change of scene, thus reducing the stresses that had brought forth the original disturbance. But even in the mid-1800s doctors were recognizing that sometimes isolating the patient from family and friends could be counterproductive.

The questions that asylum administrators asked themselves whenever a nonviolent patient was presented for admission were: (1) Is the disorder more likely to be cured by hospitalization than by staying in familiar surroundings? (2) Is the patient's comfort and safety likely to be improved by commitment? (3) Does the safety and well-being of others require that the patient be removed from home?

Unwarranted commitments were more likely to occur among this third group than among either of the others. Friends' and relatives' definitions of "safety" and "well-being" could differ radically from those of doctors. Not incidentally, patients who were committed because of an affirmative answer to the third question could produce among the inmates and staff of the hospital the same reactions that prompted families or friends to want them committed in the first place. (Dr. McFarland thought everyone would be the better if this latter group became "peripatetic reformers" because "a vagrant life" dissipated and diffused the "perversities" that set these people at odds with family and neighbors. "In a hospital," he said, "their powers of mischief are intensified by the limited area of their operations.")

A fourth question not often asked was: Could someone who was not demonstrably insane be driven over the edge by continued association with the emotionally disturbed? Or, to phrase it differently, Are mental maladies catching? Elizabeth's answer to that was an emphatic yes. She maintained that after a year in the asylum at Jacksonville she began to exhibit, by contagion, the symptoms with which she had originally been charged. She insisted that one tended to become what was expected of one.

Elizabeth's first meeting with the man who would rarely leave her thoughts thereafter came the morning after her arrival.

Dr. McFarland had returned from the association meeting late on the night of June 18 and, after a brief sleep, was up in time to breakfast heartily with Theophilus. He then set aside an hour for a preliminary interview with the new patient.

Theophilus had filled Dr. McFarland in on the basics of Elizabeth's case as he saw it. He had spent at least five years picking over his wife's thoughts and actions. His original theory, that her nineteen-year-old brain fever was an indication of insanity, had had to be scrapped when Libby came down with the same ailment. It behooved him to find another cause and, searching in his memory, he did—Elizabeth's mother, Lucy, and her fits of weeping and praying for family and friends. Theophilus's mother had never behaved like that. The more he thought about it, the more convinced he became that Lucy had been insane and that Elizabeth's problem was hereditary. (He did not carry that idea forward to include his children's future.) This information he passed along to Dr. McFarland who stored it away for future consideration.

Dr. McFarland frequently spoke before gatherings of colleagues and wrote on mental illnesses for medical journals. In the July 1863 issue of the *Journal of Insanity*, he published an article on "Minor Mental Maladies." It said in part: "A review of minor mental maladies would be incomplete without mention of that form of well-known mental disease which will be more quickly recognized from some of its leading features than by any name that could possibly apply to it. It seems to consist in love for the extreme, the eccentric, and the general opposite to the received opinions, practices and fashions of the rest of mankind."

When he wrote this, he had a patient who qualified, which may have prompted the article. By the time it appeared, she had been discharged. His amplification of the foregoing paragraph was almost tailor-made for Elizabeth. "In religion, he follows a side track, with none but his kindred motley associates, no two of whom agree, except in the common opposition to everything established by the concurrence of the rest of mankind."

One wonders whether under that definition, Dr. McFarland would have hospitalized Martin Luther and the ex-nun he married, Voltaire, Mary Baker Eddy or Joseph Smith.

Andrew McFarland was forty-three, six months younger than Elizabeth. He was a graduate of Dartmouth College and Dartmouth Medical School, class of 1840. After practicing general medicine for a few years, he was appointed superintendent of the insane asylum in his native New Hampshire. He grew increasingly interested in the workings of the human mind and psyche. In 1850 he resigned (for political reasons; he had a tendency to get embroiled in local controversies) to spend a year expanding his expertise by visiting hospitals for the insane across Europe. In 1852 he went to Jacksonville.

Because the hospital personnel were professional and clerical without a sense of the historical, no one saved medical records beyond the patients' lifetimes. No one foresaw that one of the discharged would become of historical interest. Thus, there is no documentation of Dr. McFarland's initial interview, his personal reaction or his original diagnosis. Nor is there a record of Elizabeth's hospital years. There is only Elizabeth's recollection and a copy of Theophilus's entrance statement.

The visit took place in the hospital reception room, not Dr. McFarland's office. Because of the locale, Elizabeth felt she was being *invited* as a guest, rather than summoned as a patient. The interview lasted considerably longer than the designated hour. They discussed many topics in the news, not the least of which would have been the threatening war clouds, plus, in Elizabeth's words, "progressive ideas of the age, even religion and politics." The doctor "gallantly" let her talk freely, which would have instantly predisposed her to think well of him. To her the interview was "a feast of reason and a flow of soul." She flattered herself that he felt the same way.

Elizabeth told the doctor of her "instinctive aversion to being called insane." She felt the label diminished her and cast a permanent stain on her mind and soul. He reassured her: "No, Mrs. Packard, this is not necessarily so. Even some of the most gifted minds in the world have been insane and their reputation and character are still revered and respected." He cited as examples the poets Tasso and Cowper. Elizabeth was convinced that Dr. McFarland did not find her insane. He did, in fact, suggest once (not to her) that she might not have been admitted so readily had he been present when she arrived. Much later he told colleagues that "for two years of the closest study . . . I could [not] discover any intellectual impairment at all, certainly nothing that deserves the name." And to the state legislature's investigating committee, when it was looking into her case years later, he would say: "Everybody is insane; degrees are as various as the individualism of the human family. But in Mrs. Packard's case the variation from sanity to insanity is so very slight it can only be discerned by a thoroughly educated expert! There is not one in 1,000 who can possibly detect it. In fact the variation in her case is the slightest there can possibly be." Still he had kept her.

Perhaps, Elizabeth speculated, he did not like to revoke Dr. Tenney's decision so abruptly that she would be returned to a husband who clearly thought her deranged. Perhaps he was reluctant to disappoint so eminently respected a person as a Presbyterian minister. Or perhaps (she hoped) he wanted to get to know her better. In her mind, Dr. McFarland showed possibilities of becoming the "manly" protector her husband had proved not to be.

The doctor assured her she would not be a patient for long and she believed him. She may have remembered that she spent only six weeks in the Worcester hospital and then she had truly been ill. She may have been thinking of the one small suitcase she had brought with her.

Under Illinois law the admitting doctor was almost forced to accept a married woman on her husband's say-so. Today psychiatrists who are familiar with the Packard case, thinking in terms of contemporary law and practice, contend that Dr. McFarland could have discharged her after a period of observation if he had concluded that she was not in need of hospitalization. The fact that he did not indicates to these twentieth century doctors that he recognized that she was indeed having a psychotic episode. But they drew wrong conclusions from his action—or lack of it. State law specified a two-year observation period before deciding whether a patient was curable or not. The final decision was up to the trustees, not the superintendent.

Dr. McFarland had an excellent reputation as a doctor and administrator. There was no reason to question his motives at that point in his career, although his subsequent behavior, irrespective of the charges Elizabeth would bring against him, showed, at best, questionable judgment.

Since Elizabeth had been admitted in his absence, he could not discharge her instantly even if he felt her admission was not justified. He had to seem to respect his assistant's decision for the moment. He had to obey the law. He also needed to square Theophilus's description of Elizabeth with the demeanor she showed during their first meeting. And in the event that there was a delusion or aberration lurking beneath her rational and intelligent surface, the institution itself would be a therapeutic tool. He would have to wait and watch and reserve judgment before deciding whether hospitalization was or was not legitimate and if legitimate whether it would be beneficial or counterproductive.

The preliminaries over, Theophilus came to say goodbye. Dr. McFarland tactfully withdrew. The glow from Elizabeth's interview with him dissipated rapidly. The stark reality of her forcible separation from home and family reappeared, and Elizabeth importuned her husband all over again to relent. He dozed off during her pleadings. But when the doctor reappeared he started to weep, perhaps for his sad lot in life, certainly not for his separation from his wife. Dr. McFarland later told her, "I never saw a man so deeply affected as Mr. Packard at parting from you." Elizabeth knew better. "His face was radiant with joy" as he looked back at her, she wrote.

At first Elizabeth was treated more like a paying guest than a patient. She had her own room and was allowed her own toiletries, books and papers. She received no medical treatment. She saw little of the ugly parts of the asylum or the actively disturbed inmates. She spent her hours pretty much as she chose, knitting, reading, taking walks around the grounds and farm and writing letters that were mailed uncensored.

Her letters to "My dear Husband and Children" were a mix of anguish ("May you never know what it is to be numbered with the insane within the walls of an asylum, not knowing [if] your friends will ever regard you as a fit companion or associate for them again"), hysteria ("Do bring my poor lifeless body home when my spirit has fled to Jesus's arms for protection, and lay me by my asparagus bed so you can visit my grave and weep over my sad fate in this world") and reportage ("My fare does not agree with my health, and so I have begged of our kind attendants to furnish me some poor shriveled wheat, to eat raw, in order to promote digestion").

Theophilus complained that "I often wrote to my wife at the hospital, or to the Superintendent respecting her, and urged both of them to write me often. She wrote me only once; and then refused to write me again during the three years she remained in the hospital."

Theophilus's memory played him false. Elizabeth wrote for nearly a year. Then, under severe provocation, she presented him with terms for a reconciliation. Dr. McFarland would not mail that letter and Elizabeth refused to write again until Theophilus had replied to her offer. He kept asking for letters from her; the doctor kept urging her to write; she kept refusing. It was the irresistible force and the immovable object. As for the doctor, he wrote often enough. Theophilus recorded the receipt of forty to fifty letters from Dr. McFarland during those three years "describing the marvelous *peculiarities* of [Elizabeth's] case."

Sometimes the McFarlands gave Elizabeth money and sent her to town to shop for them. Occasionally she was put in charge of carriage loads of patients out for airings. By her own count she even held the reins fourteen times. The McFarlands certainly benefited materially if not intellectually from her presence. Elizabeth made dresses for their daughters, comforters for the hospital and clothing of various kinds for the patients. She visited often with Mrs. McFarland, for whom she developed a deep affection and admiration, and she sometimes joined the family for dinner.

During this halcyon period, Elizabeth's friends, the Blessings, came from Manteno to visit, bringing with them a Dr. Shirley, a Jacksonville town dentist. Elizabeth, with the keys in her pocket, gave them a tour of the hospital (as they would subsequently testify for her defense at her trial). They went home thoroughly aroused and tried to raise money and support for Elizabeth's release. There was a public "indignation" meeting. Theophilus rounded up some medical and theological sympathizers and managed to defuse the crowd. The Manteno friends then tried for a writ of habeas corpus and a trial, but Elizabeth was legally, if unconstitutionally, hospitalized and there was little they could do. (It would be different when she came home and Theophilus locked her up in her own house.) They raised some money for Toffy to use in obtaining his mother's freedom but he was not yet of age and had no standing in the eyes of the law. However, he did go to visit Elizabeth despite his father's forbidding such visits under pain of disinheritance. All he knew was what Isaac wrote him. He wanted to see for himself.

It was the first time Toffy had deliberately disregarded a parental directive. He was now eighteen and thinking for himself; he questioned such an arbitrary order. The prospect of being disinherited didn't bother him; it was more a symbolic than an actual threat. Theophilus had little to leave. Toffy consulted the minister at Mount Pleasant who said he had a right to see his mother.

Elizabeth was overjoyed to see her eldest son but distressed at his disobedience. He wept and told her he had to see with his own eyes whether his father's charges of insanity were true "and now I see, it is just as I expected. You are . . . the same kind mother as ever." Elizabeth prayed, asking God if she should chastize her son for not heeding his father. Then it occurred to her that she should ask Dr. McFarland, whose opinion she put almost on a par with God's. The doctor assured her that a son had a right to visit his mother. (Toffy visited her secretly three more times, squeezing the train fare out of his small salary. Isaac managed to get there once.)

There were only two events during those first few months to disturb the placid surface routine of her days, one half good, one all bad.

First and worst was the arrival from Manteno of a trunk of winter clothing, effectively shattering her dream of imminent release. On examination, the trunk revealed only her oldest and shabbiest clothing. (What

Theophilus had done or was doing with her good clothes was, for the time being, a mystery.) There were no letters from the children in the trunk but there was a small scrap of paper from Libby: "We are glad to hear you are getting better, hope you will soon get well. Your daughter, Elizabeth." (Isaac later told her that Theophilus would not let them write except what he dictated; Isaac thought dictated letters would hurt her more than no letters. Her reaction to Libby's note indicated that he had guessed right.) The second incident was less clear-cut.

Elizabeth had been informally attached to the Seventh Ward, mostly married women who did not seem insane to her. (She once asked Dr. McFarland how long it took to determine insanity; was it six months? a year? Then she began to wonder if there might be an understanding between the husbands and the doctor that "subjection" of the wife was the cure the husbands sought.)

On the occasion of the second incident, she had been supervising some of the Seventh-Ward patients in the yard. Patients from one of the men's wards were there at the same time. (There is no indication that this was either routine or exceptional. Elizabeth mentioned it without comment.) She had seated herself briefly on a swing next to one of the men. One of her charges chastized her for swinging with a man and reported her to an attendant. Elizabeth went promptly to Dr. McFarland, before the attendant could, to tell him what had happened. She confessed to "improprieties" and asked what she could say to the attendant in her own defense. "Say nothing," counseled the doctor. "I will see that you are protected." Then he kissed her on the forehead. Although she professed to regard his gesture as an impulse without "evil motives," Elizabeth, the moralist, chided him. The doctor explained it as a "kiss of charity."

Elizabeth was developing a love-hate attitude toward the doctor. (There is some suggestion that his attitude toward her was equally ambivalent. At one point, he described her to the wife of one of the asylum's trustees as a woman of high intelligence, refined and polished in manner, whom the trustee's wife would enjoy meeting. Another time he told colleagues she gave him "infinite trouble" and he "got tired of her.")

The "kiss of charity" stuck in Elizabeth's mind. During her "love" phases, she interpreted it as proof of his regard for her; during her "hate" phases, it became a symptom of the doctor's base nature. The effects of her imprisonment, benign though they had been so far, were beginning to take their toll. She expanded her correspondence to include Dr. McFarland, the hospital trustees and even the governor of Illinois, protesting her confinement and treatment, making demands for reading material, objecting to being a charge of the state when her husband could pay. Sometimes her prose became quite purple.

In October 1860, after four months in the asylum, she delivered to Dr. McFarland her first petition for release. It was a hand-written twenty-one-page defense of her sanity—formal, dignified, carefully constructed and sublimely self-confident.

> Dr. McFarland—Sir: I, your sane patient Elizabeth P. W. Packard, wife of Rev. Theophilus Packard of Manteno, Kankakee County, Illinois, do hereby respectfully request that you forthwith give me an honorable discharge from this Asylum upon your own responsibility, that is, without consulting my husband in the matter for the following REASONS.

There were eight of them, ranging from a claim of a legal and constitutional right to her liberty because she had neither done nor said anything to forfeit it, through her ability (unspecified) to support herself which obviated the need for a husband, to the danger to Dr. McFarland's reputation for holding her unjustly.

She then posed sixteen questions, among them: Would it not be an example of moral courage, true Christian humanity and/or honor to come to the defense of "injured virtue and helpless innocence"? And since she had been illegally committed, could she not be illegally discharged?

She continued her petition with "An Appeal to Your Understanding." She cited Isaac's portrayal of his father as a "smothered volcano" and described the deterioration of life in the Packard household that culminated in her hospitalization. She characterized Theophilus as "the most perfect practical specimen of his own favorite doctrine, viz: 'the heart of man is deceitful above all things and desperately wicked.'" She reported her constant concern for her children and the comfort she derived from her daughter's statement: "Mother, if you are compelled to leave us, I shall always remember to do in my troubles as I know you do in yours, instead of returning evil for evil, you go and tell Jesus and get him to help you to be patient and return good for evil."

She referred at length to the Bible and God's purposes: "I expect God to help me only as I help myself"; she protested the subordinate position of women, especially the frequency with which husbands claimed the law of marriage to be the subjugation of "the weaker vessel to the arbitrary will of the stronger, rather than the protector of true womanly rights of the weak." She enumerated her grievances against Theophilus and recounted in detail her last day at Manteno. She listed the only terms on which she could return to her husband and concluded: "It is not that I am unwilling that my husband should cling to his long cherished opinions . . . but only that I claim equality with him in my individual right to my private opinion. . . . I am a martyr for the rights of opinion in women in the year 1860 in this boasted free America."

Dr. McFarland accepted this appeal smilingly without comment. Its lack of effect reinforced her developing paranoia. Her future communications would move gradually toward the hysterical, his reactions toward the intemperate.

Sometimes they clashed ideologically in person. Elizabeth recorded many "conversations" with the doctor that inevitably became debates on the definition of insanity. Dr. McFarland held that a person could be insane without "irregularities of conduct," that "moral perversity" was an institutionalizable disorder; Elizabeth maintained that "many acts appear insane that would not if we knew the reasons which prompted them." She quoted her old mentor, Gerrit Smith: "When you have done all that forebearance, kindness and intelligence can do to right your wrongs, all that is left for you to do is 'assert your rights,' kindly but firmly and then leave the issue to God."

So the difference between them boiled down to the source of the "wrong" she was trying to right. In nineteenth-century America, a husband's exercising his authority no matter how was not a "wrong"; a wife's attempting to resist it was. Today such a controversy would be considered frivolous.

In her free roamings around the hospital, Elizabeth had come across if not considerable as she claimed, certainly some, examples of mistreatment, infelicitous conditions and even cruelty. She knew she was being given preferential treatment; so did the staff and some of the patients. There were rumblings of discontent. She did not want to terminate her own favored position so she decided, as she put it, to be a Queen Esther and use the influence she thought she had to improve the lot of the others. She wrote Dr. McFarland a lengthy letter that she subsequently reprinted in one of her books as "My Reproof to Dr. McFarland for his Abuse of his Patients." (In the book it covered sixteen pages.)

She started out by saying that "I do not approve of publishing your faults to the world until you have an opportunity first, to amend your ways and your doings," and went on to charge that the principles on which the asylum was run were "the best calculated to make maniacs that human ingenuity could devise . . . even a person with a sound mind and a sound body could hardly pass through a course here and come out unharmed, without faith." She described "wrongs, oppression and received cruelties in the most expressive terms I could command"; gave names, dates and places; quoted attendants, rumors and stories arising out of the other patients' paranoia as if all were gospel; and she appealed to the doctor's intellect, humanity and conscience to mend his ways. She punctuated each point with the assurance that she was speaking out of love and respect in the hopes that he would reform. Then she tendered a bill for five dollars for services rendered to his family and signed it, "Your true friend, E. P. W. Packard."

Dr. McFarland did not take this document in the spirit in which it was offered. It must have hit him on a bad day when the man overrode the scientist. Elizabeth was instantly reclassified to patient status. Some of her friends on the Seventh Ward, to whom she had read passages from her letter, had warned her against delivering it so she was prepared for trouble. She made a copy that she hid in her mirror between the glass and the backing. (In case she were killed in the asylum, she said, it would explain why and if she were released it might vindicate her.)

The next Saturday after prayers Dr. McFarland personally escorted her to the Eighth Ward, told the nurse, Miss Tenny, to treat her like all the others and locked the door behind her. Elizabeth claimed she could not understand what had motivated the doctor despite her earlier admission that she was delivering the letter at "self-risk." She asked Miss Tenny, "I wonder if my 'reproof' has not offended him." Miss Tenny assured her that indeed it had and that everyone in the asylum knew about it. Elizabeth later claimed that the doctor could have stood all the other parts of her "reproof" if she had not mentioned that he had kissed her in his office.

Paranoia is a much used and much misused word. Webster's Third New International Dictionary defines it as (1) a rare chronic psychosis characterized by delusions of persecution or of grandeur, and (2) a tendency on the part of an individual or group toward suspiciousness and distrustfulness of others not based on objective reality but on the need to defend the ego against unconscious impulses that use projection as a mechanism of defense.

If one attributes everything that goes wrong in life to the machinations of others, paranoia is unquestionably an appropriate word. But if one is indeed being plotted against, a touch of suspicion and distrustfulness would appear to be the better part of wisdom.

Elizabeth seemed to go out of her way to invite disaster. At those moments it was more important for her to make her point, stand her ground and demonstrate her intellect even at the risk of a confrontation she could not win. Compromise or concession in the interests of harmony or finding an oblique route to the same end felt like defeat. There was nothing manipulative about Elizabeth; she had never learned, to use a twentieth-century idiom, that there are more ways than one to skin a cat. For her it was head on, straightforward, or not at all. A better question than was she or was she not paranoid at Manteno and Jacksonville would be: Should she have been institutionalized at all? And as further questions subsumed under that first one: Was her "disorder" more likely to be cured by hospitalization? Would her comfort and safety be improved by commitment? Did the safety and well-being of others require that she be removed from home? And, at bottom, what was meant by safety and well-being, and whose safety and well-being was being considered?

Elizabeth, her friends and her children saw it one way. Her husband, his sisters and some of his parishioners saw it another. Dr. McFarland was not an arbiter; he was a therapist. But sometimes he was only human, subject to spells of impatience, irritation and punitive impulses.

The Eighth Ward was a far cry from the Seventh, and "cry" was the operative word. The Eighth was for severely disturbed patients. There was no furniture (to keep potential weapons to a minimum). The patients sat on the floor. Many were incontinent. Elizabeth described it as "filthy and fetid, the patients unwashed and unattended, food and drink contaminated by the smell."

No longer did she have a private room. She now shared sleeping quarters with four to six women. There was only one tin basin for all the eighteen occupants of the ward, and she hardly had time to wash her face and hands before breakfast. Her daily cold bath went by the boards until she managed to find a new chamber pot that she kept under her bed to use as a washbowl. She had to bathe in front of her roommates, cringing every time.

Elizabeth was attacked a few times by the ward's more violent inmates.

Truly frightened, she begged Dr. McFarland first for a room of her own, then for protection from the others and finally for the removal of the most dangerous of her ward mates. He turned her down on all three requests.

Yet she still managed to achieve a favored position. The attendants, Miss Tenny and her sister (also a Miss Tenny) and the matron, Mrs. Waldo, probably realizing how misplaced she was in the violent ward, did her little favors. The Tenny sisters were the "first truly kind attendants" she found in Jacksonville; "they feared God more than Dr. McFarland." They let Elizabeth go to the storage room and collect from her trunk her sewing box and some clothing and they gave her a drawer in the ward dormitory with a key to lock it. Mrs. Waldo got her a proper washbasin and retrieved her mirror (with its hidden document) from the Seventh Ward.

Elizabeth rationalized that she had been ousted from her preferential position for defending others; she would therefore make others' wants her cares: "The best way to train ourselves to bear heavy burdens is to bear the burdens of others." She set to work at once to clean up the ward and its occupants, performing constructive functions even as she expressed "disturbed" words and thoughts.

The morning after her arrival she coaxed as many as she could to let her wash their faces and shampoo their hair. On Monday she initiated baths and clean clothes (obviously with the help of the Tenny sisters and the matron). The first to submit was returned to the ward as a "neat, clean tidy lady," to be an example to the others.

After instituting baths for patients, she moved on to baths for rooms, scrubbing them down with soap and hot water and a stiff brush. She tore apart the beds, many of which had rotted mattresses. With Miss Tenny's help, the beds were removed, the rotted parts of the mattresses cut away, replaced with fresh straw or husks and covered with new cloth. She took on one person and one room each day. Allowing for a day of rest, it took her three weeks to cleanse all the eighteen inmates. By then it was time to start over again.

Elizabeth kept up this routine for a year. The Eighth Ward was now rumored to be the cleanest and sweetest-smelling in the hospital, and other wards began to follow suit. Dr. McFarland raised no objection to her activities; he even requested that the trustees provide bathtubs for each ward so the patients need not be restricted to washbasins anymore. But he did caution the Tenny sisters not to let Elizabeth work too hard; Theophilus might object.

Elizabeth established a regimen for herself, too, starting with opening the windows each night at bedtime; her roommates were thus forced to join her in sleeping in fresh air. After the morning bell rang, there were fifteen minutes until breakfast. Wasting not a minute, she knelt for a short prayer, drank a tumbler of rain water and washed and dressed quickly. She stripped her bed, shaking the sheets and blankets and stirring the husks of the mattress, all of which she let air during breakfast. After eating she made her bed, swept and dusted, and then invited her ward mates to her room for prayers. Some came. After she finished her one-room—one-patient cleansing, she wrote in her diary, studied the Bible and then read something demanding, preferably a book on science.

Elizabeth had asked permission to go to the yard daily for fifteen minutes of unsupervised exercise in the fresh air. Dr. McFarland refused. She asked if she could work in the washhouse or ironing room, which would be a form of exercise. Again she was turned down. Mrs. McFarland finally persuaded the doctor to let her spend some time each day in the sewing room, which at least brought her a change of air. She had to create her own substitute for exercise.

Before the midday meal she took her bath and toweled herself vigorously. Then she did calisthenics before an open window. It was better than nothing. She combed her hair "thoroughly" and spent a good hour completing her toilet for the day, always hoping that Dr. McFarland would visit the ward and see her.

After that, she wrote in her journal, she could "relish" dinner. Actually she did not relish it at all. She found the meals were not balanced; they were seriously short on greens and long on starches. She tried to balance the diet for herself by leaving on her plate some of the ingredients she considered superfluous.

After the midday meal Elizabeth read "light literature" or the daily paper when she could get one. She sometimes took a nap. After that she went to the sewing room or to the common room where patients read aloud for their own improvement (intellectual or psychological, she didn't say) from whatever they could get hold of in the hospital library. There was no mention in her schedule of therapy or medication.

Elizabeth found two meals enough under her largely sedentary living conditions. If she ate supper, she did not sleep well, woke in the morning with a bad taste in her mouth and had little appetite for breakfast. So she skipped the evening meal. At the close of the supper hour she devoted herself to amusing the patients by dancing and playing with them until chapel after which they were all locked up for the night. Then she did more calisthenics, drank another glass of water and said another prayer before retiring. She managed to sleep for ten hours. "A good sleep is invaluable," she wrote. "You can stand anything with sleep."

In the Eighth Ward Elizabeth saw straitjackets for the first time and heard the screams of straightjacketed patients. She learned about the "screen" room, one of the cell-like bedrooms that had locked screens over the window and door. She saw patients shut in it sometimes naked, sometimes with clothing but no food. She heard both straitjacket and screen room used as threats for such minor infractions as talking at meals.

She herself was locked in the screen room for trying to help a patient who was being straightjacketed for screaming with pain from an injury acquired during an earlier punishment. (The nurse in charge was eventually dismissed for abusing patients and six months later reappeared as a patient herself.)

Elizabeth developed a taste for intervening by deed or by word in every situation she considered unjust. In time Dr. McFarland complained to Theophilus that she caused him "a world of trouble" by stirring up the patients to "discontent and insubordination." He occasionally threatened Elizabeth with the screen room when her intercessions and criticisms rubbed raw even his conditioned nerves. But only twice did he carry out the threat, the first just mentioned, the second on the day of her discharge.

Theophilus wrote occasionally, mostly to Dr. McFarland but once in a while to Elizabeth. Shortly after she was moved to the Eighth Ward, he informed her that he was thinking about breaking up the family. He asked to whom he should give the little children. Considering the rarity with which he asked Elizabeth's opinion, one must wonder whether the letter was designed to elicit information or distress. He then added: "Elizabeth [Libby] has had a fall and hurt her side so that it pains her most of the time, and yet [she] does all the work for the family, except when her Aunt Dole comes and helps a day occasionally." (Libby was eleven. The pressures of life without her mother and the responsibility of running the household would, according to Packard descendants, cause her emotional problems for the rest of her life.)

Elizabeth must have thought that even living with Theophilus was preferable to letting her children be scattered. She conceived the idea that

she could effect a reconciliation though there was nothing to indicate that
he had altered his attitude. At any rate, she drew up her terms for such a
reconciliation, excerpted from her first petition to Dr. McFarland a year
earlier. She wrote them to him in the letter that produced the standoff.
Since Dr. McFarland said he destroyed the letter as "worthless" (instead of
sending it to Theophilus for *him* to destroy if he chose), the only record of
the terms, which Elizabeth considered eminently reasonable, was her notes:

1. *Theophilus must publicly renounce his charge that she was insane and
   allow her her own opinion and conscience.*
2. *He must allow her to hold her own property in her own name and control
   it* (this was largely her patrimony of six hundred dollars).
3. *He must allow her to control her own children "as far as a mother's
   province allows."*
4. *He must allow her to have a hired girl and to run her own household.*
5. *Any attempt on his part to "usurp" these rights would indicate an end to
   the marriage.*

She recognized that making these demands ignored the custom of husbandly protection, but Theophilus had offered none; her only protection
lay in his acknowledgment of her identity as a person—neither insane nor
chattel. She concluded by reminding him of the marriage vows they had
exchanged "at the altar of your God" and asked if he thought he had kept
that solemn vow.

About then Elizabeth started to have nightmares.

She dreamed she had to draw a stagecoach over a bridge spanning a deep
river. She was roped so the greatest pressure was across her stomach and
breasts. Five stone steps, each five inches high, led up to the bridge. It
seemed almost impossible for anyone to pull the coach up those steps but
she "put forth a herculean effort" and surprise! the stage came up onto the
bridge. Stimulated by this stunning success, she raced across the bridge at
full speed, pulling the coach. Because she was running with her head down,
she didn't notice a gap between the end of the bridge and the far shore until
she had run off the roadway onto one of the two planks connecting the
bridge with the land. Now she must try to draw the coach so its wheels
would roll evenly onto the two planks. If they missed, the coach would
crash into the river and she with it. So she got out of the harness and walked
forward to assess the situation. But that was worse. Now she could not

return for the coach blocked the way back. Moving forward was dangerous; moving back was impossible. If she looked down she got dizzy.

Elizabeth sought frantically for help. On the shore behind her Theophilus, oblivious of her plight, was staring at the bridge trying to figure out how he could cross. On the forward bank a group of men with ropes were trying to find a way to help her. Now a new peril arose. The river was clogged with empty office chairs floating by, so no boat could be sent to rescue her. It occurred to her that if the public officers had not vacated their chairs and, by extension, their duties she could have dropped into their arms. But instead of being at their posts to help the helpless, their furnishings had become impediments. So in the absence of help from others, Elizabeth decided she must help herself. She started going forward inch by inch, looking constantly upward to avoid dizziness. On the way she stopped to remove her shoes and drop them into the river, and awoke— glad, for the only time, to be in the asylum.

Practitioners of psychiatry were not yet interpreting dreams. But the woman in charge of the sewing room didn't mind trying. Put public opinion behind you, she said; go it alone. "You must walk through Gethsemene's garden alone as Christ did. God's angels will sustain you when sorrows are too great to bear."

This explanation pleased Elizabeth and she began to use the phrase, "walking through Gethsemene's garden," in her petitions and letters of protest.

When Elizabeth was new to the Eighth Ward she was permitted out only for chapel and the sewing room. But after five months she was allowed to ride and walk with other patients. On her first outside visit, she went to one of the local stores to pay the storekeeper five cents she had owed him for those five months. She had ten cents with her and with the remaining nickel she purchased some paper for her writing.

Thus began a cat-and-mouse game with Dr. McFarland over her possession of paper and pen. Apparently her writing had become a forbidden pastime. So Elizabeth acquired sheets of paper, any kind, by stealth; Dr. McFarland found them and removed them; her fellow patients joined in the game and supplied her clandestinely with whatever they could lay their hands on. Elizabeth managed to keep up her literary output.

Her writing relieved the pressure of frustration and rage, moods of love and hate, self-pity and spunk, all boiling within her. She peppered her children, her father, her brother, Dr. McFarland, the trustees and any number of innocent bystanders who crossed her path with letters and notes. Some were mailed, some were smuggled out with visitors or discharged patients; some got as far as the asylum wastebasket; some survived as copies she made at the time, convinced that one day they could be used to prove her claim of unjust imprisonment. She also kept a journal, some of which survived in the original, some in reconstruction.

Elizabeth claimed Dr. McFarland forbade her to write to her children. Considering the efforts he made to persuade her to write to her husband, that was unlikely. Or if it was true, there must have been an added proviso that Elizabeth omitted from her grievance. Whatever the case, Elizabeth went to extraordinary lengths to sneak out her letters, but only one was answered. She never knew how many were actually sent.

In early 1861 Elizabeth wrote her first letter to the asylum trustees, then holding one of their quarterly meetings: "Gentlemen: Here, under your inspection, a Christian mother, and an Illinois citizen, has been imprisoned nearly nine months for simply exercising the God-given rights of opinion and conscience. . . . Do deliver me out of the hands of Dr. McFarland, for he has claimed to be better than God to me, in that he says to me that his judgment is a safer guide for me than my own conscience." She promised, if they set her free, to leave the country for England and become a subject of the Crown "where I can hope to enjoy my rights of opinion and conscience unmolested," and concluded with the plea: "Investigation is demanded of *you* by this appeal in order that your souls may be found guiltless."

She wrote also to Dr. Shirley, the local dentist who had come with the Blessings to visit her, begging that he too help deliver her from Dr. McFarland, repeating the words she had addressed to the trustees.

Theophilus came to visit during the second year, one of his two visits over the three-year period. Elizabeth refused to speak to him. Dr. McFarland thought Elizabeth's "hatred of her husband had something diabolical about it. Every instinct of love was banished from her." Both men seemed surprised at her attitude.

Later that year the matron left and Mrs. McFarland took over her duties. Mrs. McFarland was a kind, generous, sympathetic woman. The patients, including Elizabeth, loved her. She had read Elizabeth's "reproof" to her husband. Whatever she thought of Elizabeth's diatribe, she agreed that there were areas of asylum life that could be improved and she set about trying to improve them.

In the process she arranged for Elizabeth to have a room of her own once again and supplied her with a washbowl, pitcher, chair and curtains, all of which Elizabeth considered a "great and rare privilege." Yet even in the fullness of her appreciation, Elizabeth could not resist a little critique: "I have almost unbounded confidence in your womanly nature; I believe its instincts are a safe guide in dictating your duty so far as it goes; yet I do not regard your judgment as so mature that experience may not improve it. Will you therefore allow me to make a suggestion, when I assure you that it is made with the purest motives and the kindest feelings?"

Then, for the first time since she entered the hospital, Elizabeth wrote to her father. She blamed the long silence on orders from Dr. McFarland: "I am entombed here without cause. But I am trying to bear my wrongs as patiently as I can." She described Theophilus's charges against her, defended her homemaking and mothering which her children were now denied and cried out again for her right to her own beliefs and thoughts. She begged him to take her home with him for a visit so he could judge her sanity for himself. If he felt too feeble to make the trip, he could send her brother, Austin, and if Austin thought the asylum a proper place for her, she would consent to stay. She concluded piteously, "With no trial and no chance for self-defense, is it not unjust to leave your only daughter uncared for any longer? Father, *do something*, to get justice done to me and my precious children."

Instead of coming to her rescue, Samuel Ware sent Theophilus one hundred dollars toward her hospital bill. He did not know the state was paying for Elizabeth as an indigent and he did not know Theophilus kept the money he had contributed. (Eventually, this would be added to Samuel's list of grievances against his son-in-law.)

In time Elizabeth came to understand her father's action. "For my father's defense," she wrote, "the superintendent sent with my letter one of his own which destroyed the influence of mine. And as the superintendent and the husband both agreed in opinion respecting me, it is not so strange that a man nearly 80 years old should heed their statements rather than those of one whom he supposed insane."

The love-hate relationship with the doctor continued, but now that her circumstances had improved, the love periods seemed to predominate. "It is perfectly natural to me to love the opposite sex," Elizabeth wrote. "It need not be a matter of surprise ... if I should come to love the only man [Theophilus] allowed me to associate with, for three years, especially if I can find in him anything worthy of my love."

Toward the end of her stay she wrote that after three years of "absolute desertion," she felt no other man on Earth cared for her happiness but the doctor. She chose him as her "only earthly protector" and offered him in return "a woman's *heart* of grateful love," all she had to give. She also offered to be his wife in heaven, a symbolic statement that he chose to interpret literally and quote as evidence of her insanity, if not depravity.

There were times, apparently, when even a man trained in dealing with "distracted" minds and mental maladies found his lot too much to bear. In September 1862, two years and three months after Elizabeth's arrival, Dr. McFarland was arrested in Springfield, booked, and, according to the daily *Illinois State Journal*, fined three dollars for being "plain dead drunk."

Later that month, with a trustees' meeting pending, Elizabeth asked if she could "fire a few guns at Calvinism" before the trustees. Dr. McFarland reminded her that the trustees themselves were Calvinist but he agreed to let her do it and even gave her writing materials. She thought he was being permissive because he expected her theological differences to convince them of her insanity.

Theophilus paid his second visit coincident with the trustees' meeting. He was now unemployed. The July before he had entered in his diary, with no explanation, that he "thought it best to resign" his pulpit. This time he could not blame his job problems on his wife.

There are three conflicting versions of this meeting: Theophilus wrote in his Journal: "The Superintendent wished me to appear before the Trustees, as they held their Quarterly meeting at the hospital while I was there, and give them a more full view of [Elizabeth's] singular and peculiar case. I did so. My wife at her request appeared and stated her case to them as she pleased. The result was she was retained in the hospital."

Dr. McFarland's version was that he was "tired of her" and wanted the trustees to discharge her as "the only means of getting rid of an intolerable and unendurable source of annoyance." But her husband appeared and protested. Then Elizabeth came in with a paper "the existence of which I was not aware until she produced it. . . . It was a paper of some singularity, exhibiting a good deal of power of language and composition, and was a treatise on Calvinism (see Appendix 1 for the complete text of this paper). She was not discharged at the time."

As Elizabeth described it, she wrote out her view of Calvin by contrasting each Calvinist principle with a Christian principle, thus showing Calvinism to be a "doctrine of devils." She showed the paper to Dr. McFarland and he took her to the parlor to read it to the trustees. She made much of entering the room on his arm which she thought lent credence to her position.

Then, according to Elizabeth, after she read the first paper, she produced another paper that she had written on the sly, about "the conspiracy" of her husband and the doctor to deprive her of her liberty. The trustees allowed her to read it. They asked Theophilus to leave the room and Dr. McFarland went with him. The trustees then questioned her at length. They decided she could go free but it would be unwise for her to return to her husband. They offered to pay for her fare to her father in Massachusetts, or to her children in Manteno, or they would pay for lodgings in Jacksonville. But Elizabeth declined. Since they agreed that she had the right to her liberty, she felt she had won a moral victory. But she did not feel safe as long as she was subject to her husband and his accusations. So she concluded that she might as well spend her days in their prison as in any other. However, if the superintendent could be persuaded to give her a key or a pass so she could come and go freely, she could continue to live under inmates' rules and still be her own keeper. The trustees did not authorize a key but they did say she might confer with the doctor about her activities and do what he and she mutually agreed would be best for her.

What Elizabeth wanted to do was to expand her attack on Calvin to book-length. The doctor agreed. He had decided her writing had therapeutic value and even furnished her with pen and paper. She set to work and in six weeks had an outline of "The Great Drama," each chapter named for a car on a railroad train. The final handwritten manuscript covered 2,500 pages of notepaper.

At the July 1863 annual meeting of the Association of Medical Superintendents of American Institutions for the Insane, Dr. McFarland described an interesting case he had been treating, without mentioning Elizabeth by name. He was disputing a popular diagnosis of "moral insanity," claiming that the deep-seated root of that disorder was actually an "intellectual perversion." In the course of his talk, he made the statement, undocumented except for Theophilus's word, that his patient's mother had been insane for many years. There were many factual errors in his account. He said Elizabeth had been hospitalized at Worcester when she was twenty (her commitment papers read "19"). He said she was discharged after a term of residence "not exactly remembered" (the discharge papers said "six weeks"). He said she was married a few months later (it was three years later). He said she chose as her husband a "young clergyman of fine promise" (Theophilus was thirty-seven, far from young by early nineteenth-century or even today's standards). He said the trouble between the couple started after five or six years of marriage though, in fact, the marriage in Theophilus's own diary was happy for twice that length. He had them moving first to New York (where they only went for a visit); then to Ohio from which Theophilus was compelled to move after a few months because of Elizabeth's troublemaking (they were there for a year); and then to Iowa where again Elizabeth's behavior forced them to move in a matter of weeks (they stayed in Iowa for two years).

There was indeed friction within the church communities where Theophilus served. Elizabeth and her friends attributed it to Theophilus's intransigence and theological severity; he attributed it to his wife's raising troubling theological questions and creating the possibility of heterodoxy.

In making so many minor, careless errors in reporting Elizabeth's case to his colleagues, Dr. McFarland leaves himself open to the question of how accurate was his diagnosis of her "malady."

He described his patient as a woman of "extraordinary mental capacity and power, great charm of manner, and taste in dress, and good judgment." But along with those pluses, he said she managed to make everyone around her miserable, "set up in opposition to her husband in matters of religious belief—tore his church all to pieces and created great dissensions in his family" (not *their* family). At that point Theophilus, under the Illinois law that had done away with "due process," got her admitted to Jacksonville.

"I do not think," Dr. McFarland continued, "that for two years of the closest study I could discover any intellectual impairment at all." He found her hatred of her husband extreme; she was "thoroughly demoralized," yet only when she was sick could he find any "delusions." As he described them, they could have been delusions, but they also could have been delirium.

"She gave me infinite trouble," the doctor continued, and after 2½ years, he "got tired of her"—a remarkable statement for a psychiatrist to make about a patient—and he asked the Board of Trustees to discharge her "as the only means of getting rid of an intolerable and unendurable source of annoyance." Then he described the trustees' meeting at which Theophilus appeared to object to her release and Elizabeth read her paper on Calvinism, which the doctor claimed he knew nothing about. He then gave her permission to expand it into a book.

And at long last, in the pages of this book, he located her delusion, which had remained hidden for eighteen years. (He arrived at the number eighteen because of his errors in dating her fever and her wedding. If he placed the birth of the delusion at the time of her teenage illness and hospitalization, then it was twenty-six years later that she wrote the revealing book.)

The delusion Dr. McFarland unearthed was Elizabeth's belief that there had to be sexual distinctions in the Trinity and that she was the Holy Ghost. This, he said, lay behind all her "perversity of conduct," thus proving that an "intellectual perversion" produced what his colleagues had been terming "moral insanity."

Had Elizabeth indeed thought that she personally was the Holy Ghost, she would certainly have been delusional. But, again, Dr. McFarland was as careless in quoting her as he had been in reporting her biographical data.

Elizabeth's theory, that the Trinity should have the same sexual distinctions as the physical Holy Family, made of the Holy Ghost the Mother figure. Even the witness at her trial, the "sewing-machine salesman," Dr. Brown, was more accurate when he quoted her as saying she was the "personification of the Holy Ghost," which, by extension, meant that any spiritual woman was in her words, the "temple of the Holy Ghost." (Elizabeth also said that a spiritual or Christlike man was a personification of the Son of God. But no one quoted that.)

As in the report that Elizabeth's mother was insane which grew in the repetition to "hopelessly insane," "hospitalized for years," and finally "died in an insane asylum," none of which can be documented, so Dr. McFarland's statement that Elizabeth thought herself the Holy Ghost has become her official "delusion." Even today there are psychiatrists superficially familiar with her case who are convinced that Elizabeth *did* think she was the Holy Ghost though none of them can remember where they read it.

Between writing chapters of "The Great Drama," Elizabeth continued her barrage of letters and protest. She wrote to her brother, Samuel, whose wife had invited her to stay with them after leaving the asylum: "Thanks, many thanks, kind brother and sister, for this kind offer, for it is one I can fully appreciate. Yes, your sister Elizabeth has no place on earth she can now call home, but a prison. And I am not only homeless, but every means possible is used to impress upon my mind the feeling that I am friendless also." She wrote again to Dr. McFarland: "It is time for me to know whether you are indeed my friend or my enemy. . . . You must allow me to be my own keeper, by giving me a key or a pass, . . . If after all the love and kindness, light and reason, forebearance and trust I have so implicitly reposed in you . . . you now resist these combined influences and persist in your wrong doing, I must be true to you and unveil your character to the world."

The world outside troubled Elizabeth as much as the world within. "Daily events of the most thrilling kind were occurring and I felt it to be a great privation to be deprived of news of the war." She wrote to the chaplain, Dr. Sturtevant, and after chapel personally presented her letter to him so she knew it was received: "Dear Brother in Christ—Entombed alive as I am at present, I, an intelligent being, suffer greatly from being deprived of all communication with the world outside the Asylum. . . . I venture to ask of you an expression of sympathy, by furnishing me with the reading of the *Independent*, weekly, by bringing it to me, on each Sabbath, when I will exchange the previous one."

The chaplain did not comply; he didn't even respond. Elizabeth thought he should have offered to lend her his copy if he would not get her one of her own, and she resented the fact that he didn't even give her an excuse for not doing so.

Then she wrote bitterly to the chairman of the trustees, complaining that she had not been set free. Either she had forgotten her triumph at the September quarterly meeting or their judgment favorable to her had been a figment of her imagination.

The euphoria from working on her book could not sustain Elizabeth all the time. There were periods of bleak despair. The Christmas season, especially, was filled with gray days. In December 1862, half way into her third year at the asylum, she wrote to her son, Isaac:

> *Isaac dear, what is in store for your mother, God only knows. . . . I do feel that I am utterly forsaken of all men, except Dr. McFarland. He has promised me not to leave me desolate. . . . I never felt so much like despairing of all human help as I do now. . . . Perhaps I am to die a prisoner in my cell. . . . Kiss the precious children for me and tell them not to forget their mother, although we may never meet again on earth. My heart is almost broken and crushed from hope of seeing them once more.*

Then she had another nightmare. She and Theophilus were attending an anniversary meeting of some national benevolent institution, as they had in their honeymoon days. Theophilus had to sit on the platform; Elizabeth was in the front row facing the pulpit. Theophilus was making "eccentric" gestures and distracting the audience. She was embarrassed and worried for his reputation; she was also worried because she wore no bonnet and her hair was untidy. When it was Theophilus's turn to perform his part in the ceremony, he chose the high pulpit but, instead of climbing the few steps at the side of the altar, he descended to walk down one aisle and up another. Finally Elizabeth decided she must try to get him back on track. She followed him down the aisle and took his arm, saying, "Come, husband, let us go together and I will help you find the platform. . . . You seem to have lost your way. . . . I will set you right." Her words seemed to straighten him out. As Elizabeth sat, head down to compose her "agitated feelings," her husband whispered to her, "I am going to wash my face," whereupon he stepped upon the platform and washed in the baptismal bowl. Then he stripped off all his clothing except for his shirt which was old and torn, one she had put aside for illness. What would they think of her, letting him wear a torn shirt! She was afraid he would "disgracefully expose his person." She prayed he would at least put his pants back on before ascending to the pulpit. But he didn't. The women covered their faces or turned their backs; the men laughed. Elizabeth beckoned to the man who was occupying the pulpit with Theophilus and whispered to him, "My husband is crazy—he must be taken care of—I think it must have been coming on for some time, for some thought he was crazy when he put me in the asylum." Then she awoke.

As she sat in her little room, writing chapter after chapter, Elizabeth grew fonder and fonder of Dr. McFarland, despite an occasional backsliding into rancor. "Under the influence of these new and most joyous emotions," she looked forward to the doctor's visits. "The sound of his footsteps in the hall and his gentle knock at my door now caused my heart to bound with joy. . . . Now to be treated as a lady in this gallant manner, by this once boorish man, was to me the inauguration of a new and delightful era of my prison life."

She also wrote in her journal, "If [the doctor] should let me have my way entirely about my book, I think he would be in some danger of my gratitude growing into stronger feeling!" Apparently, the doctor did, and the result was the famous love letter in which Elizabeth offered to be Dr. McFarland's wife in heaven. She swore the letter was strictly symbolic—she could never have suggested anything that sounded like adultery or divorce—and she never forgave the doctor not only for taking it literally but for quoting it publicly. The letter was supposed to be their secret:

I don't think 'twould be best to let Calvin [her latest epithet for
Theophilus] *know I had sent you a love letter since I have been here and got
an answer, too. For he might make it an occasion against us in the eyes of his
clan. . . . Just put [it] between the folds of your shirts, in your private drawer
and not in the family drawer between the folds of the fine table linen as I did
Mr. Baker's letters. For my partner found mine and so may yours find yours,
unless you are extra wise and discreet, and I should feel very sad if I should
be the occasion to you of such a long string of disasters as Mr. Baker's writing
me has brought upon me and my children.*

Elizabeth's writing style was now considerably calmer. She seemed to feel
less embattled.

In February 1863, Elizabeth's cousin and "adopted sister," Angelina Field,
saved enough out of her board money to travel to Jacksonville from Granville, Illinois, where the Fields now lived. She wanted to take Elizabeth
home with her. She also wanted Elizabeth to divorce Theophilus. (The
Fields and her brother Samuel's wife, Mary, were the only family members
other than her children who never doubted Elizabeth's sanity.) Elizabeth
turned Angelina down on both counts. She was afraid she would lose the
children in a divorce action and without one she remained in her husband's
power.

Another version of this incident had Dr. McFarland (while he was charming and indulging Elizabeth) writing to David Field that "Mrs. Packard has
become a dangerous patient. It will not be safe to have her in a private
family." But when pressed for details, the doctor replied, "I do not deem it
my duty to answer impertinent questions."

In March 1863 Toffy turned twenty-one. He was now legally able to take
responsibility for his mother. He asked his father for permission to take her
out of the asylum. Theophilus gave it provided the trustees agreed. Coinci-
dentally they did. The trustees wrote Theophilus simultaneously with
Toffy's request, apparently finally persuaded by Dr. McFarland, that he must
remove his wife that June. So Theophilus brought his son to Jacksonville
and officially gave Elizabeth into his care.

Elizabeth, still refusing compromises, protested this action. She insisted
that the law held her subject to her husband and it was up to him to restore
her freedom; her son could not protect her despite Theophilus's agreement.
She did not trust Theophilus to keep his word; she feared he would put her
away somewhere else. She wanted to remain at Jacksonville until she

finished her book, which would then give her a means to defend herself. It would take her, she judged, another six months. She was willing to pay board at the asylum instead of elsewhere while she polished her prose and dealt with the printer. Dr. McFarland consented. The trustees did not. A month later they countermanded him and ordered Elizabeth into her husband's custody as of June 18, three years to the day after her entry. Her trunk was to be packed, her belongings gathered together by June 17. Elizabeth issued her final protest to the doctor: "In the name of Illinois and as its citizen, I claim that my right to the disposal of my own wardrobe be respected—that no hands be laid upon it without my consent. I therefore forbid you or any other person disturbing me or my things in my own hired room until I consent to such interference."

For the second time in her asylum years, Dr. McFarland ordered her into the screen room. Then he and an aide searched her room and packed everything including the mirror with the "reproof" secreted in it. The next morning Elizabeth was ordered to dress and depart with Theophilus. She agreed to dress but not to go. Dr. Tenney and "three toughs" arrived to enforce the order. She delivered a few final words to the assistant superintendent: "Dr. Tenney, I shall not go with you for that purpose. And here in the presence of these witnesses I claim a right of my own identity, and in the name of the laws of my country, I claim protection against this assault against my personal rights. I claim a right to myself. I claim a right to remain unmolested in my own hired room."

The "three toughs" were actually hospital porters. In the face of her refusal to move, two of them, under her instructions, formed a saddle seat of their hands. As she had departed from Manteno three years before, so she now departed from the asylum at Jacksonville.

According to Theophilus, the departure was even more turbulent. "June 1863 I went to the hospital to remove her; but she utterly refused to go out! and the authorities of the hospital were obligated to do it by force against her protest—breaking open the door of her room, packing her trunk and carrying her out of the hospital by main strength."

But this episode was not the finale. As she was being carried out one of the attendants said to her, "We shall miss you, Mrs. Packard, for there has never been a person who has caused such universal sensation as you have." This opinion was echoed some years later by Dr. Richard Dewey, when he assumed the superintendent's post at Jacksonville. Elizabeth was well remembered.

Months later, when Elizabeth was back at Manteno, she found a letter to her husband from the doctor: "I have laid your request for Mrs. Packard's re-admission before the Trustees and have used my influence to have them consent to take her. But they decidedly refuse to do so on the ground that the Institution is not designed for such cases." Considering Dr. McFarland's expressed desire to "get rid of an intolerable and unendurable source of annoyance," it is hardly likely that he sought to have her returned. His letter must have been a diplomatic rather than factual statement, designed to dissuade Theophilus from bothering him again.

The doctor may have thought he had thus heard the last of the Packards. He was wrong.

6.

Armistice

Theophilus took Elizabeth to the Fields in Granville. They had agreed to "board" her. Young Theophilus, now Theo instead of Toffy, paid the board. It was a quiet time for Elizabeth. Whether it was equally so for her hosts they never said. She worked continually on her manuscript, readying it for a printer.

After four months, as her story circulated, there arose in Granville a consensus that she should really be at home with her children. The risk of Theophilus committing her again still existed but the Fields' friends and neighbors apparently assured Elizabeth that they would come to her rescue. They raised thirty dollars for her travel expenses and offered their sheriff as an escort.

Elizabeth agreed to go if her "Appeal on Behalf of the Insane" were published. This was in essence a rewording of her various appeals to Dr. McFarland, the trustees and her husband written during her second and third years in the asylum. She felt that its publication would afford her some protection. One of the county papers agreed to print it. (Elizabeth subsequently had a thousand copies of the "appeal" reprinted in handbill form. She paid the printer ten dollars and sold them for ten cents each, thus establishing the nucleus of what would become a lucrative publishing business.) She accepted the townspeople's thirty dollars but declined the escort and set out alone for home.

Theophilus put the date of her homecoming at October 24. She said she arrived at the Manteno depot in November in the snow. But as Elizabeth had already noted, she could not "be safely trusted as a calendar." No one disputed that she came home in late autumn 1863 after an absence of close to 3½ years. It should have been a festive Thanksgiving and Christmas season for her and her family. It was not.

Her arrival was in stark contrast to her departure. There was no one at the depot to greet her, not even a casual passerby to help her with her trunk. But her homecoming was not without its own drama.

Elizabeth left her trunk on the station platform and began to walk home. Then, remembering her precious papers in her luggage, she started back to the station to ask the stationmaster to keep an eye on the trunk for her. A young boy was following her. She stopped him and asked if he would deliver her message to the stationmaster. The child hesitated. Elizabeth pressed him: Why would he not do her this favor? "I don't want to say anything against my Pa," he replied. It was her son George, three years older and three years bigger. Elizabeth had not recognized him. It hit her like a body blow how much she had missed during those forty-two months away from home. She dropped down on her knees in the snow to hug him but George held back.

Seeing his conflict, Elizabeth let him go. She bit back the question burning her tongue: Was he glad to see her? He obviously could not answer. He had been on his way to the post office on an errand for his father. Elizabeth went along. She was eager to tell someone of the Granville citizens' offer of protection and postmaster Labrie was the first possible person. She also had the forethought to ask that he see that her mail reached her. Under the circumstances, her fear that her husband might intercept her letters was understandable.

Word spread quickly through Manteno: Its most famous resident was home. Mr. Blessing went to the station and fetched her trunk. By the time she arrived at the Packard house friends had gathered in welcome.

The first thing Elizabeth did was to unpack her asylum papers and entrust them to her dearest friend, Sarah Haslett, for safekeeping.

Libby was the only one of her children who welcomed her with undiluted joy. George had already demonstrated his dilemma. Samuel was still torn between his parents, and Arthur, who had been only eighteen months old when Elizabeth was taken away, did not know who this strange woman was. Theophilus was obviously displeased. His first words were, "We get along better without you."

The home she returned to was far different from the one she had left. So were its inhabitants. And Elizabeth found out why her husband had been unemployed when he came to the trustees' meeting the year before. His position as preacher and the congregation to which he preached had slowly disintegrated after her commitment. His Manteno congregation had finally discovered what his parish back in Shelburne had realized earlier. There was a limit to how much fire and brimstone even the most pious could tolerate. Finally the church fathers had let his contract lapse. He explained it away by saying he "thought it best" to resign. For the past eighteen months he had been staying home, doing the cooking. He had finally made of his life what he had been deploring all along, a burden too heavy to carry.

Theophilus had appealed to the public for help in his great misfortune— an insane wife and six children to support. (He had not mentioned that the two oldest had already left home and were self-supporting, that the state of Illinois was financing his wife's hospitalization and that a rich brother-in-law, George Hastings, was supporting the three youngest.) The appeal worked. Boxes of clothing poured in from the American Home Missionary Society. There were twelve of them lying around when Elizabeth got home. In addition, a local widow had taken up a subscription as a token of sympathy and regard. She collected $113 for him.

Samuel, now sixteen, was about to leave to make his own way in Chicago. Isaac had been gone (to Mount Pleasant to join his older brother) since shortly after his sixteenth birthday. The three younger children, living for 3½ years without a mother's oversight, had developed slovenly habits of diet, cleanliness and exercise. Elizabeth was appalled by what she found.

The state of the house also shocked her. In addition to the dirt and disorder, doors everywhere were locked. Protecting his beliefs and possessions no longer gave Theophilus security enough; he now needed to keep everything under lock and key. When Elizabeth had lived there, there were no locks except on the front door and that one was rarely used. Now she could not get clean sheets from the linen closet without going to Theophilus for the key and he would give it only when *he* thought the sheets needed changing. His opinion on that point differed from hers. She could not even get to her own clothing without appealing to her husband for another key.

Elizabeth set to work with a vengeance, making her idea of order out of the chaos she found, working out her anger, frustration and resentment. Beating sheets and blankets was an almost adequate substitute for the beating she could not give her husband for her lost years. But obstacle after obstacle was placed in her way. When she hired a cleaning girl with what was left of her Granville money, Theophilus sent the girl packing. When she asked the children to help her with the heavy work, their father countermanded her request. But still she managed to air out the feather beds and wash down and dust the downstairs rooms, for, as Sarah Haslett would testify at the trial, "the house needed cleaning." Her friends (the Hasletts, Blessings, Beedys and Hanfords) as well as the neighbors, coming to visit, found her at the housecleaning day after day until, again in Mrs. Haslett's words, it looked "as if the mistress of the house was *home.*"

Theophilus then produced another key. This one was to the nursery upstairs and in it he locked Elizabeth. There seemed to be no light at the end of her tunnel. His story was that his wife withdrew voluntarily, "living in a room by herself and refusing to eat or live with the family, & refusing to speak to me." He also recorded that in October "a Manteno mob assembled to attend to her case & sent a couple of men to me, to regulate my family affairs! O what scenes were these! I cannot *here* describe them."

No one else, including the far-from-reticent Elizabeth, described them either, which raises the question, Did they indeed occur? Had Theophilus finally developed his own case of paranoia? Or was it a psychotic episode? Either is possible. After all, since his illusion that he had a dutiful malleable wife had been shattered during the past decade he had seemed to be heading in that direction. The date he gave, the October of her homecoming, was too early for anyone to have suspected mistreatment, although with hindsight, some might have anticipated it.

Elizabeth was shut up in the nursery for six weeks. Her meals were brought to her by one of the children. Her windows were nailed shut. With her addiction to fresh air and exercise, this caused her considerable mental agony and she swore it injured her health.

Theophilus did allow her to teach the children for a few hours a day and permitted them to obey her as a teacher. But he insisted that they disregard her parental instructions about their living habits, bathing, bedtime and wardrobe. During the day he would unlock the nursery door if the outer doors were locked and bolted. Neighbors who came to call had to knock and were usually turned away by George. Theophilus was preventing them from witnessing the Packards' home life, which he must have recognized was unseemly. He was also protecting himself from their wrath.

Mrs. Haslett was allowed to visit twice during the six-week period, once in the first week and once, with Mrs. Hanford, during the last week. A couple of times doctors who were strange to Elizabeth came to call and once, inexplicably, Theophilus admitted a sewing-machine salesman who stayed for what seemed to Elizabeth an inordinately long time and wandered in his talk very far afield from sewing machines. He made her thoroughly uncomfortable. She had a sudden vision of disaster in his wake.

Although she did not realize it then, this six-week period of imprisonment in her own home proved to be the stepping-stone to the freedom and vindication she had been seeking for years.

With Elizabeth locked in her room and Theophilus standing guard, there were no Christmas or New Year's festivities in the Packard home. The children probably shared in some of their friends' carol singing and Christmas tree trimming, and some of Elizabeth's devoted friends must have supplied a gift or two. But it had to have been as cheerless a holiday season as one could imagine.

One watershed day Elizabeth proposed to the children that they clean and polish the kitchen stove. Theophilus had been using the kitchen as his study but he agreed, for once, to move his books and papers temporarily to the room she would be vacating where he could read by her wood stove.

The stove cleaning became a festive occasion for the fun-starved children. They insisted that "Black Prince" now shone as brightly as he had when their mother was housekeeper. After the job was done, they cleaned themselves up and then went to Elizabeth's room to warm up before retiring. Theophilus hastily gathered up his books and papers and withdrew. In his hurry, he left behind a bundle of letters which he apparently didn't miss and Elizabeth didn't notice until later.

At first she put them aside. After all, the letters were his and she had no right to pry. But then she decided that under her present circumstances, forewarned was forearmed and anything that gave her an advantage in self-protection and self-defense was legal as well as moral. So she read them. Then, to make sure she had read aright, she read them again, and panicked.

The letters were from Dr. McFarland, Theophilus's sisters, and a Dr. Prince, head of an asylum in Northampton, Massachusetts, which did not demand curability as a condition of admission. They covered the period of her incarceration in Jacksonville as well as the months since she came home. They discussed Theophilus's past plans, which had not worked, and his present ones, which might have, had she not discovered them.

Dr. McFarland and others of his profession could well ask themselves how the determined Reverend Packard had happened to leave this revealing packet of letters where the wife he was plotting against would be sure to find them and equally sure to read them. Was he as single-minded in his head as in his heart to rid himself of Elizabeth? Did his conscience trouble him to the point of sabotaging his own intentions? The list of questions his actions could raise is long. The answers, a century later, must be guesswork and, in the long run, irrelevant. From Elizabeth's point of view Theophilus's lapse, whatever the reason, was a benefice.

Dr. Prince of Northampton had written: "I will receive Mrs. Packard as a case of hopeless insanity upon a certificate of Dr. McFarland that she is 'hopelessly insane.' " Dr. McFarland appeared to say that with such a certificate Theophilus could indeed get her entered *without any sort of trial* (Elizabeth's emphasis) and without jeopardizing either his or Theophilus's interests. His closing words were: "The dignity of silence is the only safe course for us both to pursue." Elizabeth took this statement as an admission by the doctor of wrong-doing. In fairness to Dr. McFarland, though, it must be said that he did not actually say he would supply such a certificate and that there were other possible interpretations of that cryptic last line. But in equal fairness it must also be said that Elizabeth's prior experiences at the hands of both the doctor and her husband did not condition her to seek out mitigating circumstances or alternative implications.

One of the letters, from his sister, Marian Severance, was the most alarming of all, especially since Elizabeth had no idea that Marian harbored such ill will toward her. Marian outlined an Alfred Hitchcock-like plot for getting Elizabeth to make the trip from Manteno to Northampton without knowing it.

Theophilus was to let Elizabeth go to New York by train, presumably to discuss her book with a publisher there. He was to follow in a coach behind her, assuring the conductor that she was insane and should be treated as such although she would be sure to deny it. The conductor would be directed to "switch" her off at Northampton instead of letting her continue to the New York terminus. Marian thought Elizabeth would accept all this without question, believing she was detraining at her chosen destination since her ticket would clearly read "New York." The collaborating conductor would have engaged a carriage ostensibly to take her to a hotel, but the carriage would deposit her at the asylum and Dr. Prince could then lock her up for life. Marian's letter ended with the following caution: "You will have her out of the way and can do as you please with her property, her children and even her wardrobe; don't even be responsible this time for her clothing."

Elizabeth went through the letters again and even copied some of them.

She broke into a cold sweat and for a little while she really thought her life was finished. Then she reminded herself that Right always did Prevail and God would help her if she helped herself.

Since she could not count on a visitor and her windows could not be opened for her to call out, there was no one to whom she could turn. Then she remembered that every day lately a strange man had been passing beneath her window to get water from the Packards' pump. She wrote a hasty note to Mrs. Haslett describing the trouble being brewed for her. When next she saw the water carrier, she tapped on the window until he looked up. Then she slid her letter down between the inner and outer frames of the window. It did not stick as it might have and, to her everlasting joy, Theophilus was not there to see it land, but the stranger was and he pocketed it.

This anonymous man obviously delivered the note to Mrs. Haslett. Elizabeth's plight became a subject for town discussion and a variety of solutions, from pedestrian to bizarre, were proposed. In the end Mrs. Haslett journeyed to the courthouse in Kankakee City and consulted the presiding judge, Charles R. Starr.

The way Theophilus told it: "My wife continued to live by herself up to the early part of this year [1864]. Near the first of January she tried to start off for New York City, alone, said she should never again return to the family. I told her, that I thought it my duty to prevent her going. I used no force, and she gave it up." His very next sentence recorded the serving of the writ of habeas corpus on Tuesday, January 12.

So, after nearly four years, Elizabeth finally got her trial before her peers.

On Monday, January 18, before the case went to the jury, Theophilus packed up and departed with George and Libby for the home of his sister Marian in South Deerfield, the town in which he had married Elizabeth nearly twenty-seven years before.

"The bitterest element in this cup of affliction," he wrote, "is the awful irreligious influence which my wife has exerted and is exerting over my dear children. . . . To think that my sons are taught by her and that any of them believe that morality is religion and Universalism is true, is an unspeakable grief to my soul. O, my agony of spirit on this account!"

It later developed that Arthur, only five, was being kept hidden from his mother at the Doles. When Elizabeth went there and tried to see him, Sybil and Abijah flatly denied any knowledge of his whereabouts. Theophilus eventually arranged for Arthur to be brought to him in Massachusetts.

Theophilus never knew that Elizabeth had buried a set of door keys in the garden below her bedroom window. On the Saturday before her trial ended and Theophilus fled town, she went secretly to the house. She let herself in and, with the help of the Orrs, removed her trunk. It was fortunate that she did so for two days later Theophilus mortgaged the house and everything in it, including what was hers, to his sister Sybil for the train fare to Massachusetts.

The next scene in the Packard drama comes in two versions. According to Theophilus, Elizabeth "in March 1864 brought a suit in Kankakee for *divorce*. When my counsel appeared to oppose it, she at once abandoned the case."

But the documents on file at the Kankakee courthouse, the only papers surviving to show that there once was a family named Packard with domestic troubles, indicate that Elizabeth, John Orr still representing her, filed a bill of complaint on February 8, four weeks to the day after her aquittal. It ordered Theophilus to appear before the circuit court of Kankakee County on the "first day of the next term," which would have been the second Monday of the following April, to answer her suit for divorce. On April 2, 1864, a summons to Theophilus was returned to the court with a handwritten notation, signed by the sheriff, along one side: "I return this summons the within Defendant not found in my county." There is no mention of an opposing counsel.

With no home to go to, the newly freed Elizabeth took temporary shelter with the Hanfords. But she would not stay there as a charity case for long. She had to earn some money before she could start her battle for her children, not to mention her rights. And where better to start than with her already written accounts of the abuses she had suffered. Even in the nineteenth century a woman could write, publish and sell the products of her pen.

Elizabeth recognized that she was about to take a path less traveled. Her life would be narrower in focus if wider in scope. The campaigns she planned would submerge her earlier activities around the home and in the parish. Her reading would concentrate on methods of persuasion and strategy. She would have no more time for divertissements such as her correspondence with Abner Baker. And in fact, although she referred to him occasionally in her later writings, there is no indication that they ever met or corresponded once her trial was over.

Minneapolis, Minn. Dec. 21st/86.

My Dear Daughter-in-Law Clara, Allow me to ask you to accept of the enclosed fifty dollars, ($50) as a Christmas Present from your mother-in-law.

It affords me pleasure to bestow this gift upon one so deserving of appreciation, as a Christian mother, & a ph[...]

[...] as my guest. I am anticipating much pleasure by this renewal of an old friendship, & she is very anxious to meet me once more. Should you come to Chicago while I am there I should be very happy to receive a call from you, at the "Windsor Hotel."

I hope my dear grandchildren will never forget their grandmother who feels quite proud of them. Remember me kindly to each one of them, & also your good mother, & kind sister, & ever believe me

Your Affectionate Mother,
E. P. W. [...]

The Sage of Shelburne (the first Theophilus Packard), who helped found Amherst and Mount Holyoke Colleges, and his wife, Mary Tirrell Packard (courtesy of the Packard family).

Elizabeth Packard and her husband, the Reverend Theophilus Packard, Jr., when married life was still a pleasure (courtesy of the Packard family).

Dr. Andrew McFarland, superintendent of the state asylum at Jacksonville, Illinois—perhaps victim, perhaps villain—just after the hospital's trustees had given his administration a clean bill of health (courtesy of the Andrew McFarland Center).

Four illustrations from Mrs. Packard's several books (courtesy of the Packard family).

Samuel E. Sewall, Boston attorney, abolitionist and champion of women's rights, helped Elizabeth Packard draft her first petition to amend commitment laws and campaigned on its behalf (courtesy of Massachusetts Historical Society).

Illinois Governor Richard Oglesby in his first term (1864–1868) during which he signed into law Mrs. Packard's Personal Liberty Law which became a model for other states (courtesy of the Illinois Historical Society).

General Allen C. Fuller, chairman of the committee to investigate Mrs. Packard's charges of mismanagement at the Jacksonville asylum. Known informally as the Packard-Fuller or Fuller-Packard committee, it would recommend replacing Dr. McFarland (which didn't happen) (courtesy of the Illinois Historical Society).

Below: Samuel Ware, the third son, with his younger son John, and grandson John Jr. in California in the 1920s (courtesy of the Packard family).

Ira (Isaac), Elizabeth and Theophilus's second son, named for Theophilus's younger brother, Isaac, who had died at seventeen (courtesy of the Packard family).

Clara Fish Packard, Samuel's wife,
Temperance worker, and mother of the five
children their grandmother hoped would
remember her fondly (courtesy of the Packard
family).

Samuel's daughter Stella, one of those
grandchildren, at Smith College at
the turn of the century (courtesy of the
Packard family).

Samuel and Clara Packard's fiftieth wedding anniversary, June 23, 1924. Standing (l to r): sons
Walter and John. Seated (l to r): Walter's wife, Emma, and daughter, Emmy Lou; John's son, John
Jr.; Samuel and Clara; Walter's older daughter, Clara; and John's wife, Rose Marie (courtesy of the
Packard family).

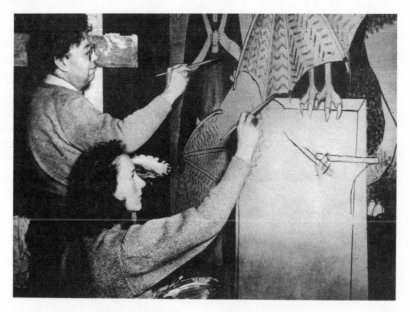

Walter's daughter, Emmy Lou Packard, studying painting with Diego Rivera in Mexico in 1940 (courtesy of Emmy Lou Packard).

Samuel's oldest son Walter, an agronomist, in Athens on behalf of the Marshall Plan in 1951 (courtesy of the Bancroft Library, University of California at Berkeley).

Ina Packard Akins in the 1930s, only daughter of the fourth Theo, who described life in their home when her grandmother and Aunt Lizzie lived with them in the 1890s (courtesy of the Packard family).

7.

The First Campaigns

The first months of 1864 were for Elizabeth a sort of limbo. She was penniless and childless but fortunately not friendless as her temporary host, Mr. Hanford, went to great lengths to illustrate. He wrote to the *Kankakee Gazette* with more or less accuracy: "From the time of her banishment into exile, . . . [her husband] has not allowed her the control of one dollar of their personal property. And she has nothing to do with their real estate." He then described the single real estate transaction she *was* permitted to participate in. She was allowed—no importuned—to sign a deed of transfer of their house and property in Iowa, "which she did at her husband's . . . promise to let her have her 'defense' long enough to copy, which document he had robbed her of three years before, by means of Dr. McFarland as an agent. Her signature *thus obtained*, was acknowledged as a valid act, and the deed was presented to the purchaser as a valid instrument even after Mr. Packard had just taken an *oath* that his wife was an *insane* woman."

Mr. Hanford then listed a number of (already known) abuses of his houseguest: Mr. Packard had reneged on a seven-year-old note he had given her for six hundred dollars that her father had once sent her to use for herself and the children; he had left Manteno with all their common belongings plus her personal wardrobe; he had "rented (mortgaged)" their house without allowing her a share of the rent "to procure for herself the necessities of life"; and, worst of all, he had "kidnapped" all their children still living at home.

Theophilus and the three younger children came to rest at the home of his sister, Marian Severance, in South Deerfield. For a while he found life there peaceful and modestly productive. He moved about the county preaching as needed, rooming where he preached if it was too far from South Deerfield for him to return at night. He finally settled in Sunderland and took a room at the home of a local widow, Mrs. Dickinson (who may have been related to his old college friend, Edward). But he still managed to spend one night a week with his children in South Deerfield.

It was his ill luck that the Reverend Samuel Ware was also living in Sunderland and that before the end of 1864 Elizabeth would come to see her father for the first time in more than a decade. It was bound to be a time of "catching up," and a lengthy list of Theophilus's misdeeds would certainly be aired. His landlady, Mrs. Dickinson, said at the time, "It is such a pity that Mrs. Packard should come to Sunderland where Mr. Packard preaches." But the parishioner to whom she spoke countered that Mrs. Packard had a perfect right to come to her father's house for protection and her father had an equal right to protect her.

Even during her first weeks at the Hanfords, basking in the triumph of her freedom, Elizabeth never forgot her intention of using her pen to become self-supporting as a step toward reclaiming her children and, incidentally, toward telling her story so just men would bring about justice for abused wives. She already had pages and pages of writing with which she could start. After several weeks of freedom and the morale lift of a legal decision that she was not insane, Elizabeth felt a resurgence of energy. She borrowed ten dollars from Mr. Hanford for train fare to Chicago. There, as a starter, she arranged with the Times Steam Job Printing House, 74 Randolph Street, to publish her November 1860 "Reproof to Dr. McFarland for his Abuses of His Patients." She paid the printer a hundred dollars, some of it left from the money the Granville people had collected for her, the rest borrowed (reluctantly) from friends. She had a thousand copies printed and sold them for ten cents each, netting ninety dollars. It seemed a fantastically easy way to make money. If she could make that much from a brief pamphlet, what could she not earn from her far more meaty "The Great Drama," all 2,500 pages of it.

She consulted with the printer and found that to print a thousand copies of her book would cost twenty-five times as much. The price sounded prohibitive, but remembering the obstacles she had already overcome, Elizabeth was sure she could find a way to surmount this barrier, too. And one night she did. It came to her in the dark of her bedroom that she could sell for 50¢ each promissory notes for her yet-to-be published work that could be redeemed for the book itself once it came off the press, and as she collected for these notes, she could make a down payment to the printer. Elizabeth was so delighted with this scheme that she entitled a chapter in one of her subsequent books "How to Commence Business Without Capital."

These promissory notes, which she called "tickets," read: "The Bearer is Entitled to the First Volume of Mrs. Packard's Book Entitled 'The Great Drama, or The Millennial Harbinger,' Price 50¢. None are genuine without my signature, E. P. W. Packard."

In anticipation of publication, she gave out a somewhat premature announcement to the local paper: " 'The Great Drama, or the Millennial Harbinger,' a work in 12 parts or volumes, is about to be issued . . . in defense of Humanity, on the common sense principles on which our Republican Institutions are based. By the persecuted Woman, EPW Packard. Manteno 1864."

Elizabeth set herself an arbitrary target of 1,400 tickets to be sold in three months. Many of her friends and neighbors offered to contribute but she refused gifts. She would take money only in exchange for the tickets. Since the price was modest and her friends eager to help, they bought.

She organized her campaign carefully. Then she set out by train to crisscross as much of Illinois as she could afford to. At each stopover she would find a "reliable agent," usually a postmaster or owner of a bookstore, whom she could persuade—as either good business or a good turn to a lady in distress—to receive the published books and deliver copies to ticket holders. Then she would seek out customers on the streets and in the lobbies of hotels, inns and rooming houses where she stayed overnight, often on credit. Obviously Elizabeth managed to arouse the latent chivalry in the nineteenth-century male. But to her, all her actions were strictly business.

The same was true of her ticket selling. People in the towns and on the trains, where she cruised the aisles with her tickets, were intrigued by this handsome, articulate, middle-aged woman, obviously a lady in the Victorian sense of the word, who told such an improbable story and engaged in such a novel and, for those days, unseemly activity. Some bought tickets out of curiosity. Some recognized her name from the lurid newspaper coverage of her trial and bought as people today seek autographs; some bought to escape her high-pressure sales talk.

Elizabeth never questioned their motives. She was convinced that she had a salable product and an acceptable sales technique; every ticket she sold reinforced that belief.

She was obviously effective. A brief paragraph in the *Illinois State Journal* of Springfield, on August 20, 1864, said: "New Book.—Mrs. E. P. W. Packard has placed upon our table a work, in pamphlet form, entitled 'Exposure of Calvinism & Defense of Christianity,' of which she is the author. Price 50¢. This is the first volume or a kind of advertisement of 11 volumes which are to follow this, and which will complete the work under the title of 'The Great Drama; or the Millennial Harbinger.' Mrs. P. [sic] is now engaged in making sales of the work in this city."

When she had sold somewhere between eight hundred and nine hundred tickets, Elizabeth went back to Chicago to find a printer. This time she chose The American Press. Wartime inflation had driven up the price of paper; her book would now cost half again as much as she had anticipated. However, lessening that blow, she learned that once the plates had been paid for, she could have a second edition for only a third as much as the first. So she continued to sell her tickets. As a concession to economics, she raised their price to seventy-five cents and her goal to two thousand.

By the time the last ticket was sold, Elizabeth had paid for the plates; she had also paid all her back bills and had some money left over. She continued to peddle the tickets if less aggressively. With money in the bank she could relax a bit and think about other problems, too, which was fortunate because suddenly a snag developed that no novice could have anticipated.

Elizabeth was downstate on one of her selling trips when she received her first proof sheets. The printer had not used the typeface she had chosen. She instantly sent him a message to stop the presses and rushed back to Chicago to set things right. She discovered that though he was a specialist in job and paper printing, he knew little about books and she had not been able to give him proper instructions because she knew even less. But the entire problem was now academic. The American Press had gone out of business.

The momentum Elizabeth had built up was sufficient to carry her over this stumbling block. Scouting around, she found a man at the *Chicago Tribune* who remembered her from her trial. He agreed to handle the job for her. At his instigation she hired a stereotyper, an engraver and a bookbinder. Then she left town again to sell more tickets. But she had to come back repeatedly to correct proofs and give her employees partial payments to keep them working. To them, a woman publisher was like Samuel Johnson's woman preacher: They marveled at her existence; they had little confidence in her competence. These travel expenses plus the hotel where she stayed in Chicago (at $17.95 a week) all came out of her ticket sales. No longer did she need to ask for credit.

Elizabeth continued her bookselling and in fifteen months had sold twelve thousand tickets. It was at the halfway point, late in 1864, that she decided to return to Massachusetts to visit her aging father. She had not seen him in twelve years; he might still think her insane and she wanted to prove to him that she was not.

She stopped first in South Deerfield where her youngest brother, Austin, lived, not two miles from Theophilus's sister, Marian. She spent two days with him and his family. After living for nearly a year with the knowledge that her sanity had been confirmed legally, Elizabeth was considerably calmer. In that two-day visit, at close quarters, her conversation and demeanor, her affection and her intelligence convinced Austin and his wife that Theophilus had misinformed them. They tried to arrange a visit with the nearby children but Theophilus refused. Austin then drove Elizabeth to Sunderland.

Old Samuel Ware was conscience stricken because he had unquestioningly accepted everything Theophilus had told him about Elizabeth and had even contributed money to defray her hospital expenses. Now he rallied to her defense. Theophilus might refuse to let the children see their mother; he could hardly deny them a visit to their aged grandfather, Theophilus's old mentor, who was approaching the end of his life. Samuel sent Austin to the Severances with this request. But all Austin returned with was a letter. "I came from Illinois to Massachusetts to protect the children from their mother," Theophilus wrote, "and I shall do it, in spite of you or Father Ware, or anyone else."

Austin, whom Elizabeth had once characterized as "slow," quickly came to Elizabeth's own conclusion, using a word he must have learned from her: "The mystery of this dark case is now solved in my mind completely. Mr. Packard is a monomaniac on this subject; there is no more reason in his treatment of Sister than in a brute."

Sunderland and its environs were not as instantaneously aware as was Manteno of the prodigal's return. Elizabeth's predicament had not been public property back east as it had been in Illinois, but word finally spread that Preacher Ware's daughter had come home and that her husband was refusing to let her see her own children. The local residents were indignant and said so. Theophilus felt that adverse public sentiment could damage his interests. In a short time he had a change of mind, if not of heart. With his sister, Marian as bodyguard and witness, he brought the children to the Ware home ostensibly to visit their grandfather, a semantic quibble for reunion with their mother.

Seeing her husband revived Elizabeth's old terrors. The law in Massachusetts concerning commitment to asylums was not much of an improvement over Illinois. Affidavits from two physicians, qualified or not, were enough to get a person put away. If Theophilus were to acquire such affidavits, neither her father nor her brother could save her from further institutionalization. Elizabeth was afraid to stay in such close proximity to her husband.

She had proved she could be persuasive in selling books to the public. Perhaps she could turn this same talent to selling ideas to legislators. So shortly after Christmas 1864, she set out for Boston to see if she could get some kind of protection for endangered wives written into the law. As fuel for her campaign, she had some six thousand more copies of her book printed locally so she could start peddling them. This upset Theophilus. He entered (retroactively) in his diary: "My wife . . . published one of her six books or pamphlets containing falsehoods and slanders respecting me, and sold them extensively . . . to my injury. In many cases papers would publish her false story, and refuse to publish the testimony of witnesses I sent them."

In many cases, perhaps, but not all. The Kankakee paper, with scrupulous fairness, printed his complaint and sent a copy, along with his corroborating testimony, to the *Boston Daily Advertiser*, which on May 3, 1865 printed it all. This in turn, infuriated Stephen Moore, Elizabeth's defense attorney, who felt personally maligned. On May 15, 1865, he sent a lengthy rebuttal to the Boston paper.

The certificates of corroboration, he wrote, were designed to prove either that Elizabeth's account of her trial was false or that Theophilus "is not so bad a man as those who read the trial would be likely to suppose him to be." Elizabeth's account, he said, was made from his own notes which had never been called into question before. "Policy and selfish motives would prevent me from making an incorrect report, if I was guided by nothing higher."

Then he discussed the aforementioned witnesses' statements, the certificates. The first was signed by the Doles, "as the trial shows [Theophilus's] co-conspirators"; by one of his deacons, J. B. Smith, "who was a willing tool"; and by Miss Sarah Rumsey.

"Let Jefferson Davis be put on trial," he wrote, "and then take certificates of Mrs. Surratt, Payne, Azteroth, Arnold, Dr. Mudd and George N. Saunders, and I am led to believe they would make Jefferson [Davis] out to be a 'Christian President' whom the barbarous north were trying to murder." Their additional statement that "the disorderly demonstrations by the furious populace, filling the Court House . . . were well calculated to prevent a fair trial is simply bosh. . . . 'The furious populace' consisted of about 200 ladies of our city who visited the trial . . . because they felt a sympathy for one of their own sex whose treatment had become notorious in our city."

The second certificate, Moore continued, was from young Samuel Packard, who was "entirely under his father's control." A third one, from Libby, "takes umbrage because I called her . . . the 'little daughter' of Mrs. Packard . . . and she was then *14*." Moore also attacked a statement in the final certificate given by one of Theophilus's lawyers that a large portion of the community was more interested in an attack on Presbyterians than on the question of Mrs. Packard's sanity. What did the "feelings" of the community have to do with the court and the jury? Moore rhetorically asked the lawyer. "You selected the jury. You said they were good men. If not good, you could have rejected them. . . . If Packard believed he could not [have a fair trial] the statute of Illinois provides for a change of venue." The publicized account of the trial no doubt presented Theophilus and his "confederates" in an unfavorable light. Moore concluded: "If they do not like the picture, they should not have presented the original."

Both Theophilus and Stephen Moore were flogging dead horses. By the time this exchange of letters appeared, Elizabeth, with the help of some crusading Bostonians, had talked, cajoled and persuaded her way to her first legislative triumph.

Elizabeth was not the first to find fault with hospitals for the insane. The few such institutions that existed in the early part of the century were poorly staffed, poorly managed and in poor repair. As their number increased, treatment of the insane became more professional and mental institutions began to offer to the professionally-trained prestigious job opportunities at good pay. By 1844 there were enough superintendents of such hospitals to warrant their forming a professional association as a lobbying and educational organization.

By midcentury, legislatures, as well as families of current and former inmates, were attacking asylum superintendents for a variety of abuses from patient care to financial mismanagement. But before Elizabeth took up her cudgel, the question of how and why those men and women had become patients in the first place had hardly been raised.

That was about to change.

Whether or not Elizabeth knew before she left Sunderland that there were champions waiting in Boston, she quickly found one, the Honorable Samuel E. Sewall.

Samuel Edward Sewall was an old-time Yankee, descended from two Massachusetts Supreme Court judges (one of whom had written an anti-slavery pamphlet as early as 1700). For twenty years, he had been battling for women's causes. In fact so well known was his stand for equality of the sexes before the law that John Greenleaf Whittier wrote a poem about him, the second verse of which read:

> And never Woman in her suffering saw
> A helper tender, wise and brave as he;
> Lifting her burden of unrighteous law,
> He shamed the boasts of ancient chivalry.

Sewall had attended Phillips Exeter, Harvard College, and Harvard Law School. He was admitted to the bar in 1821. In 1836 he married a Quaker and abolitionist. His wife's attitudes plus William Lloyd Garrison's first lecture in Boston, which he attended, converted him to the antislavery cause. It was a logical next step from supporting personal liberty for slaves to supporting personal liberty for women, a parallel Theophilus never even recognized.

In 1851 Sewall was elected to the Massachusetts Senate. As a senator he sponsored a bill to amend the law of evidence so witnesses would not be prohibited from testifying because of unconventional religious opinions, including disbelief in God. He advocated the reform of divorce laws and the abolition of capital punishment. He introduced for the first time a bill that made a wife the legal owner of her own property—all before he ever heard of Elizabeth Parsons Ware Packard.

In 1850 Sewall's wife died. After that, according to his longtime partner, "he spent almost half his time in endeavoring to protect the weak and defenseless." One of his more dramatic cases was that of a Mrs. Denny.

Mrs. Denny made the mistake of suing her husband for divorce. Mr. Denny promptly charged her with being insane and had her confined to a private asylum where she was cut off from all communication with family and friends. Like Elizabeth, she secreted pieces of paper. On these slips, she scribbled notes to Sewall that she dropped from the carriage in which she was taken for occasional airings. Some of them reached him and he charged to the rescue, gaining her her freedom. When Elizabeth came to him with a not dissimilar story, he was more than ready to do battle for the unjustly committed.

Sewall drafted a petition to the state legislature to amend existing laws pertaining to commitment and became the first to sign it (see Appendix 2). Elizabeth, certain that she was the motivating power behind the move, set out to ring bells and knock on doors at banks, mercantile establishments, courts of justice, newspaper offices, doctors' offices, and even the halls of government. In each place she told her own story; sometimes she added some embroidered stories of people she had known at Jacksonville. (The case of Mrs. Denny had already been told.) In all, she gathered 116 signatures from civic leaders, all men of property, many of them longtime abolitionists, ever ready to join a fight to expand personal liberties. She claimed she could have got hundreds more from the working classes had she needed them, and she was probably right. Boston, the cradle of liberty, was fertile ground for such as she.

Elizabeth had added to her usual run of prospective book buyers workers at the Boston Customs House and the Navy Yard. She actually spent a day and a half at the Navy Yard, talking to the laborers there. They listened and didn't seem to scoff. She sold 139 of her tickets. (She found only one, she reported, who disagreed with her and was willing to leave commitment procedures as they were.)

Opponents of her petition drive, largely doctors and hospital super-intendents, claimed that nineteen-twentieths of the signers did not know what they were petitioning for and only signed as a favor to a gracious lady. This Elizabeth disputed. She had personally witnessed every signa-ture, *after* the signer had read the document. The only exceptions were the members of the Common Council who signed the petition during an evening session at which they passed it around the table. But, though she did not witness *each* signature, she did observe the scene, and it was her distinct impression that they all *seemed* to be reading it before passing it along.

The petition with its 117 distinguished signatories was submitted to the legislature. On January 26, 1865, the representative from Charlestown introduced a bill in the House of Representatives to amend the commitment law. It was referred to a select committee. Four days later the Senate referred the bill to its Committee on Public Charitable Institutions. Both groups then held hearings of which only Elizabeth's notes remain. Elizabeth, along with Mrs. Denny and a Mrs. Phelps (also committed by her husband, a state senator, because she learned he had been unfaithful and so charged him) were invited to appear before the committees. The committees allowed Elizabeth to offer two bills of her own. The first said that no one should be considered or treated as insane (or "monomaniac") simply for expressing opinions that might appear absurd to others. The second specified that the only basis for committing and treating anyone as insane should be "irregularities of conduct" so extreme that they show the person in question to be an "unaccountable moral agent."

Elizabeth's defense of these proposals was that reformers, pioneers and originators of any new ideas were open to the charge of monomania and institutionalizing them would threaten human progress. Also, many cases that some call *monomania* others would call individuality, and unless behavior were the criterion, individual liberty was in danger.

The committees met several times. Elizabeth spoke earnestly and urgently for the proposed amendment. Samuel Sewall argued strongly for it as did the great orator and emancipator, Wendell Phillips (who was already on record as having said, "We do not seek to protect woman but rather to place her in a position to protect herself.") The firepower was strong.

Elizabeth's two proposals were not acted upon, but on May 2, 1865, the Massachusetts law concerning the insane was duly amended by the House. Nine days later, on May 11, 1865, the Senate concurred with the succinct statement, "The same ought to pass." On May 16, 1865, the last day of the session, these revisions were enacted. The key provision for Elizabeth personally was a requirement that a committed person was entitled to have ten relatives and two other people of his or her choosing notified. This would be adequate protection against conspirators (see Appendix 3).

The next day the *Boston Post* reported: "In the legislature yesterday, numerous bills were disposed of in accordance with the desire of the members to get away as soon as possible." And the *Boston Daily Journal* editorialized: "The Legislature did a rushing business yesterday as will be seen by our report. Measures of great importance were reported by com-mittees, or introduced on leave, and rushed through without debate, and with but a very few members understanding what they were voting for."

Despite this journalistic cynicism and despite the yeoman efforts of such as Samuel Sewall and Wendell Phillips, Elizabeth felt personally trium-phant, in part because the amendment was passed, in part because she had discovered and enjoyed the fine art of lobbying, and in part because she need no longer fear Theophilus's hot breath at her neck. Now, under state law her family would have to cooperate in any commitment proceedings against her, and since they were satisfied that she was *not* insane, The-ophilus's hands were tied. Elizabeth felt like her old, youthful self again. Her separation from Theophilus and the legal protection of the new Massa-chusetts law, added to the Kankakee jury's decision, washed away much of her paranoid and hysterical behavior. Her new cause was a satisfactory substitute for her old war against Calvin.

She decided to take on another state, neighboring Connecticut. For this campaign she would try a new tack. She would try to talk the legislature into legally establishing a wife as "companion to her husband and joint partner with him in the family interests," particularly in the care and responsibility of their children; a say in the running of the household, and incidentally, a right to decisions about her own body (an anticipation of today's pro-choice argument).

She drew up a petition to that effect and launched her drive for signatures in New Haven. There she sold 500 copies of her book, talked to "1000 intelligent men," and persuaded 250 of them to sign the petition. Then she went to Hartford, the state capital.

In May 1866, Representative Isaac Woolworth introduced her bill into the Connecticut legislature (see Appendix 4). The petition was referred to the Joint Standing Committee on the Judiciary, chaired by President *pro tem* of the Senate, John T. Wait. Wait invited Elizabeth to address the commit-tee. The audience included not only legislators but clergymen, Judge Henry Dutton, a professor at Yale Law School, and his students and a scattering of interested women.

It was Elizabeth's first attempt at public speaking. She drew on her youthful experience as a teacher. They listened in silence. Then there was a burst of applause. Senator Wait asked three times if there were any objec-tions to passing such a bill. No one spoke up. Finally he said, "There seems to be but one side to this question."

But in this case silence did not mean assent. The committee, according to the *Journal of the House for 1866*, was "adverse [sic] to granting the prayer of the petitioner." The Senate recommended and the House concurred that the petitioners be given leave to withdraw their petition, which presumably they did. Elizabeth was about ten years too early.

While the joint committee was considering the bill, the *New Haven Journal* printed a column that Elizabeth described as "cruel and vile slanders against my moral character." She later learned that at the same time a sort of chain letter of denigration was being circulated among the legislators and some clergymen.

These attacks on Elizabeth would become staples of her campaigns. She always suspected, and wanted to suspect, that Dr. McFarland was behind them. He may have been. But there were other antagonists. Many nineteenth-century psychiatrists felt that their practice of their profession was threatened by the laws she advocated and fought back by trying to discredit her.

Even though Connecticut represented a legislative defeat, the visit was not a total loss. Elizabeth arranged for the publication of another book, *Marital Power Exemplified in Mrs. Packard's Trial*, subtitled *Self-defense from the Charge of Insanity; or Three Years' Imprisonment for Religious Belief, by the Arbitrary Will of a Husband with An Appeal to the Government to Change the Laws as to Protect the Rights of Married Women.* It was published in Hartford in 1866.

Elizabeth returned to Sunderland as exhilarated as she could be while separated from her children. She had been gone for eight months.

Those months had not been kind to the Reverend Samuel Ware and his wife, Olive, both in their eighties. Elizabeth found "both my parents feeble and in need of someone to care for them, and finding myself in need of a season of rest and quiet, I accepted their kind invitation to make their house my home for the present."

The year 1865 had been a mixed bag for Theophilus. As minister at Sunderland, he was named a delegate to a National Congregational Council that met in Boston in June. Between sessions, the delegates took a trip to Plymouth and had their pictures taken posing around Plymouth Rock. Theophilus proudly saved his copy of the pictures so "my posterity can see ... my face in the Photograph." But the year ended sadly for him. On December 4, his "excellent & beloved mother, aged 90 years and 17 days" died. "She lived to see all eight offspring indulge hopes in the mercy of a crucified redeemer," he wrote, "and to witness five of them dying in peace, joy and hope."

In September of that year, Samuel Packard, his middle son, came east from Chicago where he had been working, to resume his schooling. His ailing grandmother gave him four hundred dollars for tuition, which he spent first at the Shelburne Falls Academy and then at the Easthampton Seminary. (He returned to Chicago in July 1866.)

"God forbid," wrote Theophilus in his diary, "that he should, under the influence of that education, *thus acquired*, forsake the religion of his *godly Grandmother*, and give up the great doctrines of the Bible, which supported and comforted her so greatly in her last sickness and took away the fear of death. . . . If he fails of the glorious religion of the Bible, how can he meet her at the final judgment! My anxiety for his soul is great!" Theophilus did not seem to have much confidence in nineteenth-century education.

Early that same September, after Elizabeth had settled in with her father and stepmother and her full account of her years in the midwest had been told, the Reverend Samuel Ware took up his pen in behalf of his daughter. He sent a letter to Theophilus:

> *Rev. Sir: I think the time has fully come for you to give up to Elizabeth her clothes. Whatever reason might have existed to justify you in retaining them, has, in process of time, entirely vanished. . . . Elizabeth is about to make a home at my house and I must be her protector. She is very destitute of clothing and greatly needs all those articles which are hers. I hope to hear from you soon, before I shall be constrained to take another step. Yours Respectfully etc.*

Within twenty-four hours of receiving the letter, Theophilus delivered the missing wardrobe to the Ware home. Shortly thereafter he lost his pulpit in Sunderland. Whether there was a cause-and-effect relationship is unclear but many thought there was. In answer to a clergyman friend who inquired about it, Elizabeth wrote on her father's behalf and at his request:

> *We have every reason to believe that my father's defense of me has been the indirect cause of Mr. Packard's leaving Sunderland, although we knew nothing of the matter until he left and a candidate filled his place.* Neither my father,*

---

* The Wares had by now returned to South Deerfield, Samuel Ware's last home.

> *mother nor I have used any direct influence to undermine the confidence of the*
> *people in Mr. Packard. But where this simple fact, that I have been imprisoned*
> *three years, is known to have become a demonstrated truth, by decision of a*
> *jury . . . it is found to be rather an unfortunate truth for the public sentiment of*
> *the present age to grapple with.*

The tone of this letter was a far cry from the frantic outbursts of her asylum years.

Theophilus made no mention of these events in either his diary or his journal. The chances are that Elizabeth's surmise was correct, that public opinion had once again turned against him because of his die-hard attitude toward his wife.

During the next several months Elizabeth was happier than she had been in many years. She reveled in the tenderness her father showed her, feeling that his "fatherly conduct" constituted the best apology he could make for not having come to her defense earlier.

Her father made several gestures that reinforced this feeling. He told her he believed she should have custody of her children; he said she had been "the best mother to them that I ever knew and were it in my power you should now have them all, and never be separated from them again."

He also redrew his will, increasing her share of his property. As a statement of confidence in her sanity, he left her share to her outright instead of "in trust," something he could legally do in Massachusetts thanks, in part, to Samuel Sewall. He told her brothers, "Elizabeth is just as capable of taking care of property as you are . . . therefore I shall leave her portion to her independent of supervision."

And, on August 2, 1866, he issued a public statement of belief in her sanity to undo the effects of statements he had made in defense of Theophilus six years earlier.

> *This is to certify that the certificates which have appeared in public in relation*
> *to my daughter's sanity were given under the conviction that Mr. Packard's*
> *representations respecting her condition were true, and were given wholly upon*
> *the authority of Mr. Packard's own statements. I do, therefore, hereby certify*
> *that it is now my opinion that Mr. Packard had no cause for treating my*
> *daughter Elizabeth as an insane person.*

His wife, Olive, and youngest son, Austin, cosigned the document as witnesses to its authenticity.

Four weeks later, as if he felt he had tied up all the loose ends, made all the restitution he could to his daughter, and could safely leave her, Samuel Ware, just short of his eighty-fifth birthday, quietly died.

In the months Elizabeth had spent with her father, they had recaptured the closeness they shared before he put her in the Worcester hospital. She could now grieve with love.

Theophilus, once again without work, was back in South Deerfield with his sister. Since Grandfather Ware was no longer there to demand visits from his grandchildren, Elizabeth saw little of her young ones. She was determined to regain custody but she was not yet prepared for a head-on confrontation. She wanted to consolidate her independence first. So she decided to go back to Illinois where her trial and book publishing had given her some public recognition, to try to achieve in Springfield what she had in Boston. And once her father's estate was settled, she would be able to finance her reformer's activities out of her own pocket.

Elizabeth did not realize that Illinois (Chicago excepted) was not Massachusetts. There were no white knights on horseback waiting for her in Springfield.

8.

Once More
into the Fray

$\mathcal{E}$lizabeth *returned to* Chicago in December 1866, ready to take on the state of Illinois. She was armed with letters of recommendation, new and old, to open doors and breach legislative walls.

The new letter was from Samuel Sewall; the others she had acquired in 1864 before she left Illinois for Massachusetts. She had been saving them for an appropriate moment.

Sewall had written:

> *I have been acquainted with Mrs. E.P.W. Packard for about a year. She is a person of great religious feeling, high moral principle, and warm philanthropy. She is a logical thinker, a persuasive speaker, and such an agitator, that she sometimes succeeds where a man would fail.*
>
> *I give Mrs. Packard these lines of recommendation, because she has asked for them. I do not think them at all necessary, for she can recommend herself far better than I can.*

The first of the earlier letters was from William A. Boardman, an old and distinguished judge in Illinois. Judge Boardman had attested (on the heels of her trial) that he was "acquainted with Mrs. E.P.W. Packard, and verily believes her not only sane, but that she is a person of very superior endowments of mind and understanding, naturally possessing an exceedingly well-balanced organization, which, no doubt prevented her from becoming insane, under the persecution, incarceration and treatment she has received."

Her other letter was from the Honorable S. S. Jones, a longtime member of the Illinois legislature: "That Mrs. Packard was a victim of a foul and cruel conspiracy, I have not a single doubt, and that she is and ever has been as sane as any other person, I verily believe. . . . Trusting through her much suffering the public will become more enlightened, and that . . . Mrs. Packard may be the last subject of such a Conspiracy. . . ."

With these testimonials, Elizabeth sought a local lawyer to help her draw up a petition to the legislature to change the commitment procedures of Illinois. She found Judge James B. Bradwell, and his wife Myra, both active in women's movements. The Judge was willing enough to draft the petition but, unlike Samuel Sewall, he was not willing to join in the battle. She also found that there had already been a change in the law, perhaps as a result of the publicity given the 1851 statute during her trial.

Two years before, during the 1865 session, the General Assembly of Illinois had amended the 1851 law to require a trial before a judge and jury for anyone accused of insanity. But the law had no teeth. There were no penalties for violating it and it was being violated regularly. So Elizabeth shifted gears. Her goal would now be the passage of enabling legislation so the 1865 law could be enforced.

Judge Bradwell drew up the petition. With Christmas approaching, Elizabeth spent a strenuous week circulating it among the best and the brightest in Chicago. She collected thirty-six signatures from the mayor, city aldermen, judges, lawyers, newspaper editors, and members of the Board of Trade and the Chamber of Commerce. But no doctors signed. She did not say whether members of the medical profession had turned her down or whether she had prudently refrained from approaching any. She did say that only one of those who signed was even aware of the contents of the current law before his encounter with her.

The *Chicago Tribune* and *Chicago Times*, which she thanked along with the Springfield papers in the prefaces to her books, ran supportive editorials like this: "Humanity, not to say Christianity, demands that special enactments shall make impossible such atrocities as are alleged in the case of Mrs. Packard."

Elizabeth spent Christmas in Chicago. Two of her sons were there. Samuel, whose teenage ambivalence about his parents had matured into acceptance of their differences and realization that those differences did not interfere with their love for him, had returned from the East to study law at the firm of Barker and Tuley. Isaac was in training at the wholesale mercantile firm of Cooley and Farwell. Cooley, in his childhood, had been one of Elizabeth's pupils in western Massachusetts. He was not bright, and she helped him to pass his exams. He remembered her, and when he moved west years later he looked her up and gave her second son his start. (Theo was now also a mercantile apprentice in Mount Pleasant, Iowa.)

The holiday season, during which so many activities, including legislative ones, came to a halt, gave Elizabeth time to continue work on her books.

At the beginning of 1867 she went down to Springfield to prepare the campaign she would launch when the Illinois General Assembly opened its regular session the second Wednesday of January. Her first stop was the governor's mansion, in the evening when she was sure the governor would be at home.

The governor was home when Elizabeth rang his bell but he was hosting a dinner party and had no time for her. She asked if he would spare a half hour to discuss her proposed bill. When he heard it would affect the insane asylum at Jacksonville, he demurred; Dr. McFarland was a personal friend of his. But after he saw the names of the thirty-six petitioners, he agreed to see her the next day in his office at the statehouse between 11 A.M. and noon.

Governor Richard Oglesby had first come to the voters' attention at the Republican convention of 1859 where he was a key figure in swinging the presidential nomination to the prairie lawyer, Abraham Lincoln. In 1864, the Republicans, together with the Union Democrats (as opposed to the Democrats who sided with the Confederacy), had elected him governor. Under him, Illinois became the first state to ratify the Thirteenth Amendment which abolished slavery.

The governor listened to Elizabeth's arguments, read the petition and, already predisposed to expanding the areas of freedom, passed her on, despite his friendship with Andrew McFarland, to Representative Elmer Baldwin.

Since the governor appeared to be sponsoring her, Mr. Baldwin thought as many members of the assembly as possible should hear her. He let her use his office for little conferences with the legislators who were now arriving daily for the imminent opening of the General Assembly. Elizabeth exercised her persuasiveness on "a reasonable number of members" who, in turn, passed her on to the House Committee on the Judiciary. Each referral gave her and her cause added weight.

The committee suggested that she draft the sort of bill she had in mind. Passage of the reform was now more important to Elizabeth than personal credit for its authorship; she persuaded Senator Joseph D. Ward of Chicago to draft a bill for her. Although she was not satisfied with his proposal, the draft did provide a basis for discussion. She wanted a stiff penalty for those who accepted patients without the required trial; the committee wrote in a monetary fine and a prison term. She wanted trials for those incarcerated without them and a time limit for such trials; the committee specified a sixty-day period from the date on which the bill became law. She wanted a tribunal before which the retroactive trials would be held; it chose a single person, the state attorney general.

It did not take long for Springfield to discover Elizabeth's presence. On January 4, the *Illinois State Register* printed on its front page:

Appeal by a Lady

An intelligent lady, whose appearance and manners indicate education and heart, has left on our table a volume containing the history of her misfortune and persecution. Her name is Mrs. Packard; her husband is a minister of the gospel, and as she alleges, procured her arrest and imprisonment as a lunatic in the state asylum because of her refusal to accept the doctrine of total depravity. The book is designed to inform the public of the power husbands may assume under the law, over their wives. Mrs. Packard designs to bring the subject matter of complaint before the general assembly to the end that relief may be provided other unfortunates who are suffering under similar persecution.

Perhaps this prominent notice called Dr. McFarland's attention to Elizabeth's activities; perhaps his friend, Richard Oglesby, had already told him. At any rate, the doctor, who had not been heard from since his testimony in absentia at Kankakee, was moved to action now that the battleground was his own backyard and his name and reputation were bound to be mentioned if not maligned. He set about organizing opposition to Elizabeth's proposed bill. Her smoothly planned campaign, off to such an auspicious start, was brought up short by newly aroused suspicions and antagonisms.

Dr. McFarland's public objection to Elizabeth's bill was that subjecting a mentally "deranged" or insane person to a jury trial would be so traumatic that many families would refrain from so doing and thus deprive the sufferers of necessary and beneficial treatment. Many of his colleagues agreed with him.*

He took his fight straight to the legislature. He sought out members of the assembly in the hotels and boardinghouses of Springfield where they stayed during the session and attempted to convince them that Elizabeth was and continued to be insane. Also, in the best twentieth-century public-relations manner, he arranged for the state press, then meeting in Spring-field, to visit Jacksonville as the hospital's guests. (There were three other state institutions at Jacksonville—institutes for the blind, for the deaf and dumb, and for "idiots"; the press would be able to visit them all.) It was a classic journalists' junket.

Transportation to Jacksonville was provided by the Toledo, Wabash & Western Railroad. The special cars left Springfield at 8 A.M. on Thursday, January 10. At Jacksonville the reporters and their wives were met by town authorities in carriages and driven to the insane asylum where Dr. McFarland greeted them. They were then divided into two groups, those over thirty-five years old and those under (largely the wives), for a tour of the facilities. Dr. McFarland led the first group; his assistant, Dr. Dutton, aided by a McFarland daughter, led the second. The tour was followed by a midday dinner (the *Illinois State Journal* called it "magnificent, to say the least") after which, according to the *Journal*, "everyone toasted everyone. They were having a high old time when they had to leave for the Deaf & Dumb Institution."

The press, in general, treated the visit as a less than serious assignment. Comments on the institutions visited were few. The *Illinois State Journal* wrote about the charms of Miss McFarland, the sumptuousness of the dinner table and the quality of the Havana cigars passed around after the meal. The *Jacksonville Journal* reported that the men were more interested in the farm, stables, cow shed and pig yards than they were in the patients. The *Waukegan Gazette* was an exception. It was surprised at the number of farmers among the inmates. "Many," it wrote, "at first would imagine the quiet life of

---

* Actually, the 1865 reform, as so often happens, was as extreme as the evil it was designed to correct, and twenty-five years later, it was amended to substitute a private hearing before a judge for the jury trial.

an agriculturist rendered him free from mania." Not so. The large proportion of farmers among the inmates was in keeping with statistics from similar institutions and should "enjoin upon farmers the necessity of more mental exercises and less monotony of life and thought—a little less care for wealth and more for mental culture."

Elizabeth had no time for entertaining or feasting. She had to expend all her energy on trying to beat back Dr. McFarland's attacks on her and her bill without lending credence to his accusations. She copied his tactics. She appealed to the hoteliers and landlords of the rooming houses to let her talk to their legislative boarders as Dr. McFarland had. Most of them agreed. She wanted to argue for the bill but, equally important, to demonstrate to them that she was not insane. She was given permission to use the front parlors to hold little meetings, which she did, night after night. Speaking mostly to House members, she was as calm and reasonable and as quick with details as possible. As Samuel Sewall had indicated in his letter, she was logical and persuasive and quite convincing. Her listeners seemed sympathetic and many of them promised to vote yes on her bill; some even agreed to speak on its behalf.

There was no doubt she was effective, and that fact in itself spoke loudly for her vis-à-vis Dr. McFarland.

Dr. Richard Dewey, who followed Dr. McFarland as head of the asylum at Jacksonville, wrote of her and her crusade in his memoirs: "Whether at any time insane or not, Mrs. E.P.W. was now a woman of fine appearance, having shrewdness and ability." And Albert Deutsch, in discussing her Illinois campaign in *The Mentally Ill in America*, echoed that view: "Her behavior following her discharge from the state hospital at Jacksonville was so intelligent, and her ability so striking, as to lend weight to her charge that she had been 'railroaded.' "

In addition to peddling her cause, her books and her pamphlets, Elizabeth wrote anonymous letters to the newspapers to draw still more public attention to the bill. There was a time lag between her writing and the papers' publication of them; the bill was already going through the legislative process by the time the letters began to appear.

Elizabeth did not save, or if she did, did not reproduce in her books, these "anonymous" letters, but it isn't hard to spot them. They bear her touch.

On January 26 the following appeared in the *Illinois State Journal*, under the heading "Dr. McFarland's Report Opposed to Jury Trials":

*He says, "What antagonisms of the most painful kind are wantonly
engendered, what violations of delicacy, and often of decency, what outrages
upon mental and physical sufferings must be the result [of jury trials]?"*

*We wish to ask . . . which course would be most likely to engender
antagonisms, the consignment of a relative to an indefinite term of imprisonment
without allowing them any hearing or any chance of self defense . . . ? the
imprisonment of an individual on the decision of 12 impartial men . . . or the
decision of one interested man . . . ?*

*Again Dr. McFarland says, "in nearly 3,000 admissions here, a question
was never seriously raised in a single instance." Has the Doctor forgotten that
the question has been once, at least, seriously raised by the Court at Kankakee
City? (signed A Lover of Justice.)*

Another, a few days later, headed "Legislative Justice" and signed *Humanity*,
said:

*If legislatures make unjust laws, have they not only a right to repeal such
laws, but are they not in justice bound to repair, as far as possible, the injuries
they have occasioned? For example, the Illinois Legislature of 1851 passed a
law allowing married women to be imprisoned at the Jacksonville Insane
Asylum at the request of the husband. . . . There is reason to believe that many
a helpless wife and mother . . . has been consigned there . . . and some . . . are
now lingering out a most wretched existence.*

On Monday, January 14, the day the legislature opened its 1867 session, the
Illinois State Journal ran an editorial entitled "Of Married Women." It noted
that Elizabeth's petition was being circulated and concluded: "There is no
doubt in our mind that the power conferred [in the 1851 law] is altogether
too broad and sweeping! and if it has not been already, is liable to be used
improperly. . . . We are sure the Legislature will not permit so unequal a law
to remain longer upon the statute books."

That same day, Senator David J. Pinckney introduced a bill for an act for
the protection of personal liberty (which would become known as Mrs.
Packard's Personal Liberty bill). It was referred to the Senate Committee on
State Institutions. On January 23, in the lower chamber, Moses W. Leavitt
introduced House bill 608, which used the same phraseology as the Senate
bill; it was referred to the House Committee on the Judiciary.

Elizabeth's bill was now official business, subject to official as well

as unofficial attack and defense. Dr. McFarland's position had its sup-
porters, too.

The day after "Humanity's" letter appeared, the *Jacksonville Journal* ran a
lengthy editorial on "Our laws relative to insane persons": "It seems to us
that the people generally, and in many cases our well informed citizens, are
not well posted relative to the laws of Illinois concerning insane persons."
The editorial then discussed the question of the "lunatic" who owned
property. Under the law then in force, the judge of the circuit court of the
county in which such a propertied "lunatic" lived could, on application of a
creditor or relative, summon a jury to determine the person's mental state
and if the jury decided he was indeed insane, the judge could appoint a
conservator. Nowhere was it indicated that the person in question must be
present. The state supreme court, the editorial continued, eventually ruled
that such a person was entitled to be informed of the charge and given time
to defend himself. It was never intended that someone with a personal
interest in the accused's property should be able to get him out of the way
without his fighting back. This, it considered ample protection, although
there were those who thought a new law with increased protection, such as
a jury trial, was called for. If insanity was a crime, it continued, then a jury
trial would be appropriate. But since insanity is a "great affliction," the law
should treat the afflicted as gently as possible. *The Journal* concluded by
saying it understood that Dr. McFarland wanted to repeal the 1865 law, and
it agreed in part; it preferred that the law be amended, not given teeth.

In early February, House bill 608 with amendments was read again and
ordered to be engrossed for a third reading. On February 16, a Saturday, it
was read for the third time. Someone proposed that it be tabled. The
motion lost and the House passed the bill handily, 66 to 6. On Monday,
February 18, it was sent on to the Senate.

From then on, Elizabeth reported, it was a cliff-hanger with the potential
for tragedy. After the second reading, the bill stalled in the Senate and she
could not find out why. She moved ceaselessly among the politicians
seeking in vain for an explanation, agonizing that someone somewhere was
sabotaging her cause. Then, as the legislature approached the close of the
session, she heard a rumor that her bill had been incorporated into an
omnibus bill.

This news was so unexpected that she hired a House employee to check
it out. He found that there was indeed an omnibus bill but "the Personal

Liberty bill is missing. The number 608 is scratched out and the bill is nowhere to be found." It was Tuesday night; there were thirty-six hours before adjournment.

Early the next morning, after a sleepless night, Elizabeth presented herself at the Leland House Hotel to see Senator Washington Bushnell, chairman of the Senate Committee on the Judiciary, but he was too busy to help her. She then went to Lieutenant Governor William Bross, the Speaker of the Senate. Bross did not see how he could help, either, but Elizabeth suggested that he not hurry the bill through while she sought help elsewhere. Then she went to the Senate chamber.

She knew few senators. Most of her lobbying had been among House members. But she now knew Senator Bushnell. She got him to introduce her to the nearest man and promptly began to tell him her story. He promised to vote for her bill *and* defend it (if it turned up). Then she got him to introduce her to the man next to *him*, and so on through the chamber. She managed to speak to fifteen senators, all of whom promised to vote yes. Five of them also promised to call up the bill. The gavel, calling the session to order, ended her lobbying. She withdrew to the visitors' gallery.

Elizabeth knew she was the focus of all eyes. She knew the senators were baffled by and not altogether pleased with this woman who had invaded their sanctum to do what was usually considered man's work. She "refused to quail before their suspicions."

There had been so much agitation and publicity about the Personal Liberty bill that the Senate gallery was filled with women. Unfortunately, they could not stay long enough to see the outcome. It was dinnertime before the House bills were called up and most of the audience had gone home to cook dinner for their lords and masters. The senators were hungry, too. There were shouts of "Lay it on the table" even before the reading of each bill was completed.

Whoever had stolen House bill 608 was either conscience stricken or contrite because suddenly it appeared and was promptly introduced. Then, instead of "Lay it on the table," someone called out, "Read it." The clerk started, then stopped and said, "There is no enacting clause."

The Honorable Murry McConnell of Jacksonville, a friend of Dr. McFarland, leaped to his feet. "Lay it on the table," he said. "There is no time for bills presented in this condition. It is of no more use than so much white paper if it's passed as is." Senator Bushnell, whose committee had considered the House version, was embarrassed. He had not noticed the defect in the bill. Lieutenant Governor Bross then suggested that the bill be returned to the House to insert the enacting clause; it could be back in the Senate in time for action before adjournment.

The bill reached the House as it was about to adjourn. James C. Conkling, chairman of the House Committee on the Judiciary, was also embarrassed at having sent the Senate an incomplete measure. He suggested postponing adjournment in order to rectify the error which the House did promptly. The messenger then returned the corrected bill to the Senate where it was duly read.

Many of the senators had never read beyond the bill's title. Now they realized for the first time the problems, costs and personal upheavals of such jury trials. Many were tempted to renege on their promises to Elizabeth and vote against it. When the vote was called, a few of the waverers looked up at the gallery where Elizabeth was sitting, by now alone. They caught her eye. She must have looked like an avenging angel. The support held. Elizabeth went back downstairs to try to shake each senator's hand in gratitude.

That was the way she recalled the Illinois campaign but that was not exactly how it happened. As she herself had said, she was not reliable as a calendar. The drama she described actually took only four days. As reported in the legislative calendar (which was printed daily on the day after each session in the *Illinois State Journal*), House bill 608 was read in the Senate for the second time on February 23, a Saturday, and ordered up for a third reading. On the following Wednesday, February 27, it was read for the third time. There was an attempt to have it tabled which was voted down. The bill then sailed through 20 to 0. Elizabeth's account of the behind-the-scenes intrigue may have been accurate; the legislative calendar reported only the tallies of votes.

Obviously those four days had seemed like forty to Elizabeth and her memory so reflected it.

Victory on the assembly floor did not mean the drama was over. The bill would not be law until the governor signed it. Normally there was a two-week delay between passage and signing. Despite the overwhelming vote for the Personal Liberty bill and the editorial support given it by so many newspapers, Elizabeth was afraid to leave Springfield before the last step had been taken.

She approached the secretary of state, Mr. Sharon K. Tyndall, asking him as a special favor if he could persuade the governor to sign it right away.

Tyndall agreed and went to the Senate engrossing clerks for a copy. The clerks said they had already forwarded the bill to the governor. Elizabeth followed it, but it was not there. She had visions of another theft but this time she was wrong. They had approached the wrong clerks. A House bill was engrossed by House clerks. A House clerk had indeed copied House bill 608 the day before and sent it on to a house committee at the State House. Elizabeth rushed there after it.

She was told the bill could not be sent to the governor until the Speakers of both houses had signed it. House Speaker Tom Corwin signed it on the spot; the Senate Speaker, Lieutenant Governor Bross, a former newspaperman who had an interest in the *Chicago Tribune*, was in Chicago for the week. Elizabeth waited until he returned and then went to his office to ask for the bill. His office told her it had already gone to the governor.

An aide in the governor's office said the bill had been received but mislaid. Again Elizabeth suspected foul play but after an hour's search, over which she presided like a mother hen, it turned up. The aide took it in to the governor. Elizabeth waited nervously for another hour. Finally, through the door, she heard the governor's private secretary reading it aloud; she heard him say as he finished it, "That is a good bill." She heard the governor reply, "Yes, it is first rate."

Then Governor Oglesby brought the bill out to her, saying, "Mrs. Packard, your bill is signed." Elizabeth took his hand, thanked him in the name of all the married women of Illinois and gave him one of her books.

Now it needed only the *pro forma* signature of the secretary of state. Elizabeth wanted to take the bill to him herself but law required that only an appointed messenger could do that. So, on March 5, 1867, she followed the messenger to Secretary Tyndall's office and watched him sign into law her Personal Liberty bill (see Appendix 5).

It was now official. Any administrator of a hospital or asylum who accepted and kept in custody anyone who had not been declared insane or "distracted" by a jury was guilty of a "high misdemeanor" and subject to a fine of as much as one thousand dollars or imprisonment for up to a year or both. In addition, anyone who had been confined since 1865 without a trial was entitled to a retroactive one, to be held within two months. Once again Right had triumphed and Justice had prevailed. Now all that remained was for Illinois to offer trials to all those inmates who had been committed without them.

Though Elizabeth took no active role in the subsequent trials, she kept an eagle eye on Dr. McFarland's performance during the sixty-day grace period. She noted that "he sent off hosts of sane patients who had been unjustly confined . . . under the specious plea that they were suddenly cured! Indeed the 'Personal Liberty Bill' became a universal panacea for . . . sudden cure." She was convinced that he released them precipitously to avoid trials which would vindicate them and incriminate him. Elizabeth had written of Dr. McFarland during her last days in the asylum: "In regard to Dr. McFarland's individual guilt, justice to myself requires me to add that the *worst* which my heart dictates toward him is that he may *repent* and become 'The Model Man' his nobly developed manhood has fitted him to become. For he is, in reality the greatest man I ever saw—and he would be the *best* if he wasn't so bad!"

His hold on her emotions had been strong. But his siding with Theophilus during her trial and his leading the fight against her bill, which she equated with a fight against her, had damaged that hold beyond repair.

At the time the Personal Liberty bill was passed, there were 350 persons in the Jacksonville insane asylum, some admitted before the 1865 revision of the 1851 law. As the new law ordered, they were offered trials to determine whether or not they should stay.

On April 6, well within the sixty-day grace period, the Springfield and Jacksonville papers reported that ten of the inmates wished to be tried in their home counties, forty-four chose trials at Jacksonville, seventy-five chose not to be tried at all and the remainder didn't even understand what they were being asked.

On May 2, Judge Herbert G. Whitlock of the county court and a twelve-man jury showed up at the hospital to start the trials. Hearings would start the next day and the press was invited. The question of whether those who did not choose to be tried or did not understand must be tried anyway had been referred to the state's superior court.

The papers listed by name and county everyone who was interviewed. In some cases they added comments; in a few they went into detail. The first case they reported on at length was Reuben White, of Lake County, who had been mentioned by a Lake County reporter in his account of the press visit to the hospital in January.

White, some years before, had murdered his wife. He was tried for murder, declared insane and confined to the asylum. The Lake County reporter had talked with him and found him in good physical and mental condition. White protested vehemently his sanity; he wanted to go home to attend to his business, his property and his children. Then the reporter talked to Dr. McFarland who assured him that White was far from sane, that he often imagined he was sole owner of the asylum and entirely responsible for its management. At White's trial for insanity in May, the papers reported, he talked sanely "except on the subject of his wife's death," which he did not remember.

Charles A. Kennicott, of Cook County, was "quite fierce" at his trial and left the jury a note beginning, "Liberty or death." Samuel Plain, of Macoupin County, had had experience with Indians, panthers, snakes and the like, but thought men the worst "varmints" living. Dr. H. Y. Foster, of Saugamon County, said he was earning $50,000 a day practicing medicine and that Dr. McFarland owed him $4,190,000. (He impressed one reporter as "the happiest man in the state.")

After examining the forty-four people, the jury decided none should be released. The next day it heard those who wanted to be tried in their home counties but lacked the fare to get there. Among them was James T. Goddard, of Williamson County, an enormously wealthy man. The jurors decided "his wealth caused his derangement." Another was Eda Hoffman, of Cook County, "a German yet no one has ever been found who can understand her language." The jury found a few who were nearly well. (These, in fact, were soon sent home.)

In mid-May the superior court decided that the new law required *all* persons at the insane asylum to be tried whether or not they wanted to be. Judge Whitlock therefore scheduled additional hearings. The *Jacksonville Sentinel* deplored the court's decision: "Aside from the unnecessary trouble and expense involved . . . these farcical trials inflict serious and positive injury on the patients." On May 29, an inmate who was about to be released hanged himself.

The *Illinois State Register* also began to find the proceedings "so manifestly farcical and absurd as to provoke only derision." The *Peoria Democrat* reported: "A commission from the legislature is trying the patients in the Insane Hospital to see whether they are more crazy than the men who got up the committee."

Elizabeth did not care what the papers were saying. She remained convinced that the law was necessary, that the harm it prevented was greater than any harm it might cause. She was also finally convinced that Dr. McFarland was an unregenerate miscreant and must be punished.

* * *

Meanwhile, Theophilus, back in South Deerfield and again unemployed, was unaware of his wife's frenzied activities in the midwest. For him the high point of 1866 was his serving on the board of the general school committee of Deerfield, for which he "received compensation." In 1867 he was a guest preacher here and there. From time to time he "received liberal aid from various friends in supporting my children." He seemed to be living primarily on charitable donations from former parishioners for auld lang syne:

> *My old Shelburne people have generously befriended me. This winter I had a visit from representatives of some 20 families who left me a liberal donation. Likewise . . . South Deerfield people left me valuable gifts. Through the great mercy of God and in his wonderful Providence, I have been able this year to pay the last dollars of my nearly $4,000 debt, which for so many years has been pressing upon me. Thanks to the Heavenly Provider! How wonderfully has he furnished support for myself and family amid years of darkness!*

He attended commencement exercises at his alma mater, Amherst, a nostalgic moment. For the rest of the year he read and reread "with greater interest than ever before" twenty to twenty-five volumes of theological and religious works.

In August 1867, son Samuel, aged twenty, was admitted to the bar in Illinois. Neither of his parents was there for the ceremony. It was not that they weren't proud of him, but Theophilus had no money for train fare and Elizabeth was in the midst of her next battle, to see that Dr. McFarland paid for his sins.

9.

Sounds and Furies

During her travels around the state in 1864, Elizabeth had come across, by accident or design, some aggrieved ex-employees of the Jacksonville asylum. Somehow, during the next three years, letters that leveled charges against Dr. McFarland got written and some of them came her way.

Now, as her Personal Liberty bill was safely launched and making its way through the legislature, she took her first step toward repaying her former idol for his perfidy. She gave one of those letters to the *Illinois State Register.*

The *Register* was receptive. Two years after Appomattox, Illinois was still fighting the Civil War. There were Republicans and Radical Republicans, sometimes called jacobins (with a small "j"), and Union Democrats as opposed to Democrats with southern sympathies. They took positions on local issues in accordance with the politics of the people involved. The newspapers attacked each other as if an opposing viewpoint were the enemy.

The *Register* was Democratic, the statehouse was Republican as were its appointees. To the *Register* (and other Democratic papers in Illinois), how the asylum was run was less important than who was running it. Elizabeth may have knowingly taken advantage of this postwar politicking. The bickering factions may have been using her. In either case, the two "wars" became intertwined.

It may not have sought out misdemeanors to hold against Dr. McFarland but the *Register* did not mind repeating others' charges, especially if it need not take responsibility for them. The paper had been printing rumors about the state institutions for weeks. They became so prevalent that the legislature felt obliged to inquire into them.

Representative Joseph Ward, chairman of the Finance Committee, while reporting out bills to support the four Jacksonville hospitals, took advantage of his having the floor to announce that his committee had looked into these rumors and they were groundless. But his finding did not settle the question.

The first mention of possible wrong-doing had appeared in a front-page editorial in the *Register* on February 5, 1867. Superintendents and staffs at the state institutions were reported to be living, eating and dressing well while the inmates were not, and one superintendent was supposedly using state funds for his own benefit.

The *Jacksonville Journal*, which supported the Republicans, charged the *Register* writer with being "profoundly ignorant of what he was discussing." The superintendent of the "insane hospital" was on a fixed salary and controlled not one additional dollar. "On all financial matters, he is but the servant of the trustees" and the way in which he chose to spend his own income was really none of the legislature's business. It asked for an "investigation, searching and thorough."

But when, on February 22, the *Register* printed the accusatory letter Elizabeth had supplied, written a year earlier by Susan Kane (sometimes spelled Kain), the charges became far more serious than whether or not the superintendent and staff "ate sumptuously" and clothed themselves "in purple and fine linen."

Mrs. Kane, who had been an attendant at the asylum for five months in 1865, wrote that the female inmates were subjected to indignities, addressed abusively, "debased like the negro." She also claimed that the "head of the institution" could be bribed to accept anyone as a patient in so secret a way that it could not be proved and she contended that the trustees could not possibly know what went on since they visited once every three weeks (she must have meant "three months" because most of them lived elsewhere and met at Jacksonville quarterly), stayed only a few minutes in each ward and saw only patients from whom restraints had been removed in anticipation of the trustees' visits.

She conceded that though the screen room was useful in securing "fractious" patients until their "spell" had passed, it was "often perverted to a different use. The patient is usually [strait] jacketed . . . and when thus tightly and firmly secured, they are thrown upon the floor, faces downward, their clothes removed or turned back, and then beaten until their flesh is often but a jelly, while their screams might be heard at a great distance but for thick walls and closely fitted door."

Her description raised some logistical questions: If the patients were as securely jacketed as Mrs. Kane said, how could their clothes be removed or turned back? But the *Register* did not ask; nor did Dr. McFarland's accusers. Mrs. Kane's letter continued:

> *The cold baths, O my God! It makes me shudder to think of it. The patient, often for a small offence . . . is taken to the bathroom, made to strip; the water is then let into the bathtub, sometimes hot but usually cold, and after being tied hand and foot, plumped into it and held there under it until almost dead, and then drawn out only long enough to catch their breath and then plunged in again and so on.*

She later claimed that one of the staff physicians, Dr. Dutton (the assistant physician who escorted the visiting journalists around the asylum in January 1867) told the attendants how long it was safe to keep patients under water.

The paper reported receiving two more such letters which it did not print, and a third letter that it did, from Mrs. Priscilla L. Graff, who had been in charge of the sewing room for 3½ years. She took the trustees to task for visiting the hospital so seldom and being so little aware of what was happening there. She enclosed a copy of a letter she had written earlier to Dorothea Dix, which ended: "Dr. McFarland, in his treatment, is more insane than any patient he has."

The *Jacksonville Journal*, a supporter of the institutions that were the economic base of the city, nevertheless could not dismiss the letters out of hand.

> *If what is here alleged has even a shadow of truth in it, the guilty parties should be forever dishonored, and if the charges can be substantiated, there is no punishment too severe for them. On the other hand, if these are fabrications, springing from motives of jealousy, revenge or a wanton spirit to injure another, the slanderer should meet with a withering execration and the severest punishment the law can inflict.*

Dr. McFarland, who was used to partisan attacks by antigovernment newspapers, was afraid these new and specific charges would create alarm among the families of his patients and prompt them to question his competence. He requested of his friend, Richard Oglesby, that the legislature undertake "the fullest and most thorough investigation into the management of the Insane Asylum."

Everyone, it seemed, for political, economic, personal, even, perhaps, disinterested motives, wanted an investigation of the asylum and by extension of its superintendent. The legislature had to oblige.

The press tended to bestow credit and blame far from even-handedly upon Elizabeth.

The *Register* credited her with getting the investigative committee established by coming to its office with "the facts in her possession" which the paper found "appeared to be true."

The *Sentinel*, a strong supporter of Dr. McFarland, said, "The agitation against the management of the hospital originated with Mrs. Packard, a former patient . . . afflicted with a special phase of insanity."

The *Journal* declared that Elizabeth manipulated the other witnesses, that their testimony was in her handwriting, and that she was "confidential advisor to the committee."

A gentleman calling himself *Nous Verons* wrote to the *Journal* that she "ransacked the whole state for some three years to trump up evidence to damage [Dr. McFarland]" (though for eighteen months of that three-year period she had been in Massachusetts). Other papers referred to "the wild ravings of a woman everyone . . . knows to be insane."

On the opposite side, the *Register's* Jacksonville correspondent, under the pseudonym, *Nemesis*, referred to the doctor as a jacobin, supported by jacobin citizenry and a jacobin administration. He concluded that the entire fight over the conduct of the asylum was among jacobins and not worth the attention of the Democrats who could wait for the next election that would be sure to alter the political complexion of the statehouse and all its appointees. (Actually, Dr. McFarland's ten-year contract, signed in 1854, had been renewed in 1864; a change in administration would not affect him.) Other Democratic papers dismissed the criticism of the doctor by asking rhetorically what jacobin administrator had ever done a good job anyway?

The committee, chaired by General Allen C. Fuller of Boone County, held its first meeting on May 14 at the Dunlop House Hotel in Jacksonville. Before a word of evidence had been taken, the trustees heard alarm bells: The taxpayers of Illinois were footing the bill, including the hotel bills for five legislators. The hospital itself had ample guest space where the trustees thought the investigators should be staying. How better to look into the functioning of an institution than on its premises? Should not the first step be a tour of the facility? What, exactly, was the committee planning to investigate?

The committee promptly made that last point clear. At its first meeting, it passed two resolutions. The first stated that the meetings of the committee would be closed to the public and that no records of the testimony given or the decisions reached would be published "until otherwise ordered." The second said that the committee would hear first all the testimony *against* the hospital management, and only after that would the portion that was "directly" damaging to the superintendent be submitted to him and he be allowed to defend himself.

The committee admitted that these resolutions might be unacceptable to the public as "opposed to that spirit of free inquiry common to our people," but it felt that if it kept a "full journal" of the proceedings, it would be doing its duty.

As the trustees were quick to point out, the committee's plan of action made the superintendent the sole defendant. In effect, the committee would be practicing the Star Chamber and Inquisition tactics of not letting the accused see the testimony that condemned him until the accusing witness had passed beyond the control of the court.

The trustees sent a delegation to the committee to ask that the Honorable H. E. Dummer, a lawyer and former trustee, be permitted to sit in on behalf of the board and the superintendent and that Dr. McFarland be allowed to meet his accusers. The committee, after some pressure, agreed to let a representative of the trustees sit in but refused to admit Dr. McFarland. The trustees then declined to have anything to do with the meetings.

The committee laid out a four-point agenda: financial and sanitary management, whether any inmates were improperly retained, whether any were illegally accepted and whether they were humanely treated.

Since the principal rumors and allegations seemed to be of cruelty to patients, the committee took up that issue first. At its opening session it interviewed three witnesses—the two former employees, Mrs. Kane and

Mrs. Graff, and a former patient, Elmer Searles, who had spent 1864 and 1865 in the asylum. "These witnesses," they wrote, "were intelligent, their deportment under examination respectable, and they appeared to the committee to be entirely worthy of credit. . . . The testimony of these witnesses was so remarkable in its character, as to excite for the first time . . . serious apprehensions."

The committee decided it was imperative to let the public know the hearings were being held (even if the testimony was kept secret) so anyone with relevant information could proffer it. It advertised in papers throughout the state for anyone "by whom it is alleged the charges of mismanagement of the insane hospital can or may be proven" to get in touch with General Fuller at Jacksonville before June 10.

Since the committee asked for information prejudicial to the asylum, that is exactly what it got. Anything else was excluded. Some of the reports were personal experiences of discharged patients and former employees; some were observation rather than experience; much of it was hearsay, conjecture and hunch. Elizabeth carefully recorded it all and used it to flesh out her books.

By now the Star Chamber quality of the investigation had come to the public's notice, and the press, Republican and Democratic, was becoming increasingly critical. The committee found it expedient to amend its *modus operandi*.

On June 6 it requested the superintendent's presence for a "special purpose." Elizabeth was about to testify and the investigators used her impending appearance as an excuse to get themselves out of what was becoming an untenable position.

The hearings lasted with periodic intermissions for nearly seven months, ending on December 3. The final report was issued before Christmas. A month earlier an item appeared on the back page of the *Jacksonville Journal*: "Crazy or what? A woman stating that she was a former inmate of the Lunatic Asylum at Jacksonville, called upon McCall of the *Freeport Journal* lately and gave him particular fits because he refused to buy a book of her. McCall thinks she was let out too soon. The woman must have been the notorious and crack-brained Mrs. Packard, formerly of Kankakee. It sounds just like her, at any rate."

One of the regulations governing the asylum was that patients should be observed for two years before a decision was reached as to their curability. The state required that incurables be sent home to make room for curables.

At the close of Elizabeth's second year, Dr. McFarland wanted to discharge her but he did not say she was incurable; in later speeches to colleagues, he said she had become an intolerable nuisance and he wanted to get rid of her. After two years, he had fulfilled the state requirement. But the trustees recommended another six months of observation. At their meeting six months later he again urged her dismissal; they again postponed their decision. They finally authorized him to discharge her at the close of her third year, at which time she did indeed depart, albeit protestingly (see chapter 5).

Five months before her discharge Elizabeth had written the doctor the so-called love letter. Presumably he used it as ammunition in his third plea to the trustees for permission to send her home because they knew about it. Now, in the face of the committee's bias, the secretary *pro tem* of the Board of Trustees, I. L. Morrison, talked Dr. McFarland into giving the letter to the committee. (It is interesting that he had saved the letter.)

It is hard to say who was more upset by this disclosure, Elizabeth who felt doubly betrayed or General Fuller who felt his star witness was in danger of being discredited.

General Fuller recognized that it was "generally supposed that these charges of abuse rest principally upon Mrs. Packard's testimony, and hence the question of her sanity is supposed to be of vital importance." But this he disputed. It was neither Mrs. Packard nor her sanity that was on trial. The charges of inhumane treatment could stand or fall on the testimony of others.

He admitted that the letter was a shock; it appeared to be a "brazen offer of marriage by a married lady to a married man and was either the production of a diseased and disordered intellect or a degrading invitation or proposal of illicit intercourse." It was only fair that Elizabeth be given an opportunity to explain.

It took Elizabeth overnight to work on her response. After he heard it, General Fuller concluded that the letter was, to say the least, "indiscreet and foolish—open to severe criticism, if not condemnation . . . unfortunate and foolish." But it made no difference to the hearings. If there was any culpability arising out of this incident, it was Dr. McFarland's for voluntarily making public a document that was bound to cause its author mental and physical anguish. That was a breach of hospital rules of confidentiality.

When the letter did not throw the committee into confusion as the trustees had expected, other writings of Elizabeth's were introduced.

In one book Elizabeth had discussed the transmigration of souls. She believed that "souls do inhabit different bodies at different periods of their existence, as really as vegetables and animal life exist in different forms." She defended this concept by pointing out that "life is one continued succession of existences:—the butterfly and the chrysalis is the same life in different forms."

In another book she had written, "I have no more doubt but that Shakespeare and Washington, and I don't know how many more of earth's noblest thinkers, have dictated portions of my book, than I have that my own mind is used as their medium of thought." Her further explanation was, "I regard God as the author of all truth. I don't make the truth; I only report it. . . . In that sense I am God's medium."

The committee asked her if she had any special aid from other minds in writing. She replied: "I don't know. . . . I have read various books; and ideas which I received from this and other sources have quickened into thought, and I reduced them into form. I believe that mind communicates with mind. . . . I get ideas from the writing of Jesus Christ, although he is not in the body."* It all seemed sensible enough to General Fuller if not to those members of the medical profession who continued to find Elizabeth's thought processes bizarre. Whether they were incapacitating enough to require hospitalization or only eccentricities was another—and unanswered—question. Her beliefs had created serious disharmony in a strict Calvinist home but, as time would show, they did not interfere with Elizabeth's money-earning ability or her prowess as an advocate. They did not interfere with her ability as a parent, either.

The renaming of the committee seemed to date from Elizabeth's day on the stand. From then on it was routinely referred to as "Mrs. Packard's legislative investigating committee" or the "Packard-Fuller" or "Fuller-Packard committee."

The press, unaware of the bombshell Dr. McFarland had dropped in the

---

* In the second half of the twentieth century, the composer Richard Rodgers was once charged with using a theme from a Beethoven symphony in one of his songs. He replied with a smile, "An unconscious influence." It can happen.

still-secret hearing, merely reported that Elizabeth had testified on June 6.

Elizabeth having spoken, the committee returned to those who would name names and misdeeds.

Its first witness, shortly after the resolutions were passed and before Elizabeth's testimony gave the committee the chance to bring in Dr. McFarland without appearing to yield to pressure, had been Susan Kane. Mrs. Kane said Dr. McFarland told her when she was hired that he wanted her to assist a Mrs. Ritter who he thought was cruel to the patients. Her examples of that cruelty: Mrs. Ritter didn't let the patients sit down, and if they did, she would lift them by the hair and choke them if they resisted; for the slightest offense she would give them the cold-bath treatment and if they resisted that, they would be straitjacketed and their heads submerged. Mrs. Kane said that she did not report any of this because it was understood that complaints were not wanted.

Under questioning, she acknowledged that as soon as she was able to manage alone, Dr. McFarland had let Mrs. Ritter go. But then, it developed, Mrs. Kane indulged in some abuse herself, though she did not consider it as such. She spanked patients with her shoe and sometimes with a broom handle "only as a child would be corrected. I dealt with all the patients as children." Mrs. Kane believed that despite the rule against striking patients, "an attendant should be the judge when to strike a blow."

The trustees pointed out that the Civil War had taken from state institutions their most qualified attendants and the average stay of an asylum employee was 8½ months. Sometimes an unsatisfactory attendant had to be kept on because there were simply no available replacements, and an unsatisfactory person minding a ward could be better than no person at all. Take Mrs. Kane's case. She replaced one whom "the superintendent thought a cruel and unkind person." When her own cruelties became known and she departed, the ward had to be closed and the patients distributed among other, already overcrowded wards because a replacement for her could not be found.

The committee's second witness, Priscilla Graff, aged fifty-two, had known Dr. McFarland when he headed the New Hampshire asylum and had come to Jacksonville in July 1858 at his request. She thought discipline was harsh but she did not think Dr. McFarland knew about it.

Mrs. Graff did give one serious piece of evidence (which would prove the inadequacy of a single view of a situation). A one-armed patient, Isaac Wyant, struck an attendant with a hatchet. She heard a lot of comings and goings and saw porters going upstairs with water, which led her to deduce that a cold bath was scheduled. She saw an engineer going up with chains. She heard Wyant's voice saying, "Oh, Doctor," three times. Dr. McFarland told her she did not understand the case. "I saved that man from the gallows," he said.

Later she saw Wyant with his hand chained to his waist and only enough slack for him to feed and dress himself but not enough for him to raise his hand in menace.

The committee found this a "dreadful punishment," a "most revolting" procedure, "almost too shocking to be believed."

The true story of Isaac Wyant was quite different.

In March 1857, Wyant was shot in the arm and his arm had to be amputated. During the operation large quantities of chloroform were administered; Wyant's mind was affected. When he recovered he went out and murdered his assailant. Dr. McFarland was called as an expert witness for the defense. He declared that at the time of the killing Wyant was not of sound mind. The jury acquitted him but remanded him to the asylum.

Wyant remained homicidal; he admitted to killing a patient one night because the man's outcries in his sleep disturbed him. Finally he managed to acquire a hatchet which he secreted for a year. After he suddenly attacked the attendant with the hatchet, the least damaging thing Dr. McFarland could think of was to fashion the arm-waist chain that would keep Wyant harmless but functioning.

The third witness that first day had been the former patient, Elmer Searles, aged forty and single. Searles had been committed in December 1863, his insanity attributed to his having lost his property. But his commitment papers also said the condition could be hereditary; his brother had committed suicide, and he himself was suicidal. Searles was discharged in July 1864 as "improved (not recovered)." The hospital's entire effort on his behalf during his stay there was to keep him alive, a goal that it reached since he was there to testify three years later.

Searles's complaint was that he was moved in the middle of the night from one ward to another and had his sleeping accommodations changed from a bedstead to a bed made up on the floor. According to Dr. Dutton, Searles screamed so much at night that they had to move him to a ward where such behavior was not uncommon.

Then the committee moved on to male attendants. George Merrick, aged thirty-four, had worked at the hospital for five months in 1866. He reported that his supervisor, one John Doan, aged twenty-one, seized a young patient by the ankles while the patient was undressing and threw him to the floor, injuring him severely; that a docile and consumptive patient was refused medical treatment by Dr. Dutton and had died, and that a "very bad and crazy" patient had his head banged against the ceiling by an attendant. (In case the reader wonders how a head could be banged against a ceiling, the report later quoted Dr. Richard Patterson of Chicago, who inspected the facilities, as recommending the abandoning of some wards because "the story is lower than is desirable.")

John C. Edmundsen, aged thirty-five, once an assistant engineer at the asylum, saw but did not report abuses because he said his boss, Samuel Eastman, had told him he would lose his job if he did. Most of his stories dealt with patients undergoing prolonged stays in the screen room or being beaten. Edmundsen did not think Dr. McFarland knew about these abuses because no one told him.

The trustees went to some lengths to locate Samuel Eastman. They found him in Maine and took a deposition from him in which he denied flatly that he had ever told his assistant not to report abuses; it was his understanding that one of the cardinal rules of the hospital was that "improper conduct on the part of employees should be reported directly to the superintendent." The trustees also established that Edmundsen had been reprimanded twice for drunkenness.

A witness on whom the committee relied heavily was neither a former patient nor an employee, but a former official, John Henry. Henry was a Morgan County pioneer, a leading citizen of Jacksonville and a state senator at the time the hospital was incorporated in 1847. When it was opened in 1851, he was named its steward and remained so until the post was abolished four years later.

According to John Henry's *Memoirs*, the early days of the hospital were marked by friction. The first medical superintendent, Dr. James M. Higgins, was elected in 1848 with a bare majority after "many contentious ballotings." He inherited, as a result, "a plentiful legacy of ill will" and a permanent division among the trustees. "Dr. Higgins . . . suffered that controversy to enter into the affairs of the institution and took strong grounds in favor of one of the parties."

The end result was that the legislature of 1853 reorganized the Board of Trustees and on June 4, fired the doctor. Higgins's assistant, Dr. H. K. Jones, was named superintendent *pro tem* while a legislative committee sought a suitable replacement. It found Dr. McFarland, and shortly before his arrival on June 16, 1854, the trustees informed Dr. Jones that his services were no longer needed. John Henry found that action regrettable; Dr. Jones was very popular among the staff.

John Henry remained as steward for another eight months during which he claimed to have seen some cases of cruelty though he could recall only one, an Englishman, whose name he had forgotten, whom he discovered in the hands of two men who were holding him on his back while a third poured water into his face and nose. Henry rescued the hapless man and reported the case to Dr. McFarland. When he saw the case was not being investigated, he reported it to the president of the Board of Trustees and threatened to take it to court. Henry stated that "Dr. McFarland . . . did not listen to [the patients'] complaints with kindness . . . and appeared indifferent when complaints of cruelty were made to him."

At the end of eight months, when the post of steward was being phased out and its duties parceled out among other departments of the institution (to its fiscal betterment), John Henry noted, "Dr. McFarland did not treat me with that gentlemanly courtesy that I had been acquainted to receive from my colleagues."

The trustees pointed out that at the time of his testimony John Henry was an old man; in fact, they rather unkindly referred to him as a "decayed politician." They remarked that if Dr. McFarland's "treatment" in terminating the office of steward was "ungentlemanly," the taxpayers "will be likely to forgive the discourtesy." They added that his opinion about the doctor's lack of sympathy for his patients did not deter Henry from placing his own son under the doctor's care at three different times, the most recent postdating his testimony.

Altogether, the legislators turned up twenty cases of undeniable cruelty perpetrated by eighteen different individuals. There was only one case to which more than one witness testified. Considering that in his tenure of thirteen years, Dr. McFarland had treated some 2,600 patients, including those already there when he took over, the incidence of maltreatment worked out arithmetically to three every two years, a record the trustees thought it would be hard to better.

They referred to what they called "the errors of superficial knowledge." The legislators, they said, were not versed in mental maladies; they could not know whether there was a cause-and-effect relationship between what the witnesses saw and why they were seeing it: "The act of administering food to one determined on suicide by starvation; of restraining the violence of the homicidal; of even putting clothes upon the naked . . . will always afford material out of which an ill disposition may construct any amount of the same kind of testimony." As for what the legislative committee consistently referred to as "punishments," the trustees said that "every accidental collision between an attendant and a patient gets this term applied to it."

The committee may have been unqualified to render judgment on the treatment of the insane; it may have been unduly influenced by the persuasive qualities of its star witness, Elizabeth P. W. Packard, but it was not wholly lacking in a sense of responsibility. It called, in addition to discharged patients and discharged employees, medical experts from among former staff members to describe the changes made over the years in the treatment of the insane. Dr. McFarland gave the committee a list of names to choose from. Among them was Dr. Jones.

The doctors testified that where formerly close confinement, chains and restraints had been customary, there was now much more free association among patients as well as between patients and attendants. This mingling was bound to produce occasional collisions, and since attendants were human with human frailties, occasional abuses. The *Jacksonville Journal* commented: "This is the same principle by which social order may in one sense be better maintained in a despotism than under a free government. We choose the free government with its unavoidable licenses and abuses, in preference to the despotism under which no collision or outbreaks can occur."

Just before it concluded the hearings, the committee invited Dr. Richard B. Patterson, of the Chicago Medical College, once head of hospitals for the insane in Iowa and Indiana, and Dr. H. A. Johnson, president of the Chicago College, to study the Jacksonville asylum and its patients. The doctors examined every inmate and then spent several days with the committee. Everyone on either side of the issue seemed relieved, and the majority expressed a willingness to accept the doctors' verdict.

Doctors Patterson and Johnson found nothing inherently wrong with the hospital except for its ventilation which, in some wards, they found inadequate. They recommended modernization, as, incidentally, had Dr. McFarland some years before in one of his annual reports to the legislature. But the legislature was in a budget-trimming mood that session and voted down the recommendation.

Dr. Patterson stated flatly, "There is no very sharp, positively well defined line of demarcation between insanity and sanity . . . there is debatable ground between the two conditions." (One hundred years later, a study by the American Bar Association on the hospitalization and discharge of the mentally ill in effect agreed with him. A person's mental health like his physical health, it said, can fluctuate depending on various internal and external circumstances. Some people are chronically mentally ill; others are fairly consistently sound. In between are those who can usually, if not always, adjust so their mental illness does not interfere with their ability to function adequately. So the study concluded, the question should not be "Who is ill?" but "Who needs to be hospitalized?")

Dr. Patterson continued: "In proportion as a patient's recovery is complete and permanent, he will be likely to speak well of the institution." The doctor said the insane distort what they see and are not always competent to tell the truth, but—and this was a significant "but"—the very fact of being institutionalized has "a demoralizing effect upon the mind" that decreases the ability to see things in proportion.

That seems an apt description of the difference between Elizabeth as patient and Elizabeth as responsible citizen.

The visiting doctors did not think anyone was wrongfully retained; there were a few "convalescents," presumably recovered from whatever mental disorder had brought them there but perhaps not as strong physically as the medical staff thought they should be.

Psychiatrists, even a century ago, talked of "the reciprocal influence of the mind over the body and the body over the mind" and believed that a person would not lapse into insanity without a physical abnormality to start with. A frail or sickly patient was more subject to relapse than a healthy one. Consequently, some might be kept longer than the state of their minds would seem to warrant. Also, the visiting doctors pointed out, some patients suffered paroxysmal or periodic bouts of insanity, what today would be called psychotic episodes; between spells they would show no symptoms. Without expert advice at hand, it would be hard to make positive determinations. However, the two doctors expressed themselves as satisfied that Dr. McFarland was running a tight ship.

The committee delivered its report, 160 printed pages, to Governor Oglesby in early December 1867. The governor was in Europe at the time.

Instead of waiting for his return, the committee allowed the *Chicago Tribune*, Lieutenant Governor Bross's paper, to publish it.

There was a howl of outrage from the legislature which had expected it to be kept secret until the governor had seen it, and from other papers charging favoritism because of the Bross connection.

Strangely, all the testimony and the committee's conclusions *had* been kept secret until then. But once the *Tribune* printed it in full, Dr. McFarland's time bomb finally exploded. The love letter and Elizabeth's response became public property. The press gleefully leaped upon it. The story had become tired; the papers had been reduced to quoting each other and criticizing each other's editorial opinions. Now they had juicy meat to feed on.

Elizabeth started the letter by quoting the president of Amherst College, Dr. Humphrey, who had advised his students not to marry until they were finished with their studies, but when they did find a *"fair tree . . . to mark it."* Then, in her best purple hospital prose, she explained that Dr. McFarland was the "manly" man her womanly nature had been seeking, so she decided to apply Dr. Humphrey's advice to herself, "marking" Dr. McFarland as her future husband. She acknowledged that though she could love his spirit and his manliness, she could not love the doctor himself because he was married. (So was she, she admitted, but she did not consider her heart to have ever been given.) He would be a husband in *"a Far-land,"* a suggestion that Elizabeth had her eyes fixed metaphysically on a marriage literally in heaven. She then urged him to burn her letter "since an exposure of it might imperil my virtue in the estimation of *perverted* humanity" and ended by saying that since her son, Theo, was turning twenty-one soon and could protect her from further persecution by her husband, she would go with him and resume her motherly function. She signed the letter, "Yours in the best of bonds, Elizabeth."

General Fuller refused to let the letter shake his confidence in his prize witness and sometime assistant. Dr. McFarland and the trustees said they were not holding it against her; she should not be criticized for it because she was insane. The newspapers showed no such forebearance. No one was yet aware of the transference of patient emotions to the doctor as a psychiatric phenomenon during treatment. It would be another eighteen years before Freud even realized it could happen and more before he realized its use as a therapeutic tool.

Said the *Journal*: "It exposes her to the public gaze as a strumpet."

It was the *Jacksonville Sentinel's* delicate opinion that "the letter is of such grossly immoral character that we refrain, at least for the present, from giving it place in our columns."

The *Peoria Transcript* wrote: "It has been a question whether Mrs. Packard is crazy or not, but if she hasn't more of the old devil in her than Mary Magdalene we are not a Yankee."

The *Chicago Post* was satisfied from the tenor of the letter "that Mrs. Packard is crazy but congratulate her friends that her insanity, though amorous, does not take an obscene turn."

Finally, for all the locals who did not read the Chicago papers, the *Jacksonville Journal* printed the actual letter (see Appendix 6).

Elizabeth's response appeared in full in the committee's report, the *Chicago Tribune* and the *Springfield Journal*. The *Chicago Tribune* also published a letter referring to "the great good" Mrs. Packard had achieved in her "intrepid and unparalleled labors for the insane," which the writer thought entitled her to some appreciation from the public. Then the writer mentioned the letter that, "in a very peculiar exigency," Elizabeth had written to Dr. McFarland and praised the committee for chastizing him for releasing it. "Suppose it was 'a foolish letter,'" said the writer, "the very fact that she wrote it in such confiding trust and honest simplicity is a proof of her innocence." Had she improper motives, she could have found any number of ways of communicating them without putting them on paper. Her defense of her letter would be her best shield against slander. Friends of Mrs. Packard need not worry, it concluded: "By her unparalleled industry she has made an indelible impression of good upon the age, and will live in enviable fame long after every mouth of malignant traducers has become forever silenced." The letter was signed, "A Friend of Justice," in all probability Elizabeth herself.

Her defense of the love letter read:

> *Truth is my only apology . . . viz: the defense of true principles.*
>
> *1st I love God. This love is spontaneous, free, independent of my own free will or choice. . . . I love Him because He is the only embodiment of the principles of justice, goodness and truth. . . .*
>
> *2nd I love myself. The primary instinct of my nature is self-protection. I instinctively fly to and trust these principles as my refuge. . . .*
>
> *Man is made in God's image. . . . And just in proportion as man is true to his type—his origin—just in that proportion do I reverence and love him as my protector.*

Her spirit, she continued, called for a personal protector, and as "man is strength and wisdom," she would fly to a man rather than a woman for protection. To the degree that this man protected her, to that degree would she love him. It had been her misfortune in life not to have found a man who fulfilled her image of protector until she met Dr. McFarland: "He became my manly protector ... [and] instinctively developed in my womanly nature, first the feeling of gratitude, then of reverence, then of love."

Elizabeth then described how he had encouraged her to write her book "as a means of defending my character, which is far dearer to me than my natural life," promised to publish it, and then seemed to break his promise.

> *Almost in a state of desperation, I ventured to make one more final appeal to this prince of manliness, which you find contained in this letter. . . . I believed him pledged to do all in his power to redeem my reputation from this most cruel brand of insanity. But the revelation of the Court Room at Kankakee revealed to my mind the traitor instead of the man. I now found he had only assumed the mark of manliness for the malign purpose of betraying my innocence to shield himself and the use he is now making of this letter demonstrated that I did not then misjudge him.*

Having done this groundwork, Elizabeth eventually wrote a slim volume entitled *The Mystic Key*, devoted to an explanation of the letter. Its title was apt. Her explanation was indeed mystical. She demanded that her letter (her explanation, too) be read on a much higher level of abstraction than most correspondence exists on. It did not diffuse the criticism of her contemporaries in the slightest.

Dr. McFarland had started out at a disadvantage. To the trustees' distress, he took the legislative investigating committee at face value; after all, he had asked for it. In addition, he seemed reluctant to cross-examine those of his former patients whose emotional balance he considered fragile.

Finally, in July 1867, the superintendent realized he needed legal counsel and asked Mr. Dummer to represent him. Because of General Fuller's stance, Dr. McFarland had to wait out the final accusatory report of the committee. Only when it had been submitted to the governor and leaked to the press was it possible for him, through the trustees' own follow-up investigation, to seek vindication.

* * *

The committee's report found nothing wrong with the business and financial management of the hospital. But it did find "gross carelessness and inexcusable irregularities in the admission of patients, without the needful evidence and papers required by law."

It charged that "148 were admitted without the proper *legal evidence* of their insanity and the security required by law." Some of these so-called illegalities were as trivial as bonds with a stamp missing or documents phrased informally instead of in legalese.

The committee found Dr. McFarland's classification of patients "fundamentally wrong." The "restraints" were as often misused as not; "his government of patients is believed too severe, and his discipline of attendants too mild." The report concluded by recommending "an immediate change in the office of Superintendent."

To Elizabeth, the committee's conclusion was Mission Accomplished.

The reaction was immediate. The Jacksonville newspapers accused the committee of having decided at the outset to file an unfavorable report and cautioned the public to withhold opinion until the trustees had a chance to rebut the charges. Papers all over the state, at both ends of the political spectrum, also urged a wait-and-see attitude and the *St. Louis Democrat* added that "Mr. Fuller had investigated insane matters till he had become afflicted with the malady himself."

The *Alton Telegraph* protested the premature publication of the report. "It was not only in bad taste but discourteous to the Governor and unjust to Dr. McFarland." The *Springfield Register* did not object to the report having been leaked; it found nothing unjust to Dr. McFarland in publishing the report as quickly as possible, whereas not publishing it, "consigning the poor unfortunates who are victims of his brutality" to his power for another year, would have been a heinous crime. The *Register* assured its readers that publication had aroused intense indignation against the doctor and his staff.

The readers of the *Register* may have been indignant at Dr. McFarland; the people of Jacksonville were outraged at General Fuller. They held a protest meeting at which they passed angry resolutions.

The day after the meeting, *Nemesis* sent his report to the *Register.* He urged the people to do their own investigating, in their own hometowns, implying that little would be found locally. He wound up: "Let us then see whether a few friends, by two or three resolutions, written *in the dark*, in two minutes, can defend . . . Dr. McFarland."

Another writer, calling himself *Vox Populi*, also questioned the value of the Jacksonville rally. He agreed with *Nemesis* that the room had been dark; gave them five, instead of two, minutes and claimed they had no writing materials.

The *Chicago Tribune* slapped the Jacksonville gathering on its collective wrist. It acknowledged that the state institutions in Jacksonville were an important source of revenue but did not think the citizens should react so hostilely to the committee's report. "We tell the good people down there to keep their undergarments on" was its sage advice.

By now it was convention time again for the state press. This year the journalists met in Jacksonville. Again they visited the state institutions and again they were wined and dined. But this time they paid more attention to the people within the asylum than they did to the food upon its tables.

The *Carlinville Democrat* "found the asylum in excellent working order and the unfortunate inmates as comfortable as possible under the circumstances."

The *Quincy Whig* looked for "those instruments of torture, the case of which had been so prominently paraded before the public of late," but found none; "what little force is used is of the mildest kind."

The *Lincoln Intelligencer* noted: "We are much more favorably impressed than before (hasty visit last time). Of course, it is to be supposed that we saw things in their best light. . . . We confess that on the occasion of our last visit . . . we formed an opinion quite at variance with what we now entertain."

The *Centralia Sentinel* reporter found "the most scrupulous cleanliness and order. . . . The inmates appeared to be well taken care of, and, so far as we could judge, were free from unnecessary restraint."

The *Marshall County Republican* reported that "if there is anything wrong in the management of the Insane Asylum it is wonderfully well disguised. If Dr. McFarland is the ghoul he is supposed to be, he wonderfully belies his humane looks and urbane manners."

Had there really been a remarkable change since the previous year's tour or were the reporters viewing the asylum differently as a result of the publicity? In either case, the investigation, whatever adjectives its detractors and defenders chose to apply to it, seemed to have serendipitously accomplished something.

In February 1868, the House Committee on State Institutions acted on the committee's report. "We are satisfied that the investigation was thorough and impartial and *adopt the conclusions arrived at*. . . . The Senate Committee on State Institutions also *adopted the abstract of the evidence* in the report, ordered the report printed and submitted it to the Senate."

Meantime, the trustees had initiated their own investigation. Since the committee's material, which they intended to challenge, was restricted to the governor's office, they had to study it there, which caused an unfortunate but necessary delay.

It took the trustees the rest of the winter and most of the spring to plough through the committee's journals. Then, before issuing their conclusions, they invited experts from asylums in Pennsylvania, Massachusetts, Rhode Island and Tennessee to examine every facet of the Jacksonville operation. In general, the doctors gave the hospital a clean bill of health, though they differed over criticism of Dr. McFarland's classification system.

One doctor thought quiet patients should be placed with other quiet ones; another thought a mix of quiet and noisy inmates could give a lift to the quiet ones and subdue the noisy ones; he thought an entire ward of depressives would drive all of them into deeper depression and an entire ward of manics could stimulate them beyond control. Still others thought that rules could not be laid down—that the decisive factor should be how the patients would interact with each other, that the placement should produce combinations that would result in the greatest benefit to the greatest number, and that this decision, in the final analysis, had to be up to each individual superintendent.

In April, as the trustees were ready to release their findings, "the genial and accomplished superintendent" (in the words of the *Springfield State Journal*) was given an "elegant gold-headed cane" with an inscription on the head conveying the high regard of one of "our citizens." The paper commented that "this must be especially gratifying to the doctor at this time when malignant enemies are endeavoring to traduce his character and thwart his usefulness."

Finally, roughly a year after the legislature's investigation had got under way, the trustees published their conclusions, ninety-eight pages and an appendix, nearly as long as the committee's report.

Their rebuttal was based more on explaining away the charges and questioning the credibility of the committee's witnesses than on their own proof to the contrary. The trustees stated that asylum employees "are numerous and ever changing . . . many are discharged for incompetency or misconduct. Thus an army of witnesses, often ignorant, unfriendly, and even hostile, may be found by any one disposed to make an attack."

They charged the committee with consulting frequently in private with Elizabeth who had ulterior motives; they suspected that the two members of the legislative investigating committee who had supported Elizabeth's Personal Liberty bill in 1867 on the assumption that most of her charges were true, felt they had to justify that vote by proving Elizabeth right. The trustees concluded: "We regard Dr. McFarland as eminently qualified . . . and believe that his removal or retirement would be a great loss to the State. . . . We not only do not believe he has been guilty of abuses, or neglect of duty, but we have a settled conviction that he has been honest, vigilant, humane, and intelligent."

The 365-day wonder was over though it would echo down asylum corridors for years to come. Everyone was happy and no one was happy.

Many twentieth-century psychiatrists base their hostility toward Elizabeth Packard, which is sometimes irrationally virulent, on the fact that she ruined the career of a great and good doctor. But she did not. She tried; she certainly caused him several years of grief—three as a patient, one as an accuser. But Dr. McFarland survived and prospered, his job and his reputation intact. Despite the legislative committee's recommendations, he stayed on at Jacksonville for two more years. Then he took some time off to travel in Europe again.

In 1872, four years after the furor, Dr. McFarland opened his own private sanitarium, Oak Lawn Retreat, on "an elevated plateau" a mile and a half from the center of Jacksonville. It housed thirty patients. Perhaps with Elizabeth in mind, he took only men. But after a destructive fire in 1887, he built a larger facility and admitted patients of both sexes.

In 1875, three years after President Lincoln's widow, Mary Todd Lincoln, had been tried for insanity and hospitalized under Elizabeth's Personal Liberty Law, her son, Robert, called on Dr. McFarland to examine his mother and advise him on whether she could be released. Dr. McFarland recommended against it—and submitted a bill for $100, which, in 1875, was quite a sizeable sum. (Robert, after due thought, took her out of the asylum anyway.) Then, sixteen years later shortly before Thanksgiving in 1891, Dr. McFarland, aged 74, hanged himself.

It turned out that some years before he had been injured by a piece of timber falling on his head and since then, in the words of the *Jacksonville Journal*, he had been "troubled with his head." On October 1, he was told he had an inflammation of the brain and would probably not recover, a diagnosis with which he agreed. Despite his skills as a doctor for the mentally ill, Dr. McFarland could not prevent a deep depression in himself. The result was predictable.

Seventy-five years later, the state named a new mental health facility near Springfield the Andrew McFarland Center. In partnership with the Jacksonville hospital, which the doctor had headed for sixteen years, it provides short-term and outpatient care for an eighteen-county area in west central Illinois and gives Dr. McFarland's name more currency to date than that of his most famous patient.

Elizabeth was not in the least discomfitted by the trustees' report. She had achieved her objective when the legislature recommended that Dr. McFarland be fired. By the time the trustees issued their findings she was at work on her next venture, trying to regain her children. She thought she was through with Dr. McFarland forever.

Theophilus, during those turbulent months, appeared to be unaware of his wife's war with the doctor. There is no mention of any letters from his sister Sybil (who must have been reading the Chicago papers), keeping him *au courant*. His primary interest and activity in 1867 and 1868, according to his diary and journal, seemed to be his readings in theology and his perennial hope that his sons would one day be as interested in them as he.

10.

The Best and Briefest Victory

One of life's little ironies is that what many fathers today must fight for—custody of their children—was the norm a century ago. Theophilus broke no law in doing what would now be called kidnapping. Except in the case of divorce, children who were past what was known as "the tender age" were automatically the property of their father, as was everything else under his roof including his wife and all she owned.

Elizabeth sounded out a couple of lawyers in Chicago, including her son, Samuel, and all assured her that unless she got a divorce, there was no way she could get her young children back from their father. She had already established, back in Manteno before her trial, that she had no intention of getting a divorce. She did not believe in divorce. She wanted a husband. She was only sorry she had not chosen a more "manly" one. The marriage vow said " 'til death do us part"; she had sworn it before God, and for better or for worse she intended to uphold that oath. So her only alternative was to get custody provisions changed.

Since she would probably have to prove she could house and support the children, too, she concentrated on her writing and bookselling and actually accumulated enough money to buy a small house and a lot in Chicago, "free from all encumbrances," which presumably meant there was no mortgage. But this purchase raised another legal problem: Her property, real and financial, was still by law her husband's. Elizabeth was terrified that he might seize it, even though in his unemployed and demoralized state, it was highly unlikely. She felt she must secure her house and holdings legally which would require still another change in the law.

With her son Samuel's help, she drafted a bill that would entitle a married woman "to receive, use and possess her own earnings and sue for the same in her own name, free from the interference of her husband or his creditors." She also worked up a bill to make it possible for husbands and wives to be partners in many areas of marriage, including parenthood.

Elizabeth paid for her rooming house in Springfield for another session of the legislature so she could buttonhole legislators and campaign for the bills. Once back in the state capital, she resorted to her time-tested tactic of writing anonymous letters to the *Chicago Tribune* and *Springfield State Journal* and "had the honor to hear [them] credited to Mrs. Livermore of Chicago." The Livermores were major local philanthropists.

One letter, dated January 29, 1868, signed "A Female Parent," commented on some of the objections to the first bill, particularly the view that a woman was not prepared for such responsibilities: "It was once argued that the negro slave must first be fitted for freedom before he could be trusted with it; but the more enlightened claimed that the very best way to fit him for freedom was to elevate him to the position of a free man. Responsibility does elevate."

Another letter, dated February 2, and signed "A Mother," addressed itself to the second bill:

> It is the unmarried woman alone who has any legal right to rear her own offspring, while the father is required to provide for it. Illegitimate children are allowed a legal right to a mother's training and guardianship, while the legitimate offspring of the married woman have no legal right to the care and training of their own mothers!
> ... this Christian government thus offers a premium on infidelity, and encourages divorce or separation....

Elizabeth did not intend to deny a father his right to custody or responsibility for the children's upbringing; she only wanted a mother to have equal parental rights.

By now Elizabeth had enough friends in high places—and the idea she was presenting was rapidly gaining favor, especially among wealthy fathers of daughters who would one day inherit from them—so her bills were introduced. The first one, dealing with a woman's property and earnings, made it through both committee and legislature, though not without more opposition than had been raised against her Personal Liberty bill. Obviously the questions raised about her mental stability during the investigations of the asylum gave some of the legislators pause. Her second bill, equalizing parental rights, faced even greater opposition. But in time some, though not all, of its provisions were approved.

Now, having achieved some protection under the laws of Illinois, Elizabeth forwarded her proposals to her old friend, Samuel Sewall, in Boston, for presentation to the Massachusetts legislature. She need not have done so. Unknown to her, and without her urging, her home state had already passed a law giving a mother equal rights to her children. So she decided to put aside her campaigns, go to Boston, sue for the three minor children and become a full-time mother.

Elizabeth armed herself for the coming battle with letters—from friends in Chicago, from the real estate agent who had sold her the house and property, and from her two oldest sons, both now in business in Chicago. (They wanted to go east with her but she was reluctant to take them away from their businesses; they gave her their letters instead.)

Theo wrote:

> To Whom It May Concern: *This is to certify that I, Theophilus Packard, am the eldest son of Theophilus and Elizabeth P. W. Packard, that I am 27 years of age, that the first 16 years of my life I spent under my mother's care and supervision and nearly fitted for college under her teachings.*
>
> *That from my own judgment and knowledge, without extraneous influence, I solemnly believe that my mother is the only proper person who has both the will and ability to take charge of and maintain her infant children.*
>
> *That she is my mother in every sense of the term, and her councils I may rely upon; that her loving care and disregard of self to minister to our best interests, merits our most filial regard.*
>
> *I do not consider her as ever having been insane.*
>
> *By her indefatigable efforts she has bought and paid for a nice little house and lot in Chicago, to which she has a good title, free from all encumbrance.*
>
> *It is my earnest and sincere desire that she may obtain possession and control of the minor children, in which case I intend to live in her family.*
>
> April 20, 1869   *Theophilus Packard, Jr.*

Isaac's letter read:

> To Whom It May Concern: *This is to certify that I am the second son of Mrs. E. P. W. Packard and Rev. Theophilus Packard. That I am twenty-four years of age. I can say that my mother is every way able and competent to take charge of my younger brothers, who are now underage, educate and bring them up.*
>
> *From my early youth until I was sixteen, I have been reared under her influence. She has always been a kind and affectionate mother, and all of her children always respected and loved her so long as she was permitted to live with them.*
>
> *She was separated from them contrary to her wishes.*
>
> *I consider the charge of insanity against her wholly unfounded.*
>
> *She is a most excellent mother, her judgment good, and her moral character without a stain. The tribulations and sufferings she has undergone in the past, I feel can be but partially atoned for, by unremitting filial love and the care and custody of her minor children.*
>
> *She has a house and lot in this city worth thirty-five thousand dollars unencumbered.*
>
> *It is my wish and desire, that she may take charge of my two brothers, George H. and Arthur D. Packard, for it is my opinion they would be better brought up under her care than under the care of anyone else.*
>
> *Should this desire of her heart be realized, I intend to make my home in her family.*
>
> *April 12, 1869*   *I. W. Packard*

Isaac, like the stereotypical nineteenth-century male, seemed to have overlooked his only sister. If his mother noticed the oversight, she did not mention it.

From Judge Bradwell, who had helped Elizabeth in her first Illinois campaign, came a brief note:

> To all whom it may concern: *This is to certify that I have known Mrs. Elizabeth P. W. Packard for many years. That she is a lady of wonderful business capacity. Is comfortable in her circumstances, the owner of real and personal estate to quite an amount. Is an able and ready writer, an energetic, capable, and worthy woman and mother.*

As a mother she is not only able and capable of bringing up her minor children in a proper manner, but I would add, that I know of few if any ladies that would excel her in taking care of and educating children.

She is a very superior lady, and in my opinion should have the aid of all good citizens in getting the care of her own children.

April 13, 1869   James B. Bradwell

There was also a letter from the man at the Chicago Tribune Company who had helped her publish her first book:

This is to certify that I have known Mrs. E. P. W. Packard personally for about five years. That I have transacted business with her as publisher and printer—printing several thousand copies of her work—and have invariably found her prompt to meet business engagements and accurate in the details of business affairs.

April 12, 1869   W. H. Rand

At this juncture, Libby was not quite nineteen. George would be sixteen in July and Arthur was almost eleven.

Thus fortified, Elizabeth went to Boston in May and, with Samuel Sewall representing her, brought suit in the state supreme court for her children.

By now Theophilus had figured out that in any tangle with his wife he would emerge the loser and probably be humiliated in the bargain. He did not fight the case. Three months earlier he had left his sister's house in South Deerfield and rented a home for his children in Greenfield, Massachusetts (for $175 a year). "We once more lived by ourselves, and enjoyed it greatly," he wrote. But he was running out of money: "Having been reduced in prosperity in supporting my children during the 9 years of *severe* trials, having evidence [Elizabeth] possessed some $10,000, having consulted with friends, I thought it best to give up the three children to her on certain conditions without having the case tried."

The conditions were that he have unlimited visiting rights and that the children be permitted to go to a church of their own choosing (which turned out to be of *his* choosing). He also quietly arranged with the Doles that if "they should be *unable* to live with her," they could go to Manteno to their aunt and uncle.

On June 14, 1869, they all departed by train for Chicago, Elizabeth and the children via Philadelphia, Theophilus via Albany. Theophilus arrived first and took up residence in the Douglas House Hotel, one mile from Elizabeth's house at 1496 Prairie Avenue. (For a while Samuel lived with him. Then he, too, moved to Prairie Avenue and stayed at his mother's home for the rest of 1869 and 1870.)

On July 3, 1869, the Packard family celebrated. It was the first time mother and all six children had *ever* been together. Theo had been at school in Mount Pleasant, Iowa, when Arthur, now eleven, was born, and Elizabeth had been in the asylum before he came home. They went together to the nearby Methodist church. After that Theophilus insisted that the younger ones attend an Evangelical church and sabbath school.

The first day their father visited them at Prairie Avenue, Theo met him at the door and reminded him that this was Elizabeth's home and that he, Theo, would not let his mother be harassed. Theophilus the elder agreed. From then on he was welcome. He thought "they got along living with their mother at her house comfortably well." Elizabeth had always insisted that the children respect and revere their father. Regardless of how *she* felt toward him, she thought they should continue to do so, although several of them were now too old to take orders. She treated Theophilus courteously but distantly, as if he were a "strange gentleman" visiting. She had not actually spoken to him in years, but now that she had her children back, she felt "polite conversation" was warranted in their presence.

In March 1870, Theophilus came down with one of his throat ailments. After having observed his children for nearly a year, he decided it was safe to leave them unsupervised with their mother. So, in early April, Theophilus went back to Manteno after a six-year absence, to live with his sister. Arthur went down to visit him and stayed till nearly the end of August.

Simultaneously, Libby, now almost twenty, took ill. According to her father, "My beloved daughter was taken deranged and continued in a sad state of mind and ill health for several months. She became greatly emaciated and her mind quite inactive. . . . To all appearances it seemed as though she would soon waste away and die. . . . On the 12th of July, she was taken down here, and soon began to mend, and in three months she seemed to have wholly recovered." Theophilus did not mention any of the usual symptoms ascribed to brain fever. From his description of Libby's condition, she was probably suffering from what is known today as depression.

Libby would be subject to these or similar episodes for the rest of her life. Present-day Packards feel that the strain of having had to take responsibility for the house and the small children when she was only ten was too great for Libby. They attributed her on-again-off-again breakdowns to the trauma following her mother's incarceration in the asylum.

Elizabeth and Theophilus between them, their personal antagonisms tempered by time and distance, managed a rather remarkable feat. They managed to keep all their children, except Arthur, who was a special circumstance, on affectionate terms with both parents.

Elizabeth had only three brief years of mothering. In January 1870, Isaac married; the following November Theo followed suit. Both returned to Iowa. Then Samuel went south briefly for his health; he really didn't like Chicago's winter weather.

To Elizabeth's great disappointment George proceeded to leave high school and go to New York to work for the uncle for whom he had been named, and finally, Theophilus took thirteen-year-old Arthur to Manteno to work on a farm there. Arthur, who had not even known his mother until he was eleven, seemed to be more comfortable with his father. Theophilus claimed, without substantiation, that Elizabeth had been "mistreating and abusing" the boy, an unlikely event. He was more eager than ever that Arthur become "a christian" and prayed with and for him daily.

Elizabeth had had high hopes of sending her two youngest sons to college. Her offer to finance George still held. She realized that Arthur was lost to her. Her heart hurt, but her head told her she could not force him to love her and want to live with her. Nor could she blame him for feeling as he did. After all, during his formative years he had known only a father. The two years with her in Chicago could not compensate for the eleven critical years without her.

On October 8, 1871, Mrs. O'Leary's legendary cow kicked over the legendary lantern and Chicago went up in flames. Samuel, back from the south, lost everything. Elizabeth's house was spared but her publishing business was in ashes. She now had to take in boarders. College for George, had he wanted it, would have been another victim of the fire.

In November 1871, Theophilus recorded in his diary, in a lapse from the armistice he and Elizabeth had established: "Today I took my daughter Lizzie from her mother in Chicago, to live at my brother Dole's with me, to prevent irreparable injury to her mind by the wrong treatment she received." She improved under "judicious treatment and my sister's kind care & attention."

In December Samuel left the ruins of Chicago for Denver. To his father, going west was heading into the wilderness. Theophilus tried to talk Samuel into staying: "My chief fear was, and is, it will be injurious to his soul's eternal well-being." In a revival in Chicago some years before, Samuel seemed to have been reached; he had joined first the Presbyterian, then the Baptist church.

Not too long after arriving in Denver, Samuel wrote to his father that he was "inquiring as to the moral & religious lawfulness of practicing Law as a Profession, in the light of the Bible." Theophilus was overjoyed. He began to hope that God would lead Samuel away from the law and into "the Gospel ministry."

On February 1, 1872, Theophilus turned seventy. He wrote in his diary: "Only 28 now living in Shelburne, Mass., my native town, who were living there at my birth! Only 28 of the 1000 people there then, and of the 1,600 people there now! Of my 30 teachers in childhood and youth, only one survives, as far as I know!"

He felt his life was nearly over. Although he still hoped *all* his children would become his definition of practicing Christians, he seemed willing to settle for two of them, Arthur and Samuel, becoming preachers. (Neither did.) Expecting every day to be his last, he wound up his diary and journal keeping in his seventy-first year with the words: "This is to be committed to my Sister Dole at my death, to be retained by her, & used according to her discretion, allowing my children *only* to read it when they are at her house—and I wish them all to read it. At my sister's death, it may belong to Lizzie and Arthur, my daughter and son."

But his anticipation of his death was premature. Theophilus lived on at Manteno for another dozen years, supported in part by financial contributions from Samuel. For some of those years Lizzie and Arthur stayed with him, Arthur working at the farm and Lizzie languishing at the Doles' house.

In her postasylum years, Elizabeth wrote several books (see the list in Appendix 7), all of them still on library shelves. She told over and over, in various combinations and permutations, the story of her troubled marriage, her years in the asylum and her lobbying activities thereafter. She talked about her husband, her children, the helpful and harmful people who had crossed her path, and her feelings about them all. She included many letters written by and to her. Her life, her actions and her motivations, as she saw them, are there for anyone to see in all their eccentricities, their justifications and their logic and effectiveness.

Theophilus left behind a diary in which he entered the events and thoughts most on his mind, more and more sporadically as the years progressed. He also left his journal for the edification of his children plus a few letters of his old age to childhood friends, largely nostalgic reminiscences. Theophilus gave a limited picture of himself—doctrinaire, insecure, oddly paternal, strongly filial and fraternal. But even so, his self-portrait indicates a person less malicious and malignant than his wife said, but also less long suffering and put upon than he said. He was clearly a man in need of help. Judged in terms of effective and constructive activity in the world, he clearly needed more help than his twice-hospitalized wife.

11.

A Reformer's Work
Is Never Done

*I*t *was not* called the "empty nest syndrome" in 1872. But that is what Elizabeth would have suffered had she not had a horizon wider than motherhood. She went back to lobbying.

She rented her house, furnished, and turned over to Samuel, now back in Chicago, responsibility for its upkeep and taxes. Since two of her sons, Theo and Isaac, were in Iowa, she selected that state as her next target.

In Iowa there was no specific evil to eradicate as there had been in Illinois. Her goal was generalized improvement and for that she developed a new, potentially powerful tool: Inmates should be able to write and receive uncensored letters from relatives and friends.

The rationale was simple. If patients had free access to the mails, attendants would hesitate to mistreat them. Patients would be able to let off steam harmlessly; families and friends would get some indication of their mental states; and if there should be mistreatment to complain of, patients could be confident that someone on the outside would know. She felt that the risk of imagined or paranoid complaints, which she recognized as real possibilities, would be more than compensated for by the benefit to the inmates. Elizabeth was developing moderation and tempered reasoning.

The first representative she approached in Des Moines warned her that such a proposal would not be favorably received. He was right. The Iowa legislature was busy voting down woman suffrage; its members were thoroughly tired of being badgered by women.

So Elizabeth followed the path she had trod in Illinois. She managed to meet the members of the legislature's Committee on Insane Asylums, one of whom introduced her to Governor C. C. Carpenter, who, as so often happened in her life, became first her adviser, then her champion. And finally she had a confrontation with the head of the state asylum at Mount Pleasant, Dr. Mark Ranney, who journeyed to the state capital to oppose her. If inmates were allowed to write home freely, he said, his task of "subduing patients" would be much more difficult. His use of the word "subdue" satisfied Elizabeth that he treated the inmates like criminals. All the more reason for her bill.

The Committee on Insane Asylums, after hearing friend and foe, voted unanimously to postpone action indefinitely. A few members advised Elizabeth privately to lobby anyhow. She spent several weeks doing just that and apparently struck a responsive chord in the committee chairman, J. M. Hovey. He decided she had been the victim of injustice. He asked if she had any literature on the subject and was promptly presented with copies of her books. In the end, he led the fight for her bill.

When the bill was brought up again, the Assembly passed it handily, 78 to 1. It had a harder time in the Senate, but it passed there, too, 32 to 16.

The next morning at breakfast, which should have been a celebration, Elizabeth discovered that some legislators had received anonymous letters attacking her character and morals. She immediately assumed that Dr. McFarland, or someone on his behalf, was circulating the "love letter." She began to cry. One of the representatives comforted her: "Never mind, Mrs. Packard. The bill is safe! They were a little too late . . . to harm your cause."

The bill, which the governor signed on April 23, 1872, established a nonpartisan committee to visit the state asylum at intervals to ensure that inmates were supplied weekly with writing materials and allowed to write and receive one uncensored letter each per week. The bill also called for a coroner's inquest in the event of a sudden or mysterious death and specified up to three years in jail and one thousand dollars in fines or both for violators. (The visiting committee, however, was given some discretion to hold back patently irrational letters.)

Elizabeth went with one of the new committee, a Mrs. M. A. P. Darwin, of Burlington, on her regular visit to the Mount Pleasant asylum. It gave her an opportunity to spend some time with her son Theo and his family.

Mrs. Darwin introduced Elizabeth to Dr. Ranney (whom she had already met in Des Moines) as "This is Mrs. Packard whom I found at the depot, and she came along with me." Dr. Ranney refused to let Elizabeth accompany Mrs. Darwin into any except the two "show" wards, and told her it was against the rules to talk to the patients. What she saw was a model of neatness, quiet and order, but was it representative?

Afterward Elizabeth wrote to the governor to complain about Mrs. Darwin's attitude toward her and toward the committee's purpose. He replied that he hoped her first impression of the Visiting Committee would turn out to be incorrect. Nevertheless, he promised to look into it.

Elizabeth was so appreciative that she asked Governor Carpenter for his picture to use in her next book. He sent it and wrote: "I think you give me entirely too much credit in reference to my connection with the passage of the 'Act to Protect the Insane.' The success of that measure was entirely due to your persistent advocacy, and the good judgment with which you presented its merits to the members of the General Assembly."

Now that Iowa was safe for asylum inmates, Elizabeth moved on to New York. She had read about charges being brought against two institutions in New York City and she wanted to be there. She also had another book ready for publication; it could easily be printed in New York. To pave her way, Elizabeth wrote to New York's governor, John T. Hoffman, with suggestions for reform.

A special committee named by the Board of Emigration was looking into the management and conditions at the city's year-old asylum on Ward's Island where insane immigrants were confined. And a three-man committee appointed by Governor Hoffman was checking on charges of unwarranted imprisonment and mistreatment of patients at New York Hospital's Bloomingdale Lunatic Asylum. The first was a state institution, the second private.

The *New York Tribune* had been carrying on an on-again-off-again campaign for years to get commitment and treatment procedures amended. It was a legitimate cause. There was always some mistreatment of patients in every asylum, and there was always the disgruntled ex-employee and the former patient who were only too happy to dish up tales of horror. The *Tribune* had assigned a reporter to feign madness and get himself committed to the Bloomingdale asylum, where he managed to find exactly what he wanted.

The day the first *Tribune* story appeared, the governors of the hospital appointed a committee to investigate. It reported no foundation for the accusations and said the ex-employee whose charges the *Tribune* had printed had been discharged for drunkenness.

That did not satisfy the governor. For several years he had sought legislation to provide both safeguards against unwarranted commitments and restrictions on who could care for "lunatics." He proposed that the State Commission of Charities supervise and recommend asylums. But the Senate would not go along, largely, according to undenied rumors, because of the efforts of the chief physician at the Bloomingdale Asylum, Dr. D. Tildon Brown. (Dr. Brown later claimed that he had not understood the bill properly; he thought it would circumscribe his choice of treatment and medication.)

The governor decided that the best interests of the public as well as the reputation of the asylum called for an objective investigation. On August 20, 1872, he named the committee: Attorney General Francis C. Barlow, President M. B. Anderson of Rochester University, and Dr. Thomas Hun of Albany. He instructed them to visit and inspect all asylums, public and private, "with or without charges being made against them."

A month earlier, the *New York Times* had reported with approval a system used in Belgium whereby the *Procurer du Roi*, the officer with legal authority over government institutions, had ordered "strong and safely-shut letter boxes . . . be provided, accessible to all the inmates, and to be opened only by his own subordinates" who would visit them every week and deliver promptly all letters (presumably of complaint) to him.

Elizabeth read this and thought it a splendid idea. She promptly wrote to Governor Carpenter in Iowa and also to Governor Hoffman asking why such a system could not be instituted in their states. Both were willing to think about it.

The first hearings of the governor's committee were open to the press and public. But on October 11, the committee announced that henceforth its hearings would be secret; the *Tribune's* coverage, it complained, was inaccurate.

Elizabeth either sat in on the early hearings or read and culled the *Tribune* articles because a few of the horror stories appeared as chapters in her next book, *Modern Persecution or Insane Asylums Unveiled*.

In November 1872 New York elected a new governor, John A. Dix. The report Governor Hoffman had requested was turned in to him in February

1873. The committee found no wrongfully committed patients in any of the asylums. But it did find some mistreatment of inmates, probably, it said, because it was so hard to find and keep qualified personnel. It urged constant vigilance by the management.

As for the Bloomingdale asylum in particular, the committee found the management satisfactory but the treatment on occasion improper; the director was not sufficiently vigilant and staff discipline was lax. It allowed the superintendent an out: He had been absent for part of that year because of illness in his family; perhaps that was the reason for the laxity.

The committee recommended that private as well as public asylums be licenced by the State Board of Charities and that a "State Commissioner in Lunacy" be appointed to visit and inspect all such institutions. The legislature acted upon these suggestions, and later in 1873 the provision the former governor had sought for so long became law under his successor. This new law set a precedent that other states began to follow. Connecticut, where Elizabeth had suffered her first defeat, was among the first. Elizabeth, in Hartford to arrange the publication of her book, was present to witness its passage.

In 1874 Elizabeth received a long letter from Samuel, now 27.

Dear Mother, I do not know where to address you. I have not heard from you for some time. . . .

I expect to get married in May or June to a young lady of 19, that I met about 9 months since—She is a good Christian girl, sensible, true, refined—and I love her with all my heart. We shall go to housekeeping at once I think—I have already rented a house . . . I mean to try & live on $3,000 a year so that I can get to be independent in 10 years.

I don't want to stay in this climate longer than that—and I hope to save at least one hundred thousand dollars salted down by that time so that I can move to a more genial climate and then devote myself to carrying on some great and noble reformation—as you do. . . .

I attended an auction sale the other day and bought over $200 worth of oil paintings for my house. I say if we cannot live in a country where we can look out the window and see fine scenery the next thing to it, is to have it represented on our walls. . . .

I have not been down to Manteno for some time: but I hear from them quite often.

Lizzie is about the same.

Ira [Isaac had changed his name] *and his wife are spending a few weeks in the City. He is working at his old place with Farwell. George is running his business [in Iowa] during his absence. I seldom hear from Theo— but I understand he is to be in the city in a few days.*

    Your house I rerented for another year to the same tenant for $30 per month. That is all the place is now worth for the furniture is pretty much all used up.

    It can't be rented as a "furnished house" any longer without buying new furniture—a thing which I know you did not want to do—

    The boxes of clothes in the basement are all eaten up by the moths. What had I best do with them?

    There will be a bill, of about $200 a year for pruning the shrubs this year besides the taxes—making the taxes amount to more than the rent probably.

    It would be better for you if you would dispose of this property & put your money out at interest—you could get an income from it then. With much love, your son Samuel.

The "good Christian girl" was Clara Fish of Lombard, Illinois, a town about twenty-five miles south of Chicago. The wedding was noted in the *Chicago Legal News* and *Chicago Tribune*. It also made news back in Franklin County, Massachusetts, where the *Greenfield Gazette* reported that on June 23, 1874, "the marriage of a son of Franklin County transpired . . . at Lombard, Ill., in the Congregational Church of that place, amid a profusion of evergreens and flowers with which a professional artist from abroad had decorated the sanctuary. The ceremony was performed by Mr. Caverno, the paster (sic), *assisted by the father of the bridegroom.*" (Italics added.)

    Only in the closing paragraph were the names of the happy couple given: The bride was Miss Clara A. Fish, of Lombard, and the "party who became her husband" was Samuel Ware Packard, a grandson of the late Dr. Packard of Shelburne. Theophilus was never mentioned by name.

    The *Chicago Legal News* reported on June 27 that "on Tuesday, the 23rd instant at Lombard, Ill., Samuel W. Packard, Esq., of the law firm of Cooper, Garnett & Packard, was married to Miss Clara A. Fish, a most esteemed and popular young lady of the former place. . . . We never attended a wedding where there was so much genuine good feeling manifested." The mother of the groom, now fifty-seven, was not there. She was in Boston, resting up from an obstacle-ridden but successful campaign in Maine and preparing to take her message to the nation's capital.

* * *

By the time she reached Maine in early 1874, Elizabeth had tackled five states with varying degrees of success and only one outright failure. The bills passed were not necessarily the ones she had proposed. But if she had had anything to do with the legislation being enacted, no matter how indirect, she claimed—and not unjustly—some of the credit.

Elizabeth had her strategy pretty well structured by now. First she would canvass a state for several months, personally seeking out movers and shakers and trying to enlist their sympathies. She would furnish them with literature, ranging from her books at five dollars each to her pamphlets at ten cents.

Once anyone expressed interest or sympathy, Elizabeth would ask permission to use his name as a sponsor. She usually headed her list of sponsors with clergymen unless she was in the home town of a judge or, better yet, the governor himself. After the clergymen came lawyers, physicians and prominent businessmen.

She would check in to a first-class hotel with a "reliable" proprietor. "Reliable" meant he would let her use his office as a depository for the books she hoped to sell and would guarantee to handle redemption of the tickets for them. She was still selling tickets that buyers could exchange for books even though the books were now readily available. Tickets she could carry with her, and experience had shown that a purchaser of a ticket almost always redeemed it while someone who simply agreed to buy a book tended to forget.

After Elizabeth had enough names, she went to Augusta for the opening of the January 1874 legislature. She printed the names of her sponsors in pamphlet form and presented it to the representatives and senators with this message:

A POPULAR BILL

Members of the Maine Legislature:

Honorable Gentlemen: As proof that the public sentiment of Maine is in favor of the passage of the bill "To place the inmates of insane asylums under the protection of the law," I place before you the names of 383 of my Maine patrons—who are voters—and these men have endorsed the provisions of this bill and desire its passage.

Mrs. E. P. W. Packard

The bill she proposed resembled Iowa's 1872 "Act To Protect the Insane" with one addition. The visiting committee *must* include one woman.

With the help of a local lawyer, former Mayor Samuel Titcomb, she rewrote her petition to meet Maine statutory requirements. The governor, Nelson Dingley, Jr., whom she met through Titcomb, gave it his blessing. So the petition was read to the Senate and referred to the appropriate committee. The committee chairman promptly called a meeting for that very day and invited her to address it. Elizabeth had no time to prepare. She hated to speak extemporaneously. It was too easy to misstate something, and if she were to be rattled, which did not happen often, it would be when she was not well rehearsed. Nevertheless, she met the challenge. The session went on for hours, adjourned until the next day and then, after more hours of discussion, adjourned again until the day after that. Finally the committee recommended the bill with a few amendments and qualifications.

While the Senate was debating, Elizabeth wrote some more of her anonymous articles for the local press, which always seemed willing to print them.

After the three required readings, the Senate passed the bill and sent it on to the House. On the day the third reading was scheduled, Elizabeth showed up as usual. But she was not greeted as usual. No one even said "good morning." Then she discovered that again there was an anonymous letter, this one in the morning paper, challenging her sanity and citing the "love letter." This was the one occurrence that could still reduce Elizabeth to tears.

By now her deportment and demeanor were so businesslike, her knowledge of legislation and lobbying so extensive, and her practice of the political art so effective that to question her sanity seemed itself insane.

A reporter from the Portland paper came over to console her: "Don't feel so bad. . . . Your bill will pass." Then one of the representatives broke ranks and spoke to her. He said he personally considered the letter writer ungentlemanly.

The bill was called up but deferred.

Elizabeth packed up and left Augusta. As far as she was concerned Dr. McFarland was proving his perfidy all over again. *Her* anonymous letters were all constructive; *his* were intended to destroy. She thought he had beaten her. She went to Boston to lick her wounds and plan her next move. The day after she arrived, she received a telegram from Augusta: "Your bill has this day passed without a dissenting vote."

In June 1874, Elizabeth asked for and received free from Governor Dingley, a letter to use in her next campaign.

> Madam,—Yours of the 18th, inquiring as to the workings of the law enacted by the last legislature of this State. . . . is before me.
>
> Thus far the law has worked well, and has been instrumental in bringing about improvements in the hospital, and in inspiring increased public confidence in its management. Especially was that feature of the law which requires that one member of the Visiting Committee shall be a woman, proved to be of peculiar advantage.
>
> Respectfully yours,
> Nelson Dingley, Jr.

The female member of the Visiting Committee, Mrs. C. A. Quimby, also wrote:

> Augusta, Maine, June 20, 1874
>
> My Dear Mrs. Packard. In reply to your question, "Is the new law, passed by our legislature, a success or a failure?" . . . as far as my knowledge goes, all say it is a very necessary law and capable of doing great good in all our insane asylums.
>
> Say to the opposers of your bill, it is not true that it has been a failure in my judgment and that of the best men and women of our city and State.
>
> Ever your friend,
> C. A. Quimby

In December 1874, Elizabeth went to Washington. She had decided to try to bypass the state-by-state route by appealing directly to Congress. And she had decided to push for federal adoption of the Belgian system—post-office boxes in every insane asylum for the exclusive use of inmates and under the direct jurisdiction of the government, not the hospital administration.

She first approached the postmaster general but he brushed her off. So, as she had in Illinois, she headed straight for the top. This time the top was the White House itself. Elizabeth asked for Mrs. Grant. When asked who was calling, she replied, "A friend from Illinois."

Presently Mrs. Grant appeared to find a strange woman in the hall.

"I thought you were a friend from Illinois," she said.

"I am," Elizabeth replied. "I *am* from Illinois and I am certainly a friend to the administration."

She then asked the First Lady to sign her petition to Congress for a bill requiring post boxes in asylums. Mrs. Grant refused; her husband was against her taking part in public affairs. But she was willing to listen to Elizabeth's reasons for the proposal, which, of course, included the story of Elizabeth's commitment. Mrs. Grant recommended that she write a book about her experiences. When she heard there were already several, she bought two. She also invited Elizabeth back the next evening to tell her story to the president. Then, despite her earlier refusal, Mrs. Grant did sign the petition.

The following evening Elizabeth returned. But she was not admitted. The president was dining with the king of the Sandwich Islands (Hawaii), an appointment which Mrs. Grant had forgotten. Elizabeth was instructed to come back at eleven o'clock the next morning.

President Grant listened, approved her mission and gave her his card with an introductory note to Congressman John B. Packard (no relative) of Pennsylvania, chairman of the committee to which he assumed her bill would be referred.

Then she went to the treasury and asked for its solicitor, Theodore F. Wilson, who was too busy to see her. But when she submitted the president's card, he let her into his office, questioned her, bought a couple of books and also signed her petition. He sent her on to the next prospect, and gradually her list of signatories grew.

Elizabeth then sought the help of Mrs. Belva Ann Lockwood, a lawyer and advocate of women's rights.* Mrs. Lockwood helped Elizabeth prepare the bill which Elizabeth showed to a variety of judges for their opinions. Then she presented it to prosuffrage Senator Sargent of California and to former governor, now Congressman Joseph R. Hawley of Connecticut, her old acquaintance from her 1866 campaign.

On January 5, 1875, Senator Sargent "asked and, by unanimous consent,

---

* Mrs. Lockwood had once sought President Grant's help in forcing the law school that had reluctantly admitted her to give her her diploma. Later when she was denied permission to appear before the Supreme Court on the ground of "custom," she enlisted the support of Senator Aaron A. Sargent of California, a prosuffrage senator who swung the decision her way.

obtained leave to bring in a bill, which was read twice, referred to the Committee on Post-Offices and Post Roads, and ordered to be printed" (see Appendix 8). On the same day under the same circumstances, Congressman Hawley introduced the same bill, now labeled H.R. 4161, to the House of Representatives.

Four days later, on January 9, the *Washington Evening Star* commented on the bill:

> . . . *facts were shown that under arrangements now existing, the inmates of insane asylums have no means of communicating with the outside world. It was also shown that there are a large number of persons in the various asylums of the country that are not absolutely insane, and are kept there only because they have no means of communicating with their friends.*

The paper concluded by quoting one witness who stated that there were many inmates charged with insanity because "of certain religious beliefs" who were not a bit insane. (The "religious beliefs" the witness referred to were probably Spiritualism.)

H.R. 4161 was read twice, also referred to the House Committee on the Post-Office and Post Roads, and ordered to be printed.

The Senate committee reported out the bill favorably and placed it on the docket. Among those whom Elizabeth was counting on to vote for it was her old friend Richard Oglesby, now a senator from Illinois. But appropriations bills, introduced at the same time, took precedence, and Congress adjourned before it reached Elizabeth's bill. That was the end of it as far as the Forty-third Congress was concerned. But it was not quite the end of Elizabeth's efforts.

On January 5, 1876, as the Forty-fourth Congress convened, the same bill was introduced into the House as H.R. 452 and again referred to the Committee on Post-Offices and Post Roads. There is no record of it after that. It was not introduced into the Senate and no such law now exists. However, Nebraska and Washington Territory passed insanity laws providing for postal rights for asylum inmates. And in recent years some states have passed legislation giving inmates uncensored access to the telephone, which could be considered a lineal descendant of Elizabeth's 1875 proposal. The state legislators behind these measures are familiar with her work.

Toward the end of Elizabeth's stay in Washington, Congressman Platt, whose houseguest she was for a while, told her that the superintendent of the Government Hospital for the Insane in Washington, D.C. (now Saint

Elizabeth's) was scheduled to testify before the House committee about Dr. McFarland's opinion of Elizabeth; the superintendent was eager to prove that Elizabeth was insane. Congressman Platt said he told the committee that he did not think *Mrs. Packard* had come to Congress to be passed; it was her *bill* that was to be judged: "Is the bill sound and reasonable? is what we, as Congressmen, are to consider, not to test the state or condition of its defender."

Although Elizabeth had come to Washington for the sole purpose of getting congressional action on mail boxes for asylum inmates, it occurred to her that if the superintendent of the Government Hospital was an activist ally of Dr. McFarland, perhaps his institution needed to be looked at more closely. There is no indication that she did or did not have anything to do with it, but the fact is that in 1875 a petition was submitted to Congress charging mismanagement, extravagance and corruption in the expenditures of the appropriations set aside for the use of the asylum; incompetence in managing the government farm attached to the asylum, which made all its products cost twice as much as those on the open market; and neglect, mismanagement and abuse of the patients. Some of the charges of patient abuse went back as far as the 1850s.

Congress did initiate an investigation but apparently it petered out because on August 8, 1876, the president *pro tem* of the Senate submitted a petition of one Alexander Moffit plus twenty-four other citizens of the District of Columbia (one of whom, treasury solicitor, Theodore F. Wilson, had signed Elizabeth's petition for mail boxes) for the appointment of a joint committee to continue and conclude the unfinished investigation of the Government Hospital for the Insane.

The Committee on Expenditures of the Interior Department held hearings but the people who had signed the original petition claimed they were unable to appear since they had not been subpoenaed. When they were subsequently subpoenaed, they refused to talk unless their lawyers were present. Eventually a couple of the petitioners did take the stand. Under questioning, despite Moffit's claim that he could produce witnesses who would substantiate the charges, they revealed that many of the allegations against the hospital were based on rumor and hearsay.

The *Washington Evening Star*, which followed the story through the month, reported, "It does not seem at all likely, unless the new examination pans out better than it has thus far, that the investigation and examination of witnesses against the hospital will be resumed." (Thirty years later, during the Fifty-ninth Congress, there was "a full and complete investigation" of the management of the hospital, based on similar charges, which produced several thousand pages of testimony. By then Elizabeth had been dead for nearly ten years. The need for constant vigilance was apparently as great as ever.)

Over the next fifteen years, Elizabeth campaigned in twenty-five more states, traveling often on railroad passes, "thanks to the New York, New Haven, Hartford, Harrisburg, Pittsburgh, Ft. Wayne and Chicago Railroad Companies." She talked to inmates of the Hartford Retreat, McLean's (near Boston), and asylums in Philadelphia, Columbus, Ohio, and Concord, New Hampshire, all of whom she thanked in prefaces to her books.

In many of those states, commitment and treatment procedures were changed. Some reports credit her with responsibility for getting twenty-one laws changed; others put the total at thirty-four. The American Bar Foundation's 1968 study gives Elizabeth credit for the enactment (or revision) of commitment laws in Illinois, Iowa and Massachusetts and an indirect hand in legislation in a number of other states. In most cases, the main focus of these changed laws was mandatory jury trials, which without the mandatory aspect remain in modified or discretionary form today.

Whatever the statistics, which are hard to come by, there were a lot of changes made in Elizabeth's wake. She may have provided the spark that ignited the embers of reform; she may have arrived on the scene in time to fan those flames; she may have simply, in the words of the late Jimmy Durante, wanted to get into the act, and because of the stir she had caused years earlier in Illinois, could always get a headline. Whatever the reason, even those psychiatrists today who are inclined to think she may have indeed had psychotic episodes that warranted hospitalization give her credit for raising public consciousness about mental illness and mental institutions.

In her later years Elizabeth concentrated on the single issue of getting inmates uncensored access to mail boxes. By the end of her life, she figured she had made fifty thousand dollars from her writings and had spent half that amount on behalf of the insane. And every inch of the way she saw the shadow of Dr. McFarland. Letters denouncing her as a lunatic kept cropping up and the now-notorious "love letter" she had written, as she said in "peculiar exigencies," would be quoted.

Dr. McFarland was a reputable and respected practitioner of the art of treating the mentally ill. It is unlikely that four years of exposure to

Elizabeth would have so radically changed his professional ethics and responsibilities that he would have stooped to attempts to undermine one individual woman, like a twentieth-century political "truth squad" following on the heels of an opposition candidate. He certainly would have been willing to let opposition to Elizabeth's proposed changes in state law rest in the hands of able colleagues in the states under her siege. There had been equally or almost equally troublesome patients in his asylum before and since Elizabeth. He must have received love letters of various kinds from other women patients in "peculiar exigencies." Even though Freud had yet to diagnose and define the transference of emotions during therapy, the phenomenon obviously existed for him to find, and Dr. McFarland must have experienced it more than once. There is even some evidence that he encouraged it as an ego trip without realizing its value.

He did make the letter available to the Jacksonville investigating committees. Once revealed, like Pandora's box, there was no way such a spicy document could become private again. He could have protested its use but there is no indication that he did. Elizabeth remained convinced that he was an active participant from border to border in attempts to defeat her bills. She was so sure that in May 1886, she made a special trip to Jacksonville to see the doctor at his new asylum, Oak Lawn Retreat. Her old friend and admirer, Stephen Moore, who had defended her at Kankakee, accompanied her. Elizabeth intended to demand that the doctor promise her in writing to stop libeling her by calling her insane. He would not see her. So Stephen Moore instituted a suit for $25,000 in damages (which, reported the local newspaper, "was quite considerate, when the claim might as easily been $50,000").

The suit does not seem to have been pursued. There is no mention of it in any of Elizabeth's writings. Considering her vendetta, had there been a trial, she would have been the first to publicize it. The press, too, would have found it as colorful as the 1867 investigation, but there was no mention of it in print beyond the original comment just mentioned.

Now that Elizabeth was again in Illinois and had a rare breathing space between campaigns, she took some time for herself and paid a long-delayed visit to the Chicago suburb of Oak Park to meet Samuel's wife for the first time. Samuel and Clara had been married for twelve years and had five children, three daughters and two sons. Elizabeth was delighted with her daughter-in-law and her grandchildren.

In December 1886, with some time to spare from her labors, she wrote to Clara from Minneapolis, where she was preparing her next legislative battle:

> My Dear Daughter-in-law Clara, Allow me to ask you to accept of the enclosed fifty dollars ($50) as a "Christmas present" from your mother-in-law.
>
> It affords me pleasure to bestow this gift upon one so deserving of appreciation, as a Christian mother, & as a philanthropist.
>
> You, like me, seem to have had your field of labor assigned, by the providence of God, and we are being consecrated to our work. It is ennobling to work for Christ, and if ever you have to suffer for him, as I have done, you will then, and only then, know how to sympathize with me. But thank God! I have learned to live without human sympathy and without appreciation. But it was so hard to learn this, for one so sensitive as I am.
>
> To have God's approval is now my sole ambition.
>
> I see you are acquiring quite a notoriety as a temperance worker, and your heart seems in this good work. I rejoice that you lift so exalted a banner as the "prohibition." Nothing short of this touches the root of this evil.
>
> I have often thought of the pleasant visit I had in your happy family, & often visit you in imagination, as I can now place you as you are.
>
> I have made an appointment to meet an old Shelburne friend at the "Windsor Hotel," Chicago, on the 27th of Dec. to renew our acquaintance . . . and then return to my field of labor at St. Paul. . . . As I have no home in Chicago to invite her into, I suggested this place for our visit. . . .
>
> I hope my dear grandchildren will never forget their grandmother who feels quite proud of them.
>
> Remember me kindly to each one of them, & also your good mother, & kind sister. . . .
>
> > Your Affectionate Mother,
> > E. P. W. Packard
>
> P.S. I leave for St. Paul, Minnesota tomorrow to find a new home for a few weeks.

Elizabeth was now sixty-nine. She showed no signs of tiring; there were still states to conquer and people to save, in and from asylums, including her own daughter.

12.

Striking the Flag

S*ometime between 1879 and 1883* Theo moved his mercantile business and his family to Pasadena in southern California. The Packards were beginning to scatter.

In 1880 Lizzie, aged thirty, who had good years as well as bad, had married Harry George Craig Gordon of Portland, Oregon, and left Illinois. Arthur, too, was married and working for the Rock Island Railway as a stationmaster in Avoca, Iowa. Ira and his wife and children followed Theo west and settled in San Diego.

In 1886 George, aged thirty-three and unmarried, developed a progressive neurological disorder, probably Lou Gehrig's disease (which had yet to be identified and named). Three years later he was dead. Only Samuel, who had not wanted to, stayed on in Chicago. His law practice ballooned. He was licensed to appear before the Supreme Court and he was on his way to building up the largest private law library in the city. He gave up his dream of moving to a "genial climate" and "carrying on some great and noble reformation," unless the law could be considered that. By the 1880s he had moved to suburban Oak Park. But he, too, wound up in southern California after his wife died, in law practice with his younger son, John.

Elizabeth's brother, Samuel Ware, had followed Horace Greeley's advice, too, moving to Garden Grove, California. (Only Austin, the youngest of the Wares, stayed on in Massachusetts.)

Elizabeth had not taken Samuel's advice to sell her house and invest the proceeds for the interest. She held on to it with a dim dream of settling down there some day when her mission would be accomplished. In the meantime it stayed rented; her home, literally, was where she hung her hat, a hotel room in whatever state capital her crusade took her to.

Theophilus finally died in 1885 at age eighty-three. Since his two youngest had left Manteno he had no further parental responsibilities and spent his days praying, reading, reminiscing about his childhood and writing occasional letters to old Shelburne residents. The aged grandfather was a far mellower person than the son, husband or father had been. His final years were peaceful, perhaps even happy. His children stayed in touch and affectionate, even if they seldom saw him. But in the end he lost his battle for their souls, except for Samuel over whom he had worried most and, as it turned out, unnecessarily.

Samuel was the only one to accept the dogma of fundamentalism. Samuel's oldest son, Walter (an agricultural expert whom the United States sent on missions to emerging nations to help them increase their crop yields), told me the *only* subject his father refused to discuss with him was religion. However, Samuel's faith was not quite rock solid. In semiretirement in southern California, he took to playing the stock market and, according to one of John's sons, to bargaining with God. If his stock went up, he would make a generous donation to the church. There were months when the church profited handsomely, but in the end Samuel died broke. Both of his parents might well have said it was God's judgment.

The other sons deliberately or unconsciously rejected Theophilus's brand of religious belief. Theo, to his father's horror, had become a spiritualist. Ira converted to Christian Science when he moved west. George and Arthur were nominal Protestants. They lived what their mother considered a good Christian life. It was not good enough for their father. As for Lizzie, her health was the major factor. Prayer was what one did on Sundays if one felt strong enough.

Unlike her husband, Elizabeth was not able to relax and reflect in tranquility. The turbulence of her children's critical preteen and teenage years had taken a greater toll on some of them than on others. Lizzie's marriage could not stand the strain of her emotional fluctuations. The Gordons separated in the early 1890s after little more than ten years together. Elizabeth, now in her seventies, took her daughter under her wing. They moved to the warm climate of Pasadena and lived with Theo.

Theo's wife had died and he was raising four teenagers, three sons and a daughter. Elizabeth and Lizzie occupied the downstairs front room of Theo's house on Lake Avenue. Theo and the children shared three rooms upstairs.

At one point Lizzie became seriously disturbed. Elizabeth was determined to keep her out of an asylum, remembering all too vividly her own asylum years and forgetting—or lacking confidence in—the improvements she had brought about since. She insisted on taking care of her daughter herself. But it was not easy.

Finally, Theo built a small enclosure of webbed wire in the corner of the downstairs front room. It measured about ten feet by five feet—just large enough for a cot and a table. In it Lizzie lived for months on end. Her meals were given to her on a tray in this enclosure and she usually ate them in silence. In fact she was silent for much of the time, but there were occasional noisy nights when she would keep her mother awake. Sometimes Elizabeth took Lizzie outside for a walk in the sunshine.

All the neighbors and the children's school friends seemed to know there was an insane relative living in the Packard house though no one in the family talked about it. Theo's children were enormously embarrassed by the presence of their "crazy" aunt; they couldn't bring their friends home and they dreaded her rare walks in the garden where the neighbors might actually see her.

In 1896, in Los Angeles, Lizzie and Harry Gordon were officially divorced.

The following year Elizabeth realized that the burden on Theo and his children was too great. She decided to take Lizzie back to their old house in Chicago. The family did not think Lizzie should travel in her condition but Elizabeth was adamant.

The train journey was disastrous, and not just for Elizabeth and her charge. Lizzie, apparently regressing to the days before she was ten when the housekeeping responsibilities had suddenly fallen on her small shoulders, crouched in an upper berth and poured water down on the heads of the passengers walking below.

Her mother got her home safely to Chicago. But Elizabeth did not weather the journey. She took ill on the way and on July 25, 1897, aged eighty-one, she died of a strangulated hernia. The funeral was held at the First Presbyterian Church and she was buried at Rosehill Cemetery in the family plot.

The *Chicago Tribune* printed a lengthy obituary which said in part: "The greatest part of her life she had been a hard worker in the cause she espoused. . . . Through the influence of her books, added to her untiring efforts, thirty-four bills have been passed by various legislatures, each benefitting the insane in some way." The *Boston Transcript* gave her an international, as well as national, reputation and concluded: "It has been claimed that no woman of her day, except possibly Harriet Beecher Stowe, exercised a wider influence in the interest of humanity."

After Elizabeth's death, "whoever was in charge at the time," according to Theo's daughter, Ina, which was probably Samuel, had no choice but to put Lizzie in an institution where she died a year later. So all Elizabeth's efforts on her daughter's behalf were in vain; the ill-starred Lizzie spent her last months in an insane asylum after all.

Longevity in the Ware and Packard families seemed to die with Elizabeth.

Elizabeth lived until 81 at a time when life expectancy for a child who survived infancy was 38 for boys and 40 for girls; and a child who reached 20, boy or girl, could anticipate living to 60. The Sage of Shelburne had died at 86, his wife at 90. Theophilus reached 83. Elizabeth's grandfather Ware had reached 82 and her own father had lived to 85.

Few of Elizabeth's children survived her for long. George was already dead in 1889. The oldest, Theo, died in 1902. Ira developed cancer, which did not respond to Christian Science readings; he took his own life. And Arthur, in Avoca, whose early years had obviously been traumatic enough to make his later ones too much for him, also committed suicide. Neither Ira's nor Arthur's death certificates are available. Only Samuel lived until 1937, but by then it was well into the twentieth century and nonagenarians were not that rare.

Despite her sons' insistence in person and in writing that they never believed their mother to have been insane, they must have had subconscious doubts and when they became parents they began to worry about their offspring.

In the 1800s it was a common belief or superstition that insanity ran in families. Theophilus had no hesitancy in attributing Elizabeth's behavior to heredity. But he didn't carry the thought forward to worry that the same genes might affect his children. He only worried about their souls.

Scientific research has made long strides since then, confirming and denying. It has actually turned up genetic components in certain mental maladies, specifically schizophrenia and manic-depressive psychosis. But for delusional or psychotic episodes, the disturbance attributed to Elizabeth, so far genetics seem to play no part. Nevertheless, on the assumption that the less their children knew about their grandmother, the less likely they would be to manifest any of the "derangements" Theophilus had charged her with, they told their children little or nothing about Elizabeth. Except for Theo's children, with whom she lived for a few years (and to whom she related at length stories about her years in the asylum, their grandfather's obsession with Calvin and her reforming activities in "every state of the union,") none of the grandchildren had any recollections to share with me. Even Samuel's children, whom Elizabeth hoped, in her letter to Clara, would never forget their grandmother, remembered nothing at all.

In fact once the obituaries were filed away and the asylum superintendents with whom she had locked horns died off, she became yesterday's news.

A daughter of the nineteenth century brought up to be the conventional wife and mother, Elizabeth confounded her heritage by battling the male establishment of her day, fighting her way out of an insane asylum and back into the community's good graces. Then she went on to earn fifty thousand dollars by her pen, campaign in thirty-one states and influence legislation in more than half of them, while retaining the love and respect of her children. Considering the magnitude of her achievement, she faded into obscurity with extraordinary rapidity. Everyone forgot Elizabeth.

Everyone except for a few people in psychiatric circles, some historians and doctoral candidates. Some psychiatrists still blame her for hampering the practice of their nineteenth-century colleagues because of the laws she inspired. A few historians have contributed inaccurate biographical sketches of her to the rare anthology of women activists.

The letter Elizabeth wrote to her daughter-in-law more than a hundred years ago was prophetic; it was indeed lonely and unappreciated "doing God's work." She wrote in that same letter, "To have God's approval is now my sole ambition." *That* she was satisfied she had.

$\mathcal{A}ppendix$ 1.

MY EXPOSURE OF CALVINISM AND DEFENCE
OF CHRISTIANITY, AS PRESENTED TO THE TRUSTEES

GENTLEMEN—I am accused of teaching my children doctrines ruinous in their tendency, and such as alienate them from their father.

I reply that my teachings and practice both are ruinous to Satan's cause, and do alienate my children from satanic influences. I teach Christianity; my *husband* teaches Calvinism. These are antagonistic systems, and uphold antagonistic authorities.

Christianity upholds God's authority. Calvinism, the devil's authority.

Calvinism befriends slavery. Christianity befriends liberty.

The kingdom of Christ and the kingdom of Satan can no longer exist in one and the same family or government. The time has come when the tares and the wheat must be separated; for the harvest of the world is fully ripe.

Calvin was a bigot—an intolerant despot—a murderer. Christ was a kind, liberal, charitable and tolerant friend and protector to all, and the Saviour of all.

Calvin trespassed upon the inalienable rights of others. Christ protected the rights of all.

Calvin hated with a deadly hate his Christian brother. Christ loved with saving power his enemies.

Calvinism is treason to God's government. Christianity is loyalty to God's government.

Calvinistic marriage requires the subjection of woman. Christian marriage requires the protection of woman.

The teachings of Christ and those of Calvin are antagonistic.

Christ taught there is but one God. Calvin taught there are three Gods.

Christ taught that he was the Son of God. Calvin taught that he was God himself.

Christ taught that the Son could not be as old as his Father. Calvin taught that they could be of the same age.

Christ taught that he was a subordinate being, subject to God's authority, and that he acted with delegated power as the world's Saviour, and that when this end was fully achieved he should deliver up his delegated authority to his Father, and he himself be subject to him, and God would then be "all and in all."

Calvin taught that Christ was God himself, and acted by his own self-derived authority.

Christ taught that God was the Father of all the human family, and as such, purposes and designs the best good of all his children; and he taught that he had Omnipotent power to carry out and accomplish all the benevolent purposes of his paternal nature.

Calvin taught that the larger part of the human family were the children of the devil, and that he had Omnipotent power to *thwart* God's purposes concerning such, and could ensure to them eternal destruction in spite of God's intention and purpose to redeem the *whole* of the human family from destruction.

Christ taught that every sin would receive its just punishment—that the law of justice was inexorable—that the only way to escape punishment was to escape the *cause* of punishment.

Calvin taught that the favorites in God's family would be exonerated from this law, simply because they believed that Christ died for sinners.

Christ taught that punishment would continue so long as transgression continued, that whenever repentance took place, pardon ensued; and that all would sometime repent, because he had purposed to *save all* in *this way alone*; and he taught that death and hell would finally be destroyed, and, of course, if the effect ceased, the *cause* must have ceased.

Calvin taught that the greater part of God's family would transcend God's ability to discipline into subjugation to his authority and obedience to his commands; and that failing in his ability so to do, he was determined to show his power over them by keeping them in endless, hopeless torment, and thus, fiend-like, manifest his despotic authority by forever torturing his helpless victims.

Calvin taught that the day of probation terminated with the death of our natural bodies.

Christ taught that there were no limits to God's mercy, that he was unchangeable, "the same yesterday, to-day, and forever," therefore, repentance will always remain a condition of pardon—the free-agency is an indispensable law of our moral nature, over which the death of our natural body has no influence—that this natural law of our *physical* being has no more influence or control over the laws of our *moral* nature than the natural law of eating or sleeping has over them—or, that putting off our natural body has no more power to change the laws of our moral nature than a change of clothing has to change the character.

Christ taught that our natures are holy—that all their God-given instincts and laws are but a type of his own nature which we cannot violate with impunity—that to disregard *nature's* claim, is to disregard *God's* claims. And he has shown us what these claims are by living a natural life himself on earth, for our example. He has shown us that sin consists in violating the laws of our God-given nature—thus depraving, or perverting it, from its original tendencies; that he came to restore human nature from its present perverted condition to its original, natural state of innocence.

Calvin taught that our natures are sinful, that to live a natural life is to live a sinful life. He taught that human nature is our worst foe, which we must conquer into subjection to his perverted standard of faith and practice, or be lost eternally.

Christ taught that to be baptized we must go down into the water and come up out of the water, as he did.

Calvin taught that to be baptized we must stand up in a house and be sprinkled.

Christ taught that to feel right we must first *do* right.

Calvin taught that to do right we must *feel* right.

Christ taught us to "overcome evil with good."

Calvin taught us to overcome evil with evil—that the first step towards becoming better was to believe you were very bad, and if you are too honest to say you were bad when you felt that you were not, it was the darkest sign of guilt—so that the upright, sincere soul felt driven to become bad, so that he could make an *honest* confession of his guilt in order to secure the confidence of his Christian brethren that he was converted.

Christ taught that to clothe ourselves with his righteousness, was to do like him, be like him, by doing right in everything.

Calvin taught that to clothe ourselves with Christ's righteousness was to act contrary to the dictates of human nature and utterly repudiate obedience as a meritorious act, or as a reason why we should be acquitted and justified in God's sight, and depend wholly upon the merits of Christ, entirely independent of our own; or, in other words, to continue in an unnatural state, depending upon a sovereign act of God to appropriate the vicarious sufferings of Christ for our benefit, independent of our accountability.

Calvin taught that the elect were all that would or could be saved, and that these were God's children, and all others the devil's children.

Christ taught that all were God's dear children—that all had good and evil in them, but that all the evil in them he came to destroy. And that for this purpose, he had elected some of his children and capacitated them by peculiar sufferings and trials to be co-workers with him for the good of the many. As if a father should bestow peculiar advantages upon one child, that he might be fitted to be the educator of his other children. This is "The economy of grace."

I believe that, with these, his educated company of sanctified ones, who have come out of great tribulation, such as he endured on earth, he will make such assaults upon Satan's kingdom as will ensure its entire overthrow and destruction.

I believe that this reign of Christ on the earth, with his elect co-workers, is about to be inaugurated; and that these troublous times are only the day of preparation for a better state than has ever been experienced on earth. The clouds which precede this bright, millennial day, will soon be dispersed by the Sun of Righteousness; and that a kingdom is about to be established, which shall never be destroyed.

Then will the great work of redeeming a lost world commence, with accelerated power and efficiency.

Christ, with his chosen band of purified ones, will then make *practical* the beneficent, self-sacrificing principles of his unselfish nature, so that no inveterate foe to His government and reign—not even the stoutest Calvinist—will be able then to resist, effectually, any one of his benevolent plans to save the whole class of Calvinists from the endless torment, by leading them to bow to his sceptre, and become kind and tolerant towards others, as Christ and his followers are toward them.

I believe that all who have died unsanctified, will live again on the earth, where their surroundings will be so favorable, that they will be able to live natural lives, and in this manner, take the *first step* to a higher spiritual life. For God says, with no exception, "First the natural, then the spiritual." And the poor deluded Calvinist, who has been led to despise nature, will not be found to have committed a sin too great for his benevolent Sovereign to pardon, on the ground of late repentance.

I believe that some incorrigible Calvinists may compel God to punish them one thousand years in what, to *them*, is endless torment, before they will be willing to renounce Calvin's creed, and adopt Christ's creed—"to do unto others as they would wish to be done by"—in its stead.

The sum of my practical theology is contained in the following stanza:
"With cheerful feet thy path of duty run,
God nothing does, nor *suffers* to be done,
But what thou wouldst thyself, couldst thou
but see
Through all events of things as well as He."

REFLECTIONS

1. This impious, Calvinistic attempt to *chain my thoughts*, by calling me "insane," for opinion's sake, and imprisoning me on this account, is a *crime* against the constitution of this free government, and also a crime against civilization and human progress. For who will dare to be true to the inspirations of the divinity within them, if the pioneers of truth are thus liable to lose their personal liberty for life, for so doing?
2. The law by which I am imprisoned, which entirely deprives a married woman of the primeval law of heaven—the right of self-defence—is a Calvinistic law, since it conflicts with the gospel—the golden rule.
3. This notorious family rebellion, is the legitimate fruit of the Calvinistic law of marriage, which enslaves the wife. And the only cure for it, is legal, constitutional emancipation, based upon the principles of God's government, which demand *liberty to all*.
4. This kidnapping intelligent moral agents of their accountability is the climax of all human wrongs to which Calvinism gravitates. An imprisonment as a criminal does not begin to compare with it in cruelty—since a criminal is regarded as an accountable being. He is not locked up to be deprived of the Godhead within him! His capacity to become a guilty, wicked person, is allowed him—and this capacity, even with guilt attending it, is less to be dreaded, than a feeling of annihilation—an extinction of human capacities and being.

Gentlemen, I claim ability to defend every sentiment herein advanced by sound argument, and I pledge myself ready now to do so, either in an extemporaneous defence, or a written discussion. And I will engage to write a volume in their defence and have it ready for publication at your next meeting, if you will be so kind as to furnish me with paper to write it upon.

It would be the greatest luxury to me, to thus be able to improve this opportunity, to advance the cause of truth and righteousness on earth, so that when called to give an account of my earthly stewardship, it may appear, that while *numbered* with the incapacitated, useless members of society, I did what I could for the cause most dear to my heart.

Dr. McFarland, please to accept my most grateful thanks for permitting me this privilege of presenting some of my most radical views of religious truth before the Trustees.

Gentlemen, Trustees of this Institution, as your friend, I advise you to follow the dictates of your individual consciences, God's secretary within you, in performing the part Providence has assigned you in this great drama. Remember, gentlemen, we are a free people, and every citizen living under this Government has a right to form his own opinions, and having formed them, he has a right to express his individual opinions wherever he may think proper. And whosoever seeks to imprison him because he does this, is a traitor to that flag and the cause which it represents.

Appendix 2.

PETITION TO MASSACHUSETTS LEGISLATURE

. . . the undersigned citizens of Massachusetts Respectfully Represent,

That the laws regarding insanity are very imperfect. If a person is only charged with being insane, all the safeguards which the law interposes for the protection of any one suspected of a crime are entirely swept away, and the unfortunate man may be committed to an Insane Asylum by the certificate of any two physicians, no matter how stupid or ignorant, that may be selected for the purpose by those who may have an interest in procuring his imprisonment.

The consequences of this state of the law is a very general impression in the community that institutions created for the most benevolent purposes are occasionally made the unwilling assistants in the greatest crimes. We hear often of wives causelessly confined in lunatic establishments by their husband, husbands by their wives, and rich old ladies and gentlemen by their expectant heirs. We do not assert that in every one of these cases the confinement was unjust, but there is no doubt that people of sound mind are sometimes shut up as lunatics! and still oftener that persons of disordered intellect are unjustly imprisoned, being incurable and yet perfectly harmless and capable of enjoying liberty. We have no statistics to show the number of these cases. But the present law being wrong in principle, we earnestly beg your honorable bodies to amend it so as to afford a better protection to personal liberty.

Appendix 3.

REVISED MASSACHUSETTS COMMITMENT LAW

Section 1: The eighth section of the two hundred and twenty-third Chapter of the Acts of the year eighteen hundred and sixty-two is hereby amended that the certification signed by two respectable physicians required by said Section shall be made according to the provisions of said section, after due inquiries and personal examination of the patient by them.

Section 2: Upon application for the admission of an insane person to any State Lunatic Hospital or to any asylum or private house for the reception of the insane, the applicant shall file with his application a statement containing the names and addresses of such insane person's father, mother, children, brothers, sisters or other next-of-kin not exceeding ten in number, and over eighteen years of age, when the names and addresses of each relative are known by the person or persons making such applications and such statements shall be filed with the order of commitment or application for admission.

And the superintendent or person in charge of such asylum or house for the reception of the insane, shall within two days from the time of the admission or commitment of any insane person, send or cause to be sent a notice of said commitment in writing by mail, postage prepaid, to each of said relatives, and to any other two persons whom the person committed shall designate.

$\mathscr{A}ppendix$ 4.

BILL PRESENTED TO CONNECTICUT LEGISLATURE

To the Honorable Senate and House of Representatives in General Assembly convened:

We the undersigned citizens of Connecticut, respectfully represent that the Common Law in relation to the social condition of married women, deprives her of any legal existence, and legal protection as a married woman, thus wholly excluding her while a married woman, from the protection in law of any of her natural rights, such as a right to herself, a right to her children, a right to her home—thus leaving the protection of all her natural rights, wholly at the will or mercy of her husband; that this unlimited power is liable to, and has become an oppressive power; that the law of divorce is one of the great evils which her present legal position necessarily entails upon society.

And further, while this licensed oppression reflects only the spirit of the common law of the dark ages, when the married woman was the mere slave of the husband; we now under the light of progressive civilization, assign her the place of companion of her husband and joint partner with him in his family interests.

Therefore, we, the undersigned, respectfully petition that your honorable body will take into consideration the present legal position of married women, and inquire by committee or otherwise, whether this slavish principle of common law, viz: *the legal nonentity of the wife,* cannot justly and profitably be abolished, or so far modified, as to protect her against the abuse of this absolute power of her husband, by granting her legally the same protection in government, which the enlightened public sentiment of the present age grants her in her social position in society.

Appendix 5.

AN ACT FOR THE PROTECTION OF
PERSONAL LIBERTY IN ILLINOIS

Sec. 1: Be it enacted by the people of the state of Illinois, representing in the General Assembly that no Superintendent, Medical Director, agent of other person having the management supervision or control of the Insane Hospital at Jacksonville, or of any hospital or asylum for insane and distracted persons in this State, shall receive, detain, or keep in custody at such asylum or hospital, any person who has not been declared insane or distracted by a verdict of a jury, and the order of a court, as provided by an act of the General Assembly of this State, approved Feb. 16, 1865.

Sec. 2: Any person having charge of, or the management or control of any hospital for the insane, or any asylum for the insane in the State who shall receive, keep or detain any person, without the record or proper certificate of the trial required by said act of 1865, shall be deemed guilty of a high misdemeanor, and shall be liable to indictment, and on conviction, be fined not more than $1,000, nor less than $500, or imprisoned, not exceeding 1 year, nor less than 3 months, or both in the discretion of the court before which such conviction is had; provided that one-half of such fine shall be paid to the informant and the balance shall go to the benefit of the hospital or asylum in which such persons were detained.

Sec. 3: Any person now confined in any insane hospital or asylum, and all persons now confined in the Hospital for the Insane at Jacksonville, who have not been tried and found insane or distracted by the verdict of a jury, as provided in and contemplated by said act of the General Assembly of 1865, shall be permitted to have such trial. All such persons shall be informed by the trustees of said hospital or asylum, in their discretion of the provisions of this act, and of the said act of 1865, and on their request such persons shall be entitled to such trial within a reasonable time thereafter provided that such trial may be had in the county where such person is confined or detained, unless such person, his or her friends, shall within 30 days after any such person may demand a trial under the provision of said act of 1865, provide for the transportation of such persons to, and demand trial in the county where such insane persons resided previous to said detention, in which case such trial shall take place in said last mentioned county.

Sec. 4: All persons confined as aforesaid if not found insane or distracted, by a trial and the verdict of a jury as above, and in the said act of 1865, provided within 2 months after the passage of this act, shall be set at liberty and discharged.

Sec. 5: It shall be the duty of the State's Attorneys for the several counties, to prosecute any suit arising under the provisions of the act.

Sec. 6: This Act shall be deemed a public act, and take effect and be in force from and after its passage.

Approved, March 5, 1867

Appendix 6.

MRS. PACKARD'S "LOVE LETTER" TO DR. McFARLAND

Dr. McFarland—My True Friend,

Rev. Dr. Humphrey, president of Amherst College, in his private letters to his students on the subject of *matrimony*—"It is not best for you young gentlemen to *marry* until You get through your studies; but, gentlemen, when you see a *fair tree* I advise you to *mark it.*"

Now, Dr. McFarland, I like this *principle.* It contains an important practical truth; and since my principles allow me, although a woman, this inalienable right of choosing my *protector,* I have concluded to apply his advice to *myself* by *marking* you as my future husband; for I have never seen a man before I saw you, to whom my whole womanly nature could *instinctively* pay homage, as my *head,* as the husband should be to the wife.

To such an one alone can I entrust the key with which to unlock the foundation of *conjugal love* within me, whose depths no mortal has never yet sounded. This key I entrust to *you,* Dr. McFarland, with all the trusting confidence of a *true woman.*

The only response I ask of you, *now,* is to *help* me carry the heavy pack of lies before the public, which *Pack-ard* has put upon me to bear so unjustly as a vindication of my assailed character.

If before I leave this institution, you issue the first edition of my first volume, however small, if not less than 25 copies, on your own risk, trusting simply to my verbal promise to pay you back the whole amount in less than three months' time after the leaving of this institution, I shall regard the act, on my part, as an engagement sealed to be yours, alone, until death do us part! You can continue to be, as you are now, a husband in a *Farland*—so far off that none but my own eyes can discern this relation in you until *God's Providence* brings you near enough to recognize the relation with my bodily senses.

I love your *spirit,* your *manliness,* now, but I must not love your *person,* so long as that love is justly claimed by another woman—your legal wife.

I am no widow, Dr. McFarland, for my *heart* has never been wedded. It is whole and sound and unappreciated, except as you, the first *true man* I have ever met, accept it.

I know this is a bold step for me to take, but you know I am dauntless in the right. I have a right to love a true man even if he is in a *far off land,* or a Farland; and if he is *the* true man I take him to be, it won't offend him or expose my *honor* or virtue to let *him know* it.

I have written my thoughts (or feelings, rather) lest a verbal utterance be overheard. I wish no one except your own *private soul* to know of this act. It must be a sacred, a profound *secret* between us, trusted entirely to your *honor,* as a Christ-like man.

This note *must* be burnt, since an exposure of it might imperil my virtue in the estimation of *perverted* humanity. But my own heart does not condemn me for the act, neither does God condemn me for *loving his image.* Theophilus, my son, will be 21 the 17th of next March, and should he offer to protect me against another outrage of my husband, I will go with him as my protector and take charge of my children at that time.

Yours in the best of bonds,

Elizabeth

Appendix 7.

BOOKS BY E. P. W. PACKARD

Marital Power Exemplified, or Three Years Imprisonment for Religious Belief. Hartford, Conn., 1864.
Great Disclosure of Spiritual Wickedness in High Places (2 vols.). Boston, 1865.
The Mystic Key: or The Asylum Secret Unlocked. Hartford, Conn., 1866.
The Prisoners' Hidden Life, or Insane Asylums Unveiled (2 vols.). Chicago, 1868.
Modern Persecution, or Insane Asylums Unveiled (2 vols.). Hartford, 1873. Reprint under a new title of *The Prisoners' Hidden Life.*
The Great Drama, or The Millennial Harbinger (2 vols.). Hartford, Conn., 1892. Final version of *Great Disclosures,* started at Jacksonville.

Appendix 8.

A BILL INTRODUCED INTO THE U.S. CONGRESS

For the protection of the postal rights of the inmates of insane asylums:

Be it enacted by the Senate and House of Representatives of the United States of America in Congress assembled, That, for the purpose of securing the postal rights of inmates of insane-asylums, the Postmaster-General, whenever requested by the authorities of any State, be, and he is hereby, authorized and directed to cause to be placed, upon or in any insane-asylum, private or public, within the territory of said State, a post-office box, into which the letters of the inmates may be dropped by the writers themselves; which box shall not be under the control or surveillance of the officers of said asylums, but subject to such outside censorship as the legislatures of the several States shall determine. The collection of the mail-matter deposited in said boxes shall be made at least once a week by an employee of the Post-Office Department.

Index

Acknowledgments

*W*ithout the helping hands of all the following, some of them only friendly voices over the telephone, this book could not have been satisfactorily completed.

First and foremost, I thank Dr. Eric T. Carlson, clinical professor of psychiatry and director of the Section on the History of Psychiatry, at the Cornell University Medical College, who not only let me use his library but steered me to articles in psychiatric journals that discussed what was clearly Mrs. Packard's story though they did not mention her name. Also, through my years of rejection and rewriting, he kept encouraging me to "rescue her from obscurity." I am also grateful to his associate director and fellow clinical professor, Dr. Jacques Quen, who gave me generously of his time to explain psychotic episodes—whether they are or are not cause for hospitalization, do or do not interfere with functional living—and whether Mrs. Packard did or did not suffer from them.

I also thank the Packard great-grandchildren, Emmy Lou, the late John, Jr. (and his wife, Betty), and Theo V and great-great-granddaughter Judy Stenovich, who supplemented the written material with family anecdotes, legends, and photographs. Special thanks to my friends of long standing, Carol Cornish of Amherst, Massachusetts, and Peggy Kovacs of Chicago, who housed me during my research in their neighborhoods.

Other helping hands were proffered by Roger Bridges, of the Rutherford

B. Hayes Presidential Library in Ohio, then of the Illinois State Historical Society, and his successor, Mary Michals; Mary Genelli of the Worcester State Hospital, Worcester, Massachusetts; Daria D'Arienzo, archivist of Amherst College; David Proper of the Memorial Libraries in Deerfield, Massachusetts; George Melnik of the South Deerfield Historical Commission; Daniel Lombardo of the Jones Library in Amherst; Lawrence Dinnean of the Bancroft Library at the University of California at Berkeley; and Loella S. Young, then director of public relations, Jacksonville (Illinois) State Hospital.

My special appreciation to those who did essential research for me: Janis Ruden and Andrea Balis, Ph.D. candidates in American history at the City University of New York Graduate Center; Zing Jung of the American Psychiatric Association's *Journal of Insanity* in Washington, D.C.; and Dorothy Mapes of the Ware, Massachusetts, library.

In addition, the following people checked out for me the presence or absence of references to Mrs. Packard's legislative campaigns in the archives of their local newspapers: Judith Lamont in Washington, D.C., Stephanie Haack in Boston, Risa Sklar in Hartford, Connecticut and Donna Hendrickson in Manteno, Illinois. Myra B. Beedy of Manteno receives special mention in my preface for her voluntary efforts on my behalf.

Finally, my deepest gratitude to these three: Lucy Freeman who introduced me to Ruth Wreschner, my agent, who sold my book, and PJ Dempsey, my editor, who bought it.

About the Author

Barbara Sapinsley studied history as an undergraduate at Columbia University and as a graduate student at New York University and the City University of New York where she is now completing her work for a Ph.D. Before returning to graduate school, she worked as a journalist for *Newsweek*, and for CBS News where she wrote scripts for the award-winning documentary series *The Twentieth Century*. She has also written documentaries for ABC, NBC, Time-Life Films, the UN and the United States Information Agency. The author of many magazine articles, she has authored two books for young adults, one on the Weimar Republic (Germany from 1919 to 1933) and the other on the history of taxes in America from the stamp tax in the 1760s to the tax revolts in the 1980s. Ms. Sapinsley is a native New Yorker who has traveled widely around America, Europe and the Middle East.